The MC5 and Social Change

The MC5 and Social Change

A Study in Rock and Revolution

MATHEW J. BARTKOWIAK

McFarland & Company, Inc., Publishers
Jefferson, North Carolina, and London

LIBRARY OF CONGRESS CATALOGUING-IN-PUBLICATION DATA

Bartkowiak, Mathew J.
　　The MC5 and social change : a study in rock and revolution / Mathew J. Bartkowiak.
　　　　p.　　cm.
　　Includes bibliographical references and index.

　　ISBN 978-0-7864-4037-5
　　softcover : 50# alkaline paper ∞

　　1. Rock music — Social aspects — United States.　2. Rock music — Political aspects — United States.　3. Rock music — United States — History and criticism.　4. MC5 (Musical group)　5. White Panther Party.　I. Title.
ML3918.R63B37　　2009
306.4'84260973 — dc22　　　　　　　　　　　　　　2009009938

British Library cataloguing data are available

©2009 Mathew J. Bartkowiak. All rights reserved

No part of this book may be reproduced or transmitted in any form or by any means, electronic or mechanical, including photocopying or recording, or by any information storage and retrieval system, without permission in writing from the publisher.

On the cover: Wayne Kramer of MC5 strikes a defiant pose, courtesy of Leni Sinclair; peace sign ©2009 Shutterstock.

Manufactured in the United States of America

McFarland & Company, Inc., Publishers
　Box 611, Jefferson, North Carolina 28640
　　www.mcfarlandpub.com

To my wife Sara,
with thanks for her infinite support and patience,

and

my daughter Ella,
who had the distinction of dancing for the first time
in her life while "Kick Out the Jams" was playing

Acknowledgments

My immense gratitude goes to all of those who helped make this book a reality. To my incredible wife, Sara, and daughter, Ella, for their patience and love, thank you. I would like to acknowledge as well my wonderful family. Mom and Dad, thanks for teaching me about the importance of music, and instilling the passion to always keep learning. We miss you, Dad. Thanks to Jus, Mark, Sandy and Aaron and family for their support. Thanks as well to Adam Nelson, Baaron Schulte, and of course, Rick.

The work contained within, I hope, is an adequate reflection of the brilliant scholars I have worked with over the years: Gary Hoppenstand, Ann Larabee, David Stowe, Maria Bruno, Jack Santino, Joe Ruff, Joe Austin, Craig Lockard, Andrew Austin, Peter Kellogg, and Russ Reising. I have been so fortunate to surround myself with such caring and gifted scholars. Thank you all so much. Thanks to Peter and Susan Rollins for your support. Thanks as well to everyone in the American Studies Department at Michigan State: a phenomenal collection of students, staff and faculty.

I would also like to thank those whom I have so completely exploited through their efforts in editing and discussion about this topic: Kathryn Edney, Dr. Jerry Goldberg, Arthur Versluis, Katherine Kalish and Don Garsow. Thanks as well to Matt Conger and Tom Smith for introducing me to the MC5's music.

I want to thank Doug Sheppard at *Ugly Things Magazine* (ugly-things. com) for the use of his interview with Rob Tyner. Thanks as well to the folks at the "MC5 Gateway." I would also like to thank the staff of the University of Wisconsin-Marshfield/Wood County Library, the staff of the Michigan State University Libraries, the Marshfield Public Library and the Bowling Green State University Sound Recordings Archive and its director, Bill Schurk. Thanks as well to the faculty, staff, and students of the University of Wisconsin-Marshfield/Wood County, the University of Wisconsin Colleges English Department, and the University of Wisconsin-Marshfield Foundation.

My humble thanks as well to the DKT/MC5 family who have been so incredibly open and kind during these interviews: Michael, Angela Davis and family, Wayne Kramer and Margaret Saadi-Kramer, Dennis Thompson and Patrice, John Sinclair, Leni Sinclair (a huge thanks for the photos), and Pun Plamondon. I hope that I have done some justice to a subject and a band that will continue to fascinate generations to come.

Thanks as well to *The Journal of Popular Culture* and *The Journal for the Study of Radicalism*, who printed earlier versions of what would become two of the book's chapters.

Table of Contents

Acknowledgments vii

Preface 1

*Introduction: Rock and Revolution—
The MC5 and Music's Political Life* 7

ONE. Fighting in the Streets:
Understanding the Undercurrent of Rebellion in Rock 21

TWO. Revolution on Your Headphones:
Charting Social Location in the Rise of
the MC5 and the White Panther Party 37

THREE. Motor City Burning:
Rock and Rebellion in the WPP and the MC5 65

FOUR. Sonic Anarchy: The Making of the MC5 87

FIVE. Guns and Guitars:
Revolutionary Style and Substance? 112

SIX. Managing the Legacy of the Sound and the Fervor 139

SEVEN. Up Against the Wall: Music's Place in Revolution 168

Chapter Notes 187

Bibliography 189

Index 195

Preface

Summer 2005: On a warm Southern California night, I lay awake, gripped in a crippling anxiety. Like any good graduate student, I had by this time been instilled with a healthy sense of self-loathing and self-doubt. Today, though, took the cake. My research was crumbling before my very eyes and here I was a couple of hundred bucks in the hole, hoping that my wife might forgive me for the plane ticket that I insisted would allow profound insight into my subject of study, the MC5. I kept hearing in my mind Michael Davis, the bassist for the group, plainly saying to me earlier in the day, "To me, as one of the founders of the White Panther Party, one of the people who were sitting around the table when the joints were going down and the WPP was founded, it was just a joke! It was one of our, like, let's goof on the audience things! This is just a cartoon!"

I wondered how I had got here. Where did it all go wrong? With his words searing themselves into my brain, I thought back to the sense of romanticism that led me to this place — a happier time when there where no shades of grey. It was a time of immense discovery. It was a time of immense political awareness. It was college.

On a cold Green Bay night four or five years before my night of anguish in L.A., I was about to put a new disc in the player at the record shop where I worked. This was the most contentious time during the day in the shop. Small wars had been fought over what was next to receive in-store play. As it was down to two of us, in the dead of a slow night, I let my compatriot put on a disc by a band that sounded like it had named itself after a car part. In went the MC5's *Kick Out the Jams*. He knowingly turned the volume up and as the band assaulted — assaulted — my ears, he told me what he knew about it and something called the "White Panther Party (WPP)." He assured me it was not a white supremacist group. He didn't know too much more.

It didn't matter; I was hooked. The thought of a band that combined a musical battering with a political, even radical organization, swelled my newly politically alive and aware soul. It was perfect timing. The music was the perfect soundtrack for the college-induced sense of political righteousness that I possessed. It felt great to finally have it all figured out, and even better, to be *right* in what I was seeing as an increasingly hypocritical world, reflected in musical form.

Jumping a few years later, and across the lake to Michigan, I sat enthralled in an American studies course looking at contemporary radicalism. Figuring that the MC5 could be a wonderful term paper topic that could marry my continued interest in popular music history with radicalism, I set out to prove the wonderful authentic expression of a band that took revolution to the stage. I was sure that I had unearthed an interesting term paper at best.

Soon, the study became engrossing. Eventually, I shelved another idea for my dissertation and pushed ahead with research on the band and the MC5. I had figured out an incredibly profound thesis: the MC5 was the real deal—guns and guitars working together! It was proof that popular music could do something. It could even dance (the pun is completely intended) with notions of revolution. It was a wonderful feeling of authenticity and power that I hadn't felt since I listened to Public Enemy's *Fear of a Black Planet* as a 10-year-old. I read *Guitar Army* by the band's manager and countercultural guru, John Sinclair. The rhetoric and the passion matched the music, and proved this passionate authenticity was going to be a mark that I could easily measure.

And here I lay, my careful plans cut off at the shins with my first interview of a band member. It didn't match up. The music was powerful! The rhetoric was powerful! I had phenomenal access to the players in this historical narrative, and the interview had only confused what I saw as a clear thesis. It was so much easier to judge the entire MC5/White Panther relationship from afar. Now in the trenches, I was left with a fear that the project was dead in the water. Several hours into an epic sleepless night, a phrase from one of my professors in graduate school, Jack Santino, came to mind: "Don't let your thesis guide your research; let your research guide your thesis." It was one of the most simple but profound sentences I had heard in my academic life. Here it hit me. I was as confused and perplexed by Davis's interpretation of the WPP relationship of the band as he was perplexed by the reactions of those who invested, or trusted that this threat was a real one. I was not the first person to buy into the revolutionary potentiality of the band, and I certainly will not be the last. A whole host of fans, government officials, and others have bought into this potential, just as other idealistic and passionate individuals will surely do in the coming years when introduced, like I was, to the MC5. Others like Davis will view this "revolutionary" potential as merely a facade or a devil's trick that doesn't promise all that much.

I bring this story up because this is truly the point where this study took shape. Left behind was any kind of desire for a biographical narrative, with proof of authentic political dissidence. The next day, I talked with guitarist Wayne Kramer, who further complicated this study by expressing his desire not only to be a rock star, but also to be a model for creating revolutionary social/political change. I was going to let this study, and my access to the players in this historical/musical event, shape what this project would mean. It was only after my first round of interviews that I could begin to fathom the phenomenal story of popular culture and its power in creating a wide range of usable interpretations. From disdain to fear, rock was a place where people could engage and use popular culture to their own means. The connection of the band to this "revolutionary" organization furthers the spectrum of thought as to the validity of rock's place in the march to social change, or to the status quo, depending on your interpretation.

The legacy of the 1960s, the baby-boomers, and the New Left is being actively negotiated. As the young people of the Sixties look back on their legacy and influence on the world, it is easy to see a need and desire to offer a sense of narrative, meaning, or definitive understanding of a complex and easily romanticized time. As much as I would like to offer such a definitive statement, especially for all of the participants involved in this study, and for people looking for an absolute in terms of understanding this band and its political/musical legacy, I can't. As much as I would have liked it, history rarely offers absolutes. Stepping outside of the comforts of researching in isolation, I found a much more complex approach was required.

My isolation in the library was challenged by the harsh reality of talking to numerous actors that helped to create the story. In some cases they themselves were still befuddled by the narratives that have developed. No longer would it be possible to have a thesis guide the research. To do so would not only marginalize the actors involved and the numerous perspectives they possessed, but would also be detrimental to gaining understanding of a group with concerns in media, popularity, politics, and radicalism, and which, in a charged atmosphere, tested the possibilities of music being an agent of social change and development.

To figure out how all of these pieces fit together, I organized several levels of inquiry. I have employed numerous sources on the band, including larger biographical works, like Brent Callwood's *MC5: Sonically Speaking: A Tale of Revolution and Rock 'n' Roll* and David Carson's seminal *Grit, Noise and Revolution*. I also used academic work on the band and academic works on larger theories of power and control, as well as on popular, political, and urban culture. Also consulted were primary documents that include material collected by the FBI and other law enforcement agencies obtained under the Freedom of Information Act, and extensive interviews.

The interviews were done over a period of several years, with numerous key players. When possible, they were done in person, but were also done over the phone, and occasionally through e-mail correspondence. The interviewees included band members, management, members and officers of the White Panthers, as well as the band's photographer. Unfortunately, two of the five members of the band passed away years before this project was undertaken, Rob Tyner and Fred "Sonic" Smith. I've tried to include their voices where possible through prior interviews or secondary sources, but realize the hole that both of these men represent in terms of this research.

I quickly learned after my interview with Davis that the process was better when it was open-ended and allowed for subjects to interpret and expand as they wished. The interviews were very much focused on the relationship to the White Panthers instead of simple biography. Often follow-up questions would be asked of participants about their interpretations of events. This allowed for more contextual insight into their views, and also helped to measure the investment and meaning the MC5/WPP relationship possessed for these participants, supporters, and critics of the band and organization.

All of these voices, no matter how distanced they were from my own interpretations (or from each other's interpretations at times) are included. It is a necessary methodology that allows for some significant and in-depth insight into a creation that, due to its dependence on the media and the need to frame the MC5/WPP, was far beyond the control or capabilities of a single agent. The reader may inevitably choose a side or form an opinion about the MC5 and the White Panthers. But the discussion and debate offer a narrative of their own. It speaks of the difficulties of political significance, and illuminates the role of popular culture in helping to shape, challenge, and reaffirm our beliefs and practices in everyday life. It's a lot to juggle, but the payoff has been, at least for me, a more holistic understanding, versus a narrower and more limiting view of a contentious gathering of subjects. Although I am sure that there is much more to be done with the subject, it is a methodology that, unlike that fateful night in L.A., has allowed me to sleep much more soundly.

Introduction:
Rock and Revolution—
The MC5 and Music's Political Life

In March of 2003, the surviving members of the Detroit-rock outfit the MC5 played at London's 100 Club. An international audience of fans and fellow musicians watched the former organizing force for the White Panther Party (WPP) take the stage. Press coverage would focus on the devoted following in tow for the show, as well as detractors claiming that the band had sold out. The group, which called itself "DKT-MC5" (DKT for Davis, Kramer, and Thompson), brought the music of the band to the live stage, a rare event. The members did so with the Levi's brand name featured prominently behind them. According to manager Angela Davis, this was somewhat less than a clearly orchestrated plot:

> In 2002, Levi Strauss Vintage Clothing U.K., a small, boutique style division of the Levi Strauss Company, chose the MC5 at random when looking for a late 1960s rock band whose style most closely matched a line of clothing that they came to call Sonic Revolution. In doing their research, they came across one of Gary Grimshaw's posters, and contacted him about licensing the rights to the artwork to use on a shirt. It is unclear whether Gary was aware that he cannot license works which contain MC5 in them because this is a registered trademark. The company should have obtained two licenses, one for the copyrighted art from Gary Grimshaw, and one for the MC5 TM from the owners of the mark (the band members). At any rate, Margaret Saadi Kramer, who represents Wayne Kramer, Ben Edmonds, who was unofficially representing the interests of Rob Tyner via a loose arrangement with Tyner's widow, and I, as management for Michael Davis and Dennis Thompson, all became aware that Levi's was using the mark. After a lot of discussion, Margaret and I agreed that rather than suing Levi's and Gary Grimshaw for trademark infringement, we

would rather have the Levi's corporation set things right regarding licensing, and then see what we might do to "make lemonade" as it were.

She continues,

Shortly after, Alec Samways, a publicity executive hired by Levi's to promote the line, contacted us to inquire about the possibility of the surviving members of the band reuniting for a one-off show in London to launch the advertising campaign for the line. All three agreed that it was something they would like to have a go at [Angela Davis Interview].

Members of the group and the management made very little out of the resulting discussion in the press about selling out. They had been dealing with this for a long time. Thanks to the band's affiliation with a supposed political organization, fans, critics, and numerous other audiences had engaged in that debate from the band's outset. These questions of commerce vs. art and rebellion against capitalism have for better or worse followed those associated with the band and the White Panther Party. Although the band was only associated with the Party for a short time, and for one album, the WPP in many ways set the standard for conversation about the band and its place in musical and social history.

Released in 1969, the MC5's *Kick Out the Jams* was a new measure of the relationship between music and cultural and political change. Although rock's entire history has been based in an inherent sense of rebellion, the MC5 was seen as the "house band" for the White Panther Party, a group which advocated an end to capitalism and full support of the Black Panther Party's initiatives and other revolutionary aims (which would become the target of local state and federal authorities). The band formalized for various perspectives the threat, the promise or the parody that music could promise within larger societal spheres. The complexities of the MC5's career and its revolutionary potential are hard to fully collect and ascertain.

Scholars within popular music history and cultural studies have struggled to determine these parameters and their practice in everyday life. Debates over the validity of popular texts range from the pessimistic paranoia of Frankfurt School thinkers to conceptualizations of positivistic self-assertion through popular culture considered by Birmingham School thinkers, with numerous other polarities to boot. Often though, theoretical concerns of power and control often abstract very real human practices. This gap in consideration in determining cultural texts needs to be filled in by talking to the actors themselves, along with considering the theoretical frameworks that guided the realities of a musical creation like the MC5. Talking with those involved over the course of almost four years revealed an experiment in rock, an experiment in determining the power of media and spectacle, and an experiment in determining the role of music in cultural and political change.

My interviews with band members Michael Davis, Wayne Kramer, and Dennis "Machine Gun" Thompson (the other two members, Rob Tyner and Fred "Sonic" Smith passed away in the 1990s); their manager John Sinclair; WPP Minister of Defense Pun Plamondon; and their photographer, Leni Sinclair; opened up a world of multiple interpretations of the music. Was it a call to revolution? Was it about becoming a big rock and roll band? Was it parody? Was it serious? Was it meant to spark cultural or political revolution (or both)? The answer to all of these questions was an emphatic "yes." Framing an entity like the MC5 and the WPP, which sought to make the most of mass media, is difficult, as individuals and the media themselves all look to determine and communicate specific meanings to the targeted audience. For some, the group was a means to sparking a revolution of political and social consciousness through the use of the media and rock and roll. For others, the group was a means to begin a career and make a living through the production of musical works. Many other perspectives existed between these two.

This study does not seek to reveal the goal of the White Panther Party and the MC5. Instead, it will demonstrate the complexity of interactions and perspectives that determined the parameters of an experiment in power. This experiment and the desired goal of this book is to understand, through a case study of the career of this band, the potentialities and contradictions that occur in the relationship between music and social change. The MC5 is an example of the possibilities of audiences, performers, producers and others to engage in a space of usable rebellion.

"Usable rebellion" refers to the inherent, rebellious nature of rock that has allowed producers and consumers to partake in questioning social mores and ideas in a safe spot secured by the price of concert ticket or CD. It also allows dominant power structures and major corporate interests to find immense profit, by blending social rebellion into the very consumer fabric of rock and roll. The MC5 allows this dichotomy of subversion and profit to be better understood. The MC5 tested where these borders begin and end. By mobilizing the powers of subversion built into rock and roll from their inception, the band and the WPP were able to test the potentialities of music within the realm of social change. They also left questions about the role of dominant corporate power in harnessing this energy within rock and roll, as it has successfully done since the 1950s. Hence, this study does not seek to deny or accept the MC5 and the White Panther Party as either a legitimate or illegitimate countercultural power in the late 1960s and early '70s. It will center on how the band was able to harness the power of the counterculture and rock and roll to create a mediafriendly space in which rebellion could be explored and enacted for artists, audiences and others in a frameable model.

Such an interdisciplinary study requires an interdisciplinary framework. Issues of the media, popular music and popular culture studies come into the fray along with perspectives from history and political thought from the New Left and other radical forces. These conceptual frameworks allow for a balance from which to gauge the products and perspectives of the MC5 and those involved in its creation and maintenance. This multiplicity of perspectives will offer new critical insight into biographical works like David Carson's *Grit, Noise and Revolution*, which views the MC5 as one of numerous players within a larger Detroit rock scene, and Brett Callwood's *MC5: Sonically Speaking: A Tale of Revolution and Rock 'n' Roll*, and Michael Simmons and Cletus Nelson's *The Future Is Now!: An Illustrated History of the MC5*, which both chronicle, to some extent, the life of the band from its inception to its demise. The aforementioned works provide a biographical layout of the group's career but do not focus as intently on the relationship of music to cultural and social change, nor do they offer extended insight into the ramifications of the band's association with and disassociation from the White Panthers. Jeff Hale's article on the band, "Total Assault on Culture," which focuses on the band as a countercultural force pushed into radical extremism, leaves the musical life of the group behind and focuses on an intense view of the band and the White Panthers as a formalized entity. Don McLeese's *The MC5's Kick Out the Jams*, another major work on the band, also veers towards the biographical, but allows some perspective into the band as a musical entity, with its definitive influences on the punk and heavy metal community. Steve Waksman's *Instruments of Desire* examines the group with a focus on the history of race and the band's "explicit enactment of the racialized nature of rock's favored mode of phallocentric display, with the electric guitar as a privileged signifier of white male power and potency"

(5). Such a focus on racial identity and posturing will not be the case in this study, but Waksman's *Instruments*, like each of these works, makes some reference to the WPP. The need for a more detailed study that focused on music's role in culture and in politics was what drove *this* study.

This book is not intended to be a comprehensive biographical work. Instead, the research will be an intensive case study looking at the interaction of music with possibilities for cultural and political change. The very real pressures arising from the political and social climate of the time, the music industry and media's framing methods all contribute to the complexity of the MC5 in myth and musical practice. After numerous trips to Detroit and throughout Michigan, phone conversations, and many flights, this study reflects diverse research and insight that has been the result of actively questioning players in a production that undercuts any single intent or perspective. There is much more to the MC5 story than politics, dissent and consumable rebellion. Only a small part of the equation is being dealt with in this book, which is not intended to be a definitive treatise on a group that will continue to demand the attention of scholars, musicians and fans alike.

The spectrum of usage and possibility within the MC5/WPP relationship is really at the heart of this book. Products of popular culture can be texts of immense investment and meaning to those who choose to participate. They can also be left behind simply by turning the dial, flipping channels, or, in the case of the MC5, missing their small section as one browses in a local record/CD shop. This variance in usage would be the one constant that ran across the four years of research represented in this book. Government documents, music reviewers, fans, and the band members themselves differed greatly in how seriously they took the MC5's fronting of a "revolutionary" organization during a highly volatile time in the United States and the world. Their tenure as a band occurred during a time when the powers of the media were being harnessed by those in power and those desperate to have their voices heard.

Due to this plethora of perspectives, the following is far from a linear tale. Instead, numerous key occurrences and themes will be revisited throughout various chapters. This is done to manage the fractures and interpretations of the group that exist both within and outside the group.

In order to begin the examination of the band specifically in the frame of usable rebellion, Chapter One offers a short history of the investment by fans and by producers in an inherent sense of rebellion within the advent and life of rock and roll. Much as jazz had done earlier in the century, rock and roll offered a potentially subversive wealth of anti-authoritarianism and sexuality, and thanks to rabid consumerism, the creation of clearly delineated generational gaps in the musical fabric of the United States. Audience use, as much as marketing forces, created a space for subversion in the nation's ears and minds. These influences affected the MC5 as its members grew up in the Detroit area (a hotbed of popular performers including John Lee Hooker, Bill Haley and others). Attempts to institutionalize these musical forms by producers into more marketable and less threatening forms (e.g., Pat Boone) were eventually rejected, as groups like the Rolling Stones came to depend on an aura built on bad behavior and bad attitudes. The link between rock and rebellion continued to develop, even as it became a standard in American popular culture.

It is an open question how much this meant in everyday life. Did the potential empowerment of music as rebellion contribute significantly to the debate over the massive social issues of the 1960s like race, class, Vietnam and agency? Indeed, music was seen as a common referent in social change movements in the 1960s. "We Shall Overcome" or "Blowin' in the Wind," for instance, were common references that allowed people to unify their voices in the streets and on college campuses. The violent offspring of the Students for a Democratic Society (SDS), the Weathermen, took their name specifically from a Bob Dylan song, "Subterranean Homesick Blues" on the *Bringing It All Back Home* album. Through such examples we can see that music was a touchstone for a generation that pushed record sales to new levels and found a voice in these expressions that are now inherently connected to the rise of the New Left and countercultural movements. These musical texts became the soundtrack of a generation coming to age in volatile times.

Yet how much change could this common culture effect? Was it meant to do anything more than be a soundtrack of the times? Rebellion was alive and well in the music industry in the decades chronicled in this study, as it is today. But it's hard to comprehend its effects. Regardless, market forces and audiences delighted in the process of subversion, pushing acts like Jefferson Airplane and Country Joe and Fish in front of hundreds of thousands both on records and in live performance, whether in ballrooms or in massive concert festivals across the nation. Scholars who have written on the interaction of music and social forces such as Reebee Garafalo, Simon Frith and Keith Negus among others provide a conceptual framework from which to begin to understand this interaction of rebellion and rock. The rise of the MC5 and its affiliation with the White Panther Party pushed this discussion of music's place in cultural and political change to a more immediate level, as a band became its own organizing political force.

The 1950s and 1960s, decades in which rock and roll formalized itself as a genre, are tied to the rise of mass media forms in a new era of consumerism after World War II. Understanding the power of this media force in the constitution and life of the genre (models that the MC5 and WPP would invest in) is a first step into this discussion of meaning and power in rock and rebellion. Robert Benford, David Snow and Todd Gitlin give insight into the realities of media and labeling, marketing and naturalizing popular culture products in the post-war age. Conversely, Gitlin's work especially contextualizes the intersection of politics (of the New Left) and music: two entities whose success was based on the post-war media onslaught and the spectacle of rebellion. Theories of media framing and how the media make sense communicating information about events also point to the need for a holistic interpretation of one of popular culture's great false binaries: art versus commerce.

This intersection and the continued debate over authenticity highlight the continued investment of individuals and groups in music as an agent of identity formation. Did rock really mean to subvert? Did it mean to sell? Conversations between now-institutional names in music scholarship such as Reebee Garafalo and Simon Frith in works like *Rock and Roll Is Here to Pay* and *Performing Rights,* respectively, point us toward understanding the relationship of media to creative and artistic expression, and how much these factors are determined from above or from below. Keith Negus in *Music Genres and Corporate Cultures* links these discussions of authenticity and the realities of media power, providing a main theoretical framework from which to look into the history of rock, roll and rebellion. It no longer is a case of art versus commerce, but instead is a process. This process entails not only industry producing culture, but also culture producing an industry. Here the true nature of rock and its relationship to rebellion can best be understood.

Chapter Two, "Revolution on Your Headphones: Charting Social Location in the Rise of the MC5 and the White Panther Party," begins the complicated discussion of the varying perspectives of the group's members in relationship to WPP officials and among themselves. These varying perspectives are explored as foundations for the band members' political and musical mindsets. Chapter Two looks to ascertain the social location of group members in an attempt to understand their goals for the life of the band and its role in the White Panther Party. Most studies concentrate less on these voices than that of their manager, John Sinclair, who is often viewed as the supposed dictatorial svengali of the White Panthers. While Sinclair was a major influence, we will see that the party was born from numerous individuals, including band members.

Here, the MC5 reflect on historical events, musical foundations, and the realities of local, national, and international concerns that shaped the band musically and politically. There is not necessarily any grand narrative that is identified in these processes: instead an interaction of social and musical events and practices intertwine in the formation of the group's musical and social/political views. These views are highlighted especially through the help of meso-level guides. These deal with the social, political and cultural history of the metro Detroit area (including Sugrue's *Origins of the Urban Crisis*), which directly influenced the creation of the band and the WPP in their direct experiences and by shaping their ideas and approach to national and international issues. Issues of race, shifts in the demographics of the population, and a changing job market created a slew of influences on everyday life in the Detroit metro area. Exposure to these issues and to specific events formed, to varying extents, members' commitments to political and social causes. For instance, the perceived injustices witnessed in the 1967 riot were a call to order for several involved to commit themselves more fully to issues of social change. The Detroit area was their common heritage, and it would be an active agent in creating the sound and image of the band and the WPP.

The chapter also looks to national issues that helped formulate individual and band mentalities, as the members came into young adulthood. More nationally focused debates on politics, the Vietnam War, and race cemented and challenged notions of life that they had faced as youth in the greater Detroit area. The rise of the New Left, however each defined it, also took hold of these young men and shaped their worldviews. Groups like Students for a Democratic Society and the Black Panthers provided vivid representations of rebellion in the streets. Such views were made even more clear for individual members as different drug use patterns emerged nationally and eventually among themselves. From a locally-constructed and nurtured taste for alcohol to the significant use of LSD (and later, even harder drugs), the use of these substances played a central role in creating the MC5 and WPP mythos.

Also examined are the various influences coming from the popular culture of the time. The continued spread of media in the time period testified to the centrality of forms like television, film, and music in shaping public opinion and everyday life. Musically, the band increased its fan base while crossing musical boundaries. The British Invasion, free-jazz, folk, and other musical forms took the band from its humble origins as an R&B cover band to the sonically assaulting entity it became at the height of its popularity. The band's artistic development also owes a great deal to a rich Detroit music scene. This atmosphere embraced and made sense of the music the MC5 would become known for.

Chapter Three, "Motor City Burning: Rock and Rebellion in the WPP and the MC5," begins a detailed examination of the White Panther Party and the MC5 as a musical and potentially a social force. The chapter reflects the first phase of research conducted with individuals within the organization. John Sinclair, the band's manager and head of the White Panther Party, was interviewed numerous times over an almost four-year period beginning in the spring of 2005, as was his former wife and band photographer Leni Sinclair. These interviews were done for a perspective on the group from the Sinclairs' viewpoints. They were some of the most potent forces behind the band's rise to fame and the development of the party itself. Pun Plamondon, a co-founder of the White Panther Party, was also consulted. Plamondon, as the study will show, was one of the more radically motivated forces behind the WPP. His role as minister of defense, like other leadership roles, caused some discomfort among several band members (this is further chronicled in later chapters as well). The writings of Sinclair, the progressiveness of Plamondon in word and action, and semiotic messages put forth by the band and the collective point to numerous influences that can allow us to gauge various modes of reception. Their trials, like the "Keith Case," showcased that the cultural was political to many interested parties, and attracted repression from governmental interest especially.

There was, for many involved, a sense of authentic expression; they believed they could change the world. Although written off by critics and organizations now considered part of the New Left, many, including the FBI, took the WPP seriously. For those who bought into the WPP as a promise or as a threat, John Sinclair especially became a cause célèbre. Like the Black Panthers, like the Yippies, like SDS and the Weathermen, the WPP functioned through key figures, who became celebrated orators and proponents of the revolution. In the case of the WPP, a rock band was literally the semiotic and musical force driving the group, with Sinclair considered its guiding guru. Interviews reveal that the WPP was a group effort, and although a focus fell on Sinclair, the responsibilities rested among many, with numerous divisions of power and control.

John Sinclair, as one of the most sincere and sure proponents of the path the band and the party were taking at the time, provides immense insight into the realities of the life of the organization and the band's role in it. Instead of a formalized political organization, the party came into being from an organic base, according to Sinclair. He discusses the way in which the WPP and the MC5 were working without a concrete plan of action and calculation. Part of the chapter looks as well to the perspectives of the Sinclairs and Plamondon on the groups that preceded the WPP and that led to its formation: the Detroit Artists' Workshop and Trans-Love Energies. Building on Chapter Two, this chapter examines the organizations in much greater detail and chronicles the historical narrative essential in understanding the WPP/ MC5 relationship. Music was seen as the real tool of enlightenment to Sinclair; the MC5 was the catalyst for change against the perceived totalitarian control of the United States government. The reaction to the group by local and national authorities was swift and severe. Sinclair would serve several years in a federal penitentiary because of, in his view, his role as the manager of the MC5.

In the end, those in high positions in the WPP looked to the MC5 as a media spearhead for open questioning of and rebellion against societal norms. Like many other groups, this one framed itself through the media. The groups' propaganda along with dominant media portrayals created a frame from which the government and the public made sense of the group. This very much was the case for groups like the Black Panthers, the Weathermen, and the Yippies. Even though some would deny the connection of the "cultural" into the "political" counterculture, the structures and strains remained remarkably alike across the supposed divide. Far beyond politics, the band was representative of a program of "rock and roll, dope and fucking in the streets" (Sinclair 1) that challenged political and cultural lines. Rebellion had found a comfortable and usable home.

Chapter Four, "Sonic Anarchy: The Making of the MC5," focuses on this disagreement among the political and musical visions of the surviving members of the group, individuals who are often forgotten when looking at the life of the WPP. Perspectives vary significantly as to what the revolution was to mean and what the outcome was to be for those involved. Formalized conceptualizations of the group's political aims have proved difficult to construct when determining an overarching frame for audiences, the WPP, and band members themselves. This is due to these differing perspectives on intent. The uncontrollable power of myth that took over has left some members of the group amazed and some frustrated that politics became their legacy instead of their music.

The White Panther Party and the MC5, as the determinate power within the organization, were used by varying groups and populations. Some members of the band were very much active agents in determining their careers and roles in the WPP. Others were along for the ride and became increasingly concerned with the political fallout from the MC5/WPP, as a mobilizing force for dissent. Audiences, the government, and others to varying extents bought into the space of usable rebellion created by the group. Sometimes dismissed and sometimes feared as a threat to national security, the potentialities of meanings took on lives of their own and continue to do so today. This has created an almost mythical vision of the group within the counterculture and within rock and roll history. Some of those who have bought into the vision need to measure or authenticate the level of purity and dedication to revolutionary action. Although a level of sincerity was present in several members of the band, the number one concern for all, unapologetically, was to become rock stars. A common belief in the power of music was something all shared, but that was difficult to translate in terms of action and dedication to social change. Eventually, such pressures pushed the band away from John Sinclair and from the White Panther Party.

Coming back to Chapter One, it focuses in part on the confounding nature of creation in the media age, especially through Gitlin's work on media framing. Here the polysemic nature of intent versus appearance presents great problems. The band, like other groups perhaps considered more a part of the "New Left" by some purists, was cutting its teeth in terms of figuring out media use and manipulation. Like these groups, the instigators of this manipulation could be in awe of and disappointed by levels of media framing. Their participation in the media could create a sense of romantic rebellion as well as negative sensationalism of very small groups with loud voices.

Chapter Five, "Guns and Guitars: Revolutionary Style and Substance?," examines the career of the band in terms of how much it was seen in a revolutionary potential as an accessible product of usable rebellion. Interestingly, the band, for all of its political baggage, addressed political issues only in certain songs. More prevalent was an overwhelming sense of hedonism: traditional fare for rock music by this time. This chapter looks to the other "revolutionary" potentialities of the band and its career. Critics and other musicians commonly cite the group as a powerful influence in the development of both punk and heavy metal (two more musical forms that continued the formalized tradition of spaces of usable rebellion). What, then, made the MC5's music and its message a revolutionary one for other artists and audiences?

The MC5 understood the importance of performance. Numerous areas of "performance" including the music itself, onstage antics, and media propaganda were utilized to present and sell the image and reputation of the band. These arenas of performance presented representations of rawness and rebellion to a sometimes-believing, sometimes-suspect audience. Here the message would be conveyed. But as with the Yippies, the call to revolution could only equal a call, with no absolute response possible. Still, it took many along for the ride, including the government, and cultural critics like Norman Mailer. The band's focus on intensity of performance and spectacle seemed to begin numerous fires, but without a lasting, cohesive narration through the process.

Such levels of performance, along with the media assault orchestrated by Trans-Love Energies and the White Panther Party, created an image that no one involved in the band or the WPP was ready or able to comprehend. Thrust into the national spotlight of both popular culture and government surveillance, the myth of the MC5 quickly eclipsed any single actor, confounding those who thought they were at the controls. In essence, authorship was lost, as the 5 and the WPP became usable public texts to be embraced or merely cast aside. To return to a recurring theme, framing models create a method from which to examine this confusion of possibilities and, ultimately in terms of political change, the group's failure.

Chapter Six, "Managing the Legacy of the Sound and the Fervor," focuses on providing a postscript to the MC5/WPP story on personal, musical, social, and political levels. The fracturing of the group depended on and reflected these issues poignantly. The lasting influence of the group as a musical and potentially political text is still hotly debated. What did this all mean and how much can we learn from the life of a band now in the annals of musical and countercultural history?

At a personal level, the band succumbed to numerous problems. Drug use, conflicts among band members about direction, lasting criticism over their authenticity as musical rebels, and continued difficulties arising from their WPP connection all followed the group. Like it or not, members of the band, the Sinclairs, and Plamondon were to be marked by the WPP association for decades to come. The chapter measures these lasting influences on the individuals that were at the center of this experiment with music and social change.

The continued influence of the band musically is also an area of concern. As movements like punk and heavy metal found their way into the popular vernacular, one can see a continuation of aggressive, loud and politically influenced music. This is not to say that the MC5 is solely responsible for this. But the MC5/WPP relationship has maintained a centrality with bands from the Sex Pistols to Rage Against the Machine and Sonic Youth.

Also of note is the WPP's relationship to other groups considered part of the New Left or the counterculture. Again, many would dispute the mixture of the popular with the political, but it is incredibly apparent that many similarities existed in how the MC5/WPP dealt with the downfall of this movement. The MC5/WPP will thus be measured against this backdrop of the social and political milieu of the early to mid–1970s, as a generation tried to make sense of and measure the "revolution," wherever the parameters lay.

Chapter Seven, "Up Against the Wall: Music's Place in Revolution," then takes the lessons of the MC5 case study and looks to larger applications, exploring the realities and shortcomings of music's place in dissent and social change movements. The case study does not aim to extend itself into universals concerning this interaction, but instead examines the potentialities of music's role in social and political change through the success and failures of the MC5. The case study acts as a measure for the applicability and reality of mass media frames, potentially constituting a tool for said programs of change. Stanley Aronowitz's *The Death and Rebirth of American Radicalism* contends that there are two countercultures. The political and the cultural will occupy a central place as the lesson of the MC5's career points to a blurring of these neat lines. Yet, as a tool in itself, one can see an inherent weakness in terms of reception and use. Because of the complex interactions of media frames, group members, management, WPP community members, audiences and critics, the music could not stand on its own in terms of enacting a lasting program of social change and development.

Never, before or since, has the line between political and cultural life been as blurred as it was with the MC5. Sex, drugs and rock and roll became a call for revolution in the streets that was heard and feared by some and embraced by others. Music, as Christopher Small contends in *Musicking: The Meanings of Performing and Listening*, is a daily, human process through which we create identity and find social location. Music plays an important part in creating ideology and social norms. A complete separation between culture and politics, therefore, is a problematic notion.

Numerous wiretaps, a federal prison or two, and thousands of albums later, the MC5 myth grows. It is time to look past the myth and instead to the realities and perspectives of its participants, and weigh these against critical thought and perspectives on the power of media, and the power of music in social change and development. Single producers quickly lost their voices in the creation of the MC5/WPP relationship. No single author was able to cement its specific vision. The point of reception, especially in viewing the MC5 through media frames, whether viewed by audiences, critics, or the government, is where meaning was or is created. It is also indicative of the levels of investment that can come with popular culture texts, no matter how much one may write them off.

Far from a top-down method of ideological control, the potentialities were actively negotiated among numerous interests, benefiting from a sense of usable rebellion. In an era of equally contentious political and social times, music (the renewable resource that it is) continues the tradition of supplying audiences and fans with a place to rebel and openly take part in collective dissent. The immense success of Green Day's politically charged album *American Idiot*, along with albums from Neil Young to the Dixie Chicks, proves that the public is listening to voices of dissent within the music industry. Perhaps by examining a group that dealt with the problematic borders of commercialism and dissent, we can be provided some insight into the role of music in revolutions of all sizes to come.

CHAPTER ONE

Fighting in the Streets: Understanding the Undercurrent of Rebellion in Rock

In many ways the career of the MC5 can best be described as an experiment in power. This not only refers to the band's hard-driving sound, but also to its role as a countercultural force that tested the parameters of rebellion, as the band sought to create broad social and political change. The group was at the forefront of the White Panther Party (WPP), whose Manifesto and "Ten Point Program" challenged the foundations of American political, economic, and cultural life. These brought the band to the attention of local, state and federal authorities. For these authorities, the band became a symbol of a threatening, amorphous youth rebellion. For other observers, the band represented either the promise or the failure of music as a tool of social change.

Through their music, the members of the MC5 consciously articulated the meaning of rebellion in the youthful expression of rock. Although rebellion had been associated with rock from its very inception, the connection was implicit, rather than an explicit program of social change. From its beginning following World War II, rock had been an instrument of youth resistance and rebellion to the social mores of the 1950s and 1960s, but it was also embedded in a market system that reinforced social hierarchies. The MC5 also faced this contradiction of art versus commerce as its members openly fostered a sense of usable rebellion already located, to some degree, in the history of rock.

"Usable rebellion" refers to the inherent rebellious nature of rock that has both allowed producers and consumers to partake in rebelling in a safe spot that can be secured for the price of a concert ticket, t-shirt or album. However, this space is owned by dominant power structures and major corporate interests, who make immense profits from selling rock as both a social and economic practice. "Usable rebellion" is a process promised by and contained within rock, in which participants including audiences, artists, and critics use music to differing extents to actively question the world around them. This rebellion is no more directed than Marlon Brando's response in *The Wild One* of "Watcha got?" to the pressing question of the film, "What are you rebelling against?" This foundational and often times generic ethos of rebellion in rock can be momentary, or lasting and subversive, or reinforcing of the dominant power structures on which it depends for its distribution and reception. Despite this fluidity, some kind of reification of identity through questioning and challenge takes place for those investing themselves. Rebellion is alive in rock because through it the music maintains its freshness. The viability of rebellion is debated, showing itself in discussions of authenticity and "selling out," youth culture, sexuality and, in some cases such as that of the MC5, politics.

This is the process that was tested through the MC5's association with the White Panther Party. Here rock's constant, but often broadly articulated sense of challenge and subversion upon which it had been depended, was given a public testing ground with the MC5 and the White Panther Party. Though the WPP was not intended by its creators to be a formal, revolutionary political party, the band found itself at the center of foundational concerns about how far rock music could really go in mobilizing dissent, and how much a product of popular culture could mean to its audience.

Because the MC5's members were highly conscious of the contradiction between rebellion and consumption, they are an interesting lens through which to view the meaning of rock in the late 1960s and early 1970s. By mobilizing the powers and energies of subversion associated with rock from its birth, the band and the WPP were able to test the social and political possibilities of music. The Party and the MC5 also raised questions about the role of capitalism by harnessing this subversive energy within rock, as had been done successfully since the 1950s. Because of their dependence on a major record label, a contentious debate ensued among their critics, who wondered if such expressions of dissent could be valid when contained within the same system of capital it supposedly sought to destroy.

The long-standing debate among musicians and critics concerning the social possibilities of music, caught between commerce and authenticity, is the focus of this chapter. A historical perspective on rock's ties to a market system gives us perspective about the music's power in challenging conceptions of social identity and about its ability to create moral panic. The history of rock also demonstrates how this rebellion was successfully sold to youth, including the members of MC5 and other important figures in the life of the band and the White Panther Party, such as Minister of Information and countercultural guru John Sinclair. The chapter will also examine the role of authenticity in the debate about the viability of rebellion in rock. Authenticity, especially in relationship to major corporate interests, still elicits debate as to the role of bands and rock in shaping a challenge to dominant structures like capitalism. Notions of purity and degeneration in the face of capital have often been tied to discussions of the lineage and place of rock in society.

The MC5 could not escape this criticism, even as it articulated its version of youth rebellion. Along with its cohort the WPP and members of the surrounding youth community in Michigan, the MC5 became an experiment in semiotic and sonic warfare, challenging local, state and national authorities while attempting to inspire countercultural values in audiences. Contingents of that audience and some critics viewed the MC5's political music as a meaningless marketing ploy. Between these polarities, social locations were dynamically challenged and reified by the band and its listeners.

The Revolution Will Be Televised, Recorded and Appearing at a Venue Near You

Changes in the music industry and in media technologies in the postwar period allowed for the widespread introduction of rock. The breakdown of the monopoly created by the American Society of Composers, Authors and Publishers (ASCAP), the introduction of television and the transistor radio, and the successful creation and marketing of the 33⅓ and 45 RPM record allowed for a recontextualization of music in everyday life. With more venues for music and the opening of the music publishing and recording industries, more music was needed. Here the independent record companies came into play. Such labels as Sun Records and Atlantic began to provide artists with a less centralized recording and distribution system. Geoffrey

Hull chronicles this watershed in the recording industry in the post-war period when "rock and roll jolted record sales into ever higher gear," which resulted in "rising profits" and an increasingly formalized distribution system (Hull 71, 2). Compared to album sales of $189 million in 1950, the rise of rock and targeting of the newly anointed "teenage audience" pushed total album sales in 1960 up to $600 million dollars (Hull 2). Hull discusses how "mom and pop operations" benefited initially from this economic boom, in effect marking a breakdown of the major recording interests' oligopoly. This economic shift to the independent labels reached a pinnacle in 1958 when their recordings represented an astounding 76 percent of singles on the music charts (Hull 29). These market developments and a new generation of consumers in the mass media age caused upheaval in the music industry. A generational rift was developing because of the introduction of new technologies and the creation of the "teenager" as a cultural identity. The independent labels could exploit this rift in their marketing strategies.

Now able to compete on a national scale for radio play, the independent labels could sell to a large, upcoming niche market, the baby-boomer generation, now anointed by market interests as "teenagers." This youth market had extra spending cash, supported by a Gross National Product which rose from $200 billion to $360 billion between 1940 and 1954 (Szatmary 23). This niche market ultimately made rock a successful multi-media phenomenon.

Because of economic, technological, and social change, the recording industry made rebellion a central dimension of rock's success, a message delivered through film, television, radio, and record sales. Robert Albrecht, in *Mediating the Muse*, explains that the newborn genre was difficult to contain, especially semiotically: "The staid performances of swing bands — musicians in tuxedos sitting behind monogrammed shields and waiting for their turn to blow a few notes — would have hardly made for good television. But rock 'n' roll was different. Here was youth, action, and unbridled excitement. Taking their cues from the flamboyant performances of rhythm and blues musicians, the artists of rock 'n' roll whirled and whined, screamed and jumped across the stage and into the American living room" (159).

He further points out that especially with new development of the visual turn in society brought on by the vast success of television, rock was a new and semiotically fascinating form. Rock effectively made the image as important as the message.

If rock could be considered a revolution, the revolution was most certainly televised. Rock harnessed the potentiality of a multi-mediated world. Performers like Elvis Presley, who gyrated his hips to the beat, or Jerry Lee Lewis, who pounded the piano with various appendages, encouraged a new perspective on popular music especially aimed at the emerging buying power of the baby-boomer generation. David Szatmary sees this visual turn as intrinsically linking rock with moral panic over youth rebellion. Elvis's television appearances highlight this connection. Szatmary writes: "By the end of the year [1956] Ed Sullivan, who earlier had condemned Presley as 'unfit for a family audience' agreed to pay the new rock star $50,000 for three appearances on his show, one of the most popular television programs in America at the time" (51). Reactions to the performances were harshly received in numerous circles, including the American clergy. Much of this focus remained on the signifiers of Presley's sexuality and his violation of racial taboos. Rev. William Shannon wrote in the *Catholic Sun*: "Presley and his voodoo of frustration and defiance have become symbols in our country, and we are sorry to come upon Ed Sullivan in the role of promoter. Your Catholic viewers, Mr. Sullivan, are angry." Evangelist Billy Graham, who had not seen Elvis, commented that he was "not sure I'd want my children to see" him (Szatmary 55).

It seems the creation of this post-war notion of "teenager" allowed both successful marketing as well as a successful othering/exoticizing of youth. Presley, as rock's gyrating poster child, represented to the American populace the face of this newly established music. Combined with the raucous sounds of the music, Presley, as a visual embodiment of rock, provided a neatly packaged target for those fearing rock's influence on youth and on American culture.

Szatmary argues that the image of the rebellious youth, as embodied in Elvis Presley, was also personified in major films of the time that stoked moral panic. *Rebel Without a Cause* (1955), *The Wild One* (1953), and especially *Blackboard Jungle* (1955) were the most important of these. *Blackboard Jungle* was the first motion picture to use a rock song, "Rock Around the Clock" by Bill Haley and the Comets. If the "image of the alienated, shiftless, and violent street tough in [a] black leather jacket who dangled a cigarette from his lips" (Szatzmary, 54) was becoming a symbol of collective fear, then rock was the soundtrack for these icons of rebellion, with jazz in many circles now taking on a stodgy traditionalism or at least aura of formality.

Fears of juvenile delinquency were joined by fears of deviance and of a disintegration of class, race, and gender hierarchies as rock became more and more popular. Michael Ochs, a leading musical archivist, states: "If rock was the soundtrack to our lives, then these soundtrack albums had to encapsulate any of the teen topics of interest — automobiles, assorted fads, sexuality, rebellion, escape, energy, life, death, loneliness, dancing and dating" (Ochs 10). Rock seemed to ignore all notions of societal taboo, an image conveyed through the mass media. Boundaries of race were of special interest as rock unashamedly brought together black and white audiences and artists in a time of racial upheaval. In an examination of popular music in Britain, Dick Bradley contends that racial boundaries especially created a joyous space of subversion for youth: "It is the nature of the developing codal fusion over the years that young people should be more familiar with, and less puzzled or affronted by, the Afro-American elements in popular music than their parents and elders. This fact gave rock 'n' roll, rhythm 'n' blues, soul and Beat their shock value and their capacity to act as a 'secret for the young'" (121). Violations of class hierarchies also played a role. Primarily in the United Kingdom, but also somewhere in the American mindset, youth culture and rock were a fundamental challenge to class boundaries. Most labels and artists popularized in the early life of rock reflected a southern, working-class aesthetic: challenging dominant conceptions of what performing artists should sound and look like. A youth audience was attracted to a working class aesthetic, and found its way to this aesthetic through middle-class consumption. "This leisure style was created through the appropriation of consumption goods — clothes, haircuts, records, etc...." (Bradley 85). Hence, youth could purchase a challenge to racial, sexual and class lines simply by investing in a record.

Youth, rock and rebellion fused into a semiotic system, to which many people reacted with hostility. Frank Sinatra stated that rock was "sung, played, and written for the most part by cretinous goons, and by means of its almost imbecilic reiteration and sly, lewd, in plain fact dirty, lyrics it manages to be the martial music of every sideburned delinquent on the face of the Earth" (quoted in Altschuler 6). In their tell-all investigative report of youth culture at the time, *U.S.A. Confidential*, journalists Lait and Mortimer wrote,

> With tom-toms and hot jive and ritualistic orgies of erotic dancing, weed smoking and mass mania, with African jungle background. Many music shops

purvey dope; assignations are made in them. White girls are recruited for colored lovers.... We know that many of the platter-spinners are hopheads. Many others are Reds, left-wingers or hecklers of social convention.... Through disc jockeys, kids get to know colored and other musicians; they frequent places the radio oracle plug, which is done with design ... to hook juves [juveniles] and guarantee a new generation subservient to the Mafia [quoted in Altshuler 6].

One can see in *Confidential* a book hoping to provide some insight to a generation of perplexed parents, who looked to youth/rock culture as a supposedly bordered and segmented area where societal ideologies and values were openly questioned. Here was a "folk devil" that could be a focal point of societal fears of testing dominant, white, patriarchal ideologies. As Dick Hebdige stated in his now-classic study of subculture, *Subculture: The Meaning of Style*, "The struggle between different discourses, different definitions and meanings within ideology is therefore always, at the same time, a struggle with signification: a struggle for possession of the sign which extends to even the most mundane areas of everyday life." He continues that stylistic transformations "go 'against nature' interrupting the process of 'normalization.' As such, they are gestures, movements towards a speech which offends the 'silent majority,' which challenges the principles of unity and cohesion, which contradicts the myth of consensus" (18).

Rock was a tool of style and signification. The economic challenge put forth by smaller companies against the dominant record industry, the confrontation of new technology in the hands of a new generation, the challenge to social boundaries, and issues of sexuality provided the wellspring of value-laden arguments for and against the rise of rock. These ideological challenges allowed a fundamental identity for rock to emerge that would operate as a framework from which validity and authenticity would be gauged even as rock became an international industry.

Making Sense of the Rebellion

Obviously, the complex history of rock and rebellion warrants much more attention than is allowed in these last few pages. However, the MC5 provides a concrete case for seeing these forces in action. Against this backdrop, the band emerged in the 1960s to push the foundations of rock's relationship with rebellion.

This helped to sell the music to a youthful audience, which would or would not buy into the inherent values already discussed. This was a successful strategy as the '60s music industry saw a reclamation of the charts by major corporate interests as rock proved to be a continuing revenue producer. Vanilla-ized (a term used by Pat Boone) rock proved that the music, the visuals and the messages of the music, whether a potential corrupting force or not, could sell. The White Panther Party's call for "rock, roll, dope and fucking in the streets" was a promise to partake in the full potential of youthful rebellion seemingly evidenced in rock's early life prior to the Boone era. It was a realization of the power of youth and its ties to the music. Tied to political and culturally revolutionary ideals, it also tested how authentically one could be tied to rebellion and how much one was beholden to corporate hegemony.

As a test case, the MC5 provoked debate among music critics, artists, audiences and scholars over the conflict between authenticity and commerce in popular music. The 1950s set the standards for expectations and ideas about the role of rock. Conceptions of authenticity can be traced to the conflict between rebellion and commerce, as audiences rejected or accepted the music as a cultural form. As Bradley postulates, "Teenagers and young adults engaged in 'resistant' and rebellious cultural practices, which defined them as youth or sub-cultural members. And music-use, including music-making, was tied up with the process from the beginning" (99). The more potentiality to reaffirm a rebellious youthful identity through products of rock, the more authentic the product is seen by those taking part. The economic, technological, social, and cultural questions issued at rock's inception would set the standards as to what "real" and "authentic" rock music and culture would be. The further the music supposedly steps away from youth and rebellion, the more it is suspect and the more degeneration is seen from an ideal level of purity.

Rebellion, Degeneration and the Dance of Authenticity

In "Concerning the Progress of Rock & Roll," Michael Jarrett examines what he calls "conventionalization" as the "foundational myth of popular music" (167). He describes the tendency for rhetoric of "degeneration" to enter our understanding of popular music in everyday life (168). Jarrett contends rock lives with an ethos where "bad (commercial) things [happening] to 'authentic' music is sufficient to generate the real/fake distinction that has become musical common sense. It creates a consumer who understands the history of rock as a series of authentic moments that deteriorated into conventionalized moments, transforming the music into a field of 'commercial' imitations of some real thing, and it prompts histories organized around the proper names of acknowledged innovators" (172). Degeneration is at the "heart of all distinctions that attempt to delineate a boundary between the authentic and the commercial, in whatever guise that may take: rock vs. pop, black vs. white, modern vs. postmodern, art vs. commerce" (168).

Usable rebellion is a practical tool from which to gauge the alleged process of degeneration. Rock's foundational ethos is one that depends on supposedly authentic challenges to the status quo, predominately from a youthful perspective. Deviation from a youthful voice or deviations from themes or styles connoting dissent are seen as suspect. In *Rock 'Til You Drop*, John Strausbaugh sermonizes, "*Rock is youth music*. It is best played by young people, for young people, in a setting that is specifically exclusionary of their parents and anyone their parents' age. It is music of youthful energies, youthful rebellion, youthful anxieties and anger" (2). He continues later, in reference to older artists' continuing commercial appeal, "Colostomy rock is not rebellion, it's the antithesis of rebellion: it's nostalgia." He adds, "And nostalgia is the death of rock. We were supposed to die before we got old. Now look at us. Woo woo, Mick! Rock on Bruce!"(10).

One can stand witness here to the pervasive and continuing power of youth rebellion in evaluating the authenticity of rock music. Strausbaugh warns us about nostalgia as being the death knell of rock. Nostalgia is, in effect, creating a stasis in a music that depends on its ability to subvert societal lethargy. Strausbaugh, far from being alone, is part of a much larger societal perception that true rock is not nostalgic, but always cutting edge. The reality of thinking that nostalgia is a death knell to a youthful and dissident music is to partake in a form of nostalgia itself; Strausbaugh is pining for a form that supposedly once was in an idealistic time and place.

One of Strausbaugh's targets is the MC5. His discussion of the band reflects his broader contention that "the movers and shakers of rock were always exemplars of hip capitalism, paying empty lip service to social change and 'the revolution' but always far more focused on money and glamour and personal gratification" (15). The connection of degeneration and rebellion is further evident in the author's claim that "it wasn't just the hairlines that had receded: the political commitment, the anger, the will to change that permeated the original music was also gone" (14). His examination of the MC5, The Jefferson Airplane and the Fugs rates the subjects based upon an absolute, regenerating, fundamental nostalgia of youthful rebellion that Strausbaugh has said is the essential foundation of rock. The key issue for Strausbaugh is the authenticity of the band's political commitment. In the end his judgment is: "They made the media look and sound more cool, the better to market their products and their advertisers" (91).

The debate over authenticity and rebellion, as witnessed in Jarrett's and Strausbaugh's history of rock, is a lasting one. Simon Frith matter-of-factly states that rock is a commercial form of music. It, like jazz, the pre-eminent music of rebellion before rock, has grown and developed within the realities of an economy based on capital (54). What has been successfully sold to audiences, he says, is the aesthetic of rebellion. "The 1950s images of rebellion without a cause merged with the 1960s images of rebellion with a cause" (64). This was not done, though, without understanding the needs of the audiences. Rock from its inception has had to understand its audiences and offer them products that met their needs as youth living in the post-war American landscape. "Rock," explains Frith, "is a capitalist industry and not a folk form, but its most successful products do, somehow, express and reflect its audience's concerns" (62).

The hope is that music can be a usable counter-hegemonic force in which social dissatisfaction can be communicated and control and mastery in one's life can be reasserted against the pressures of the outside world (Frith 262). Frith states that one of the reasons audiences and critics can ignore the realities of capital is that audiences in the end are able to control and manipulate these texts within their individual lives. In Frith's perspective the interplay of collective and personal needs even within the context of commercialization can still be seen as potentially revolutionary or authentic in terms of audiences' uses of the music itself (264–265). In the end, this search for authenticity gave listeners a "sense of freedom that was, simultaneously, a sense of rootlessness and estrangement" (262).

Steve Chapple and Reebee Garofalo criticize Frith for putting too much emphasis on audience reception. Instead, the authors see economics as the determining factor that shapes the ability of audiences to receive and make use of music. To Chapple and Garofalo this very notion of rebellion is less a real tool that audiences use within the music and is more an autonomous zone that can be reached through consumption: "The creation of a teen culture was clearly not a revolutionary development, but it did distance young people to a certain degree from home and church, and provided a wedge from which inchoate rebellion could be expressed, if not yet directed *at* the establishment" (298). As rock evolved as a musical form associated with youth, it also evolved as a commercial product. "The position of the music as an increasingly important cultural commodity within a consumer economy weakened any of the explicit antimaterialist content of the music. The sexually liberating aspects of the music remained, but sexual liberation itself was integrated into the system as an important selling tool for the 'liberated' economy" (300).

Chapple and Garofalo continue that sexuality was not the only topic subsumed by a march to capital: "And finally, the music became separated from the political ferment that had provided it with its critical edge (as well as themes and images) in the earlier sixties. Musicians and the creative personnel within the music industry were integrated into an entertainment business now firmly part of the American corporate structure" (300). The music was so effective in reaching youth that it was hegemonically subsumed into the capitalist world (306, 308). The authors consider this a cooptation in which audiences had very little input and which is demonstrative of the top-down realities of power and control in modern musical practice. They emphasize production over Frith's focus on consumption. However, Chapple and Garofalo as well as Frith are aware of the important role of capital no matter how much they believe that audiences construct their own meanings. Both believe that audiences possess the ability to claim music as their own, even as a tool for constructing social locations and identities.

To counteract this top-down view of the masses and their relationship to authenticity, one can look at the work of Keith Negus to explain the complex intricacies of the industry in its relationship to the concept of authenticity. Instead of industry corrupting culture or exploiting dissent and rebellion, Negus asserts that a false binary is created between the industry and the people. Instead, the music industry is built upon larger cultural values and beliefs, which are essentially shared. Rather than a threatening edifice, the industry is composed of ordinary people who represent the larger culture. Through these participants, the industry both shapes and is shaped by the culture around it. (18, 30).

The creation of genres in Negus's perspective is a way for corporate cultures to make sense of and to market musical forms. It is a resource for audiences to make sense of and consume authenticity and to partake in potential subversion in ideology or action. Genres are "unstable intersections of music industry and media fans and audience cultures, musician networks and broader social collectives informed by distinct features of solidarity and social identity" (174). Genres allow us to affirm our beliefs and wants concerning who we are and what our past is. They provide comfort in an immense and unfamiliar world. They also allow the pleasure of breaking these boundaries. In the case of the MC5 it was possible to feel a sense of community with the band and its embracing of rock as a subversive form, as well as enjoy the group's progressive and heavy sound that challenged genre conventions of the time when compared to the dominant San Francisco psychedelic acts of the time like Jefferson Airplane.

The use-value of genres and their ability to help us discern and consume popular culture is accomplished through successfully communicating authentic feelings and experiences for audiences. The discussion of authenticity that Negus, Frith and Chapple and Garofalo engage in revolves around notions of purity. A key aspect of rock's purity is how much audiences, artists and the industry create a music that is able to overcome corporate influence. Like country and jazz, which are often understood as authentic forms emerging organically from distinct communities, rock is a music that supposedly found its voice and its power in an emerging youth culture with its own mores. The music is then, as Jarrett explains, held to romantic notions of purity and eventual degeneration. The ability or inability to overcome corporate power and to harness the energy of the music is the focus of these conversations, demonstrating the lasting influence of usable rebellion for those taking part in it.

The MC5 was heralded both as a revolutionary force and as a corporate sham because of its abilities to draw in these foundational elements of the discussion of rebellion and hence, authenticity. This was done in an incredibly intense and combative fashion through its association with the White Panther Party. The affection and disregard the band garnered often centered on this ability to test these parameters of rebellion within rock. A question loomed over its short association with the WPP about what happens when a band attempts to cash this promissory note of usable rebellion in rock. In this autonomous zone one could rebel with a cause, politically, culturally or musically through the music of the band. One could also rebel without a cause, partaking in rock's favorite hedonistic topics of sex, drugs or just momentary release when encountering the music. One could also miss any significant insight, or be overtly dismissive of this generic rebellion as something that could be written off as meaningless drivel.

The MC5 and those associated with the band soon were to learn that these modes of reception could not be controlled among their fans, among the authorities or even among themselves. The foundational themes and promises of rebellion that rock offered to the public en masse would find a spectrum of interpretations and uses. Included were impassioned concerns about authentic youthful expression, the identity it provided to those invested, and rock's possible effect on national security and the American way of life. Discussion of commerce versus authenticity would be of central concern during the tumultuous years of protest and dissent in the late '60s and early '70s and beyond. How much of a role music could play, if any, in the charge for social change highlighted these continuing debates about rock and what it has come to mean to the many that have heavily invested in it in order to develop their own levels of social location and belonging.

Media Frames and Their Importance in Measuring the MC5's Authenticity

Adding to this discussion of authenticity within music scholarship, the notion of media framing can provide a larger perspective for what Negus describes as the complexity of interactions among audiences, musicians and producers. The MC5 and its association with the White Panther Party elicited a great deal of press, from coverage in *Time* to Sinclair's self-generated press in the *Fifth Estate* and the *Ann Arbor Sun*. These media outlets negotiated the meaning of the band and its mission and provided a picture of the group for a general audience. While the band and the party didn't necessarily have a coherent plan for self-representation, these media frames could control that representation through vilification or romanticization. The use of familiar cultural frames by media outlets provided audiences with a limited understanding of what was happening with the youth in their communities. The following chapters will demonstrate that the MC5 is a textbook example of this process. Frames used for the band were many in number: it was a spearhead for a cultural revolution, a way for ordinary young men to become rock stars and pick up girls, a hollow sham to sell records, a radical threat to national security, a recruiter for the counterculture, a major or minor influence in rock, and an exploiter of mass media outlets for purposes of dissent and the promotion of anarchism.

The historical influence of the media on social movements and their role in the creation of ideology is important in garnering a full understanding of usable rebellion. This power was especially visible in the 1960s as the mainstream media's presentation of Vietnam and the anti-war movement helped sway public opinion. Todd Gitlin, a former head of Students for a Democratic Society (SDS) and a significant name in the New Left, sees the media as the primary means for the promotion of dominant ideologies (2). He explains that social movements such as SDS were made digestible and consumable through the mainstream media's use of framing techniques. This created simple binaries. As they were represented in the media, the MC5 and the White Panther Party often reflect a binary in representation, making them either authentic dissidents or dismissible fakes. In essence, the media influence social movements much more than their leaders would like to admit. Mainstream media demand spectacle, and group leaders gain visibility for their causes through spectacle. The band and the White Panther Party well understood the importance of spectacle and media assault, but like Gitlin could not, frustratingly enough, control their representations within the media completely. Sinclair especially attempted to present the band and the WPP in numerous independent newspapers as revolutionary heroes. These did little for the general populace when compared to features in major publications like *Time* and *Newsweek*.

Like Gitlin, Benford and Snow have been leaders in the development of framing theory when looking at political and social movements. According to the two, frames "help to render events or occurrences meaningful and thereby function to organize experience and guide action" (Benford and Snow, 614). The association of rock with youth and rebellion was accomplished primarily through what Benford and Snow have called "adversarial," "prognostic," and "motivational" framing. The first of these frames, "adversarial," seeks to "delineate the boundaries between 'good' and 'evil' and construct movement protagonists and antagonists" (616). Commentaries in major press sources used this framing technique to pit rock and its audience against the prevailing social mores. The MC5 was held to adversarial frames, especially from critics of the band like Lester Bangs, who looked at the group as a countercultural fake that hid a sub-par musical vision. He wrote in *Rolling Stone* about "the hype, the thick overlay of teenage revolution and total-energy-thing which conceals these scrap yard vistas" (Bangs 34).

Other public commentaries used "prognostic framing," issuing a "plan of attack" which put cultural activists and supporters of the music "on the defensive, at least temporarily" (Benford and Snow 617). As a potential force of change, rock successfully subsumed youthful rebellion in reaction to the moral condemnation that it received from prominent public figures like Billy Graham and Frank Sinatra. The audience and industry were able to create successful spaces of rebellion set apart from condemnation, and in a Hebdigian sense, take pleasure in a display of otherness. The MC5 found itself on the defensive from prognostic frames. In *Disc and Music Echo*, Caroline Boucher wrote, "The reaction they achieve is such that the MC5 seem to have earned the reputation of being the enfants terribles of America." Guitarist Wayne Kramer complained that the MC5's reputation in the press had compromised its ability to deal with promoters. He told Boucher: "Promoters think we're going to go out and burn things. They hear incredible rumors of how we kill cats on stage and run around stark naked." The band's propaganda machine, put together by Sinclair, used prognostic frames to combat its detractors and to progressively quell such negative press that might compromise their ability to be heard.[1]

Finally, through "motivational framing" the media can provide "socially constructed vocabularies" that give audiences "compelling accounts for engaging in collective action and for sustaining their participation" (Benford and Snow 617). Thus, the band's promoter, John Sinclair, produced an aggressive propaganda campaign in various publications. Through descriptions of the band's performances and run-ins with the police, Sinclair created an image of members of the band as heroic countercultural heroes capable of bringing about the revolution single-handedly. Such a call evoked the possibility of a mystical experience that Frith described as the "magic that can set you free," as "some mythical adolescent moment against which all subsequent rock moments can be judged" (Frith 176).

These framing models are effective in understanding cultural movements such as the creation of youth culture in the post-war period and the construction and maintenance of rock, a form that the New Left looked to for insight and inspiration. The question might be asked as well, is rock inherently political because of its ability to recycle the presence of youth and rebellion? With the great popularity of rock, could social change actually be effected whether or not the music is perceived as organic or authentic? This is the question that the MC5 can help us understand, since they blurred the lines identified by scholars like Stanley Aronowitz, who contend that there "were really two countercultures in the '60s." First, there was "the political counterculture, those who engaged in the politics of direct democracy, who organized traditional constituencies in new ways." Secondly, were "the cultural radicals, the artists, writers, and, above all, the rock musicians and their audience, for whom the erotic revolution was a political movement" (36). Is it possible that music can ignite social change in political and cultural spheres? How powerful are audiences and bands when used as symbiotic organizing forces?

The association of rebellion and youth in rock were realities for individual members of the MC5 and the WPP. Within the band and among community members, some looked to music as an organizing force for dissent and action. Others found music as a stepping stone for financial gain and notoriety through a sonic assault on audiences. Often, these perspectives were mixed. Often as well, the band and the Party were surprised at how effective they could be at using the recording industry and the mainstream media to attract interest, both positive and negative. Audiences, musicians, producers, politicians and the federal government were all interested in this experiment and what it was to mean. For whatever political, commercial or "authentically" created aims, the band was to enter into a continuing debate on rock and rebellion, remaining a cornerstone of this debate for decades to come.

CHAPTER TWO

Revolution on Your Headphones: Charting Social Location in the Rise of the MC5 and the White Panther Party

The interaction between popular culture and society is a constant struggle. From the studies of Theodore Adorno and the Frankfurt School, which viewed popular culture as a potential opiate for the masses, to Michel De Certeau, who claimed that the masses were able make their own worlds with the raw materials popular culture provided, the dividing lines between popular and other forms of culture are a contested domain. The rise of the MC5 and the revolutionary entity for which its members acted as organizers, the White Panther Party, are demonstrative of this complex interplay. In the collective, a musical act and a radical movement were intertwined.

Popular culture of the time was infused with national and local politics and a desire for social change as represented in the MC5's music. The Party was meant to be a channel through which the band and associated individuals like John Sinclair, a leader of various housing collectives and workshops around the City of Detroit, could express frustrations with the political and social realities of their time (Sinclair 1972, 104). The MC5 acted as the Party's sonic organizing force, bringing together audiences through music.

This chapter examines how this political and musical force came into being, and why the MC5 and the White Panther Party would become potent organizations in popular music and radical politics. Here they created a space for usable rebellion, a concept arising from the advent of rock, and especially from the "British Invasion." Interviews conducted with band members, although reflecting disparate notions of what the MC5 and the White Panther Party symbiosis was supposed to mean and how far it was hoping to go, have revealed that a commonality existed among the band's five young men. They shared a common background and upbringing in post-war Detroit. This background fundamentally shaped how individual members came to view the world around them. The interviews reveal that numerous factors came into play in the formation of the band and the party. Civil rights, anti-war sentiment, technological innovations, drug use and musical influences combined to make a product unique to its time and context. These numerous concerns were linked through the band's affinity for rock as a potential site for rebellious discourse and action. The band actively consumed rock and eventually found a voice of rebellion in rock that called for both hedonism and revolution.

That rebellion was deeply tied to the local milieu of Detroit. The group and the Party had their roots in the late 1960s Detroit landscape and eventually would find fame there, where such nationally pertinent issues like race and class would confront members through immediate experience. The message would spread and many voices would join in shaping the WPP. At its pinnacle the WPP possessed 30–40 core members, hundreds of local participants and chapters across the country and in Europe (Kramer 2006).

This assessment focuses on perspectives from surviving band members about the life of the White Panther Party and its relationship to the career trajectory of the MC5. These perspectives, although featured in some studies of the band, are often overlooked in favor of the perspective of John Sinclair, who is more often viewed as the overwhelming force behind the development of the WPP.[1] Responsibility for the WPP's life and work was spread among more individuals than has been popularly thought.

The following pages examine the views of the surviving band members. Of course time has probably reframed their views. One concern about looking back at this time is that the surviving players may want to manage their legacies. The band and those associated with it still have not come to a common understanding of the life and legacy of the MC5's and the WPP's political and revolutionary associations. Media frames and reactions from critics over time have presented the band as either an organic hope or an exploitative ruse, which eventually pushed the individuals involved into different realms of intent and hope and folded back into their self-perception. Nevertheless, the invaluable interviews upon which this chapter are based are surprisingly telling, frank and aware of folly when discussing political and revolutionary thought. The MC5's members hope to build their legacy on music. The revolution is the theme that often has gotten in the way of this hope.

Detroit Divided: Race and Class and Their Effect on a Music Movement

Before beginning to understand the contextual framework of the late 1960s and early 1970s in Detroit, we have to reach back several decades to grasp fully the intensity of racial and class discord in everyday life. These social realities would come to shape significantly the political and musical expression of the band. Detroit historian Richard Thomas describes the first four decades in the twentieth century as a period of massive change in Detroit's population because of immigration and migration. According to Thomas, arguably the most significant influence on Detroit was the "Great Migration" of African-Americans hoping for opportunities in the industrial sector (24–25).

The demand for cheap labor during World War I and numerous immigration restrictions during the first three decades of the twentieth century pushed poor southerners, African Americans, North, where they were heavily recruited by the industrial sector until the beginning of the Depression. Because of automakers' need for labor, Henry Ford promised the famous five dollars a day to potential laborers in the hope of bringing numerous demographics into the auto industry. The needs of the automobile industry coupled with demands from the iron, rail, and steel industries, pushed Detroit to become one of, if not the most, popular destinations for migrating southerners (25–26). In his *The Origins of the Urban Crisis*, Thomas J. Sugrue explains that the increased demand for labor extended through the Second World War and into the decades following (Sugrue 23). Union and civil rights organizations further opened the labor market to the black populace in this "Second Great Migration," lasting from 1940 to 1970. Especially during the war, unions "opened many locals to black membership, lobbied for civil rights protection, and supported the hiring of black workers." The United Auto Workers in the early 1940s "forged an alliance with black churches and reform organizations, especially the NAACP," that firmly established new levels of representation in the workplace and in the community for African-Americans of the time (26).

Due to this rapid expansion of the black community, the population of the Detroit area changed significantly. The influx of African Americans was seen as a threat to white industrial workers as the black population more than doubled in the 1940s from 149,119 to 300,506. This change created a thriving environment for racial and class conflict due to competition for jobs and changing ethnic and racial lines in neighborhoods. These issues were exacerbated by the eventual economic downturns that plagued the city through periods of recession and deindustrialization. White homeowners and real estate agents created and reinforced strict racial covenants in Detroit neighborhoods (Sugrue 44). A de facto racial segregation persisted due to these covenants and other racial practices in the real estate market.

The members of the MC5, Wayne Kramer, Fred "Sonic" Smith, Rob Tyner, Dennis "Machine Gun" Thompson and Michael Davis, grew up in this climate, the greater Detroit metropolitan area, mostly Lincoln Park. The economic and social realities of the area would be a constant influence on the future band members, as living in Lincoln Park (also referred to as living "down river") "was to reside within the spitting distance of Rouge, the Ford Motor Company's central plant" (Simmons and Nelson 15). The neighborhood was one dominated by white and black autoworkers. Guitarist Fred Smith's parents, who were white natives of West Virginia, reflected the labor migration, moving to Detroit in the hope of finding better opportunities for employment (Simmons and Nelson 16).

Drummer Dennis Thompson sees this industrial background as one that greatly influenced his music. By the time the MC5 coalesced in the mid- to late 1960s, Detroit had already been home to numerous musicians who reflected the intrinsically connected working class aesthetic of rock. These included John Lee Hooker, Highland Park native Bill Haley and many others (Barnett 9–11). David Carson sees such figures as Haley and Hooker leading to a Detroit sound that embraced their identification with a "tough, gritty, unheralded metropolis." *Time* magazine linked the urban industrial scene to the music, describing a "real Detroit sound, pulsating with the belch of its smokestacks and the beat of its machinery" (Carson ix). Suzanne Smith, in her *Dancing in the Streets: Motown and the Cultural Politics of Detroit*, asserts that Berry Gordy, who founded the infamous Motown label, actually used his familiarity with the production methods of companies like

Ford. "Gordy implemented his idea of inserting the assembly-line process into the recording studio as soon as he founded Motown" by creating divisions of labor throughout the company including creation, management, quality control and marketing (14). Thompson claims that the working class background weighed heavily on the members of the band's musical careers not only in their teenage years, playing in various groups, but also in their rise to fame and the radical politics of their later years:

> Detroit is a working class, blue collar and at that time, primarily an industrial town. These are people who were coming from parents who worked in factories. These were children that were coming from working class backgrounds ... where it's a tough life. It's a hard life ... you work your 40 or 60 hour week and it's boom, bang, crash and you're turning out parts in a factory and basically you work very hard. You have callused fingers and dirty fingernails ... so you want music that is pretty rough-and-tumble [Thompson 2005].

This rough-and-tumble aesthetic, born from industrial realities of life in urban Detroit, provided the MC5, along with numerous other acts, a distinct musical voice representing America's "Arsenal of Democracy." This ascription, from Thompson, makes sense in reference to artists like Hooker and Hank Ballard, as well as figures like Gordy, who had put in time at Detroit assembly lines or in Detroit steel factories before making music their careers (Carson 1–9, 35). Machine operatives and crafts workers overwhelmingly dominated the face of employment opportunities and positions in the Detroit area in the 1950 and 1970 census data (Farley 72). These jobs were fragile and highly susceptible to economic downturns due to the reliance on manufacturing. For example in 1950, 56 percent of all auto manufacturing in the United States was in Michigan. A decade later this number would fall to 40 percent, drastically affecting the Detroit and Michigan area workforces (Sugrue 128). Less a romantic ideal and more an everyday fact of life, the working-class lifestyle would be hard to escape in post-war Detroit and was reflected in the cultural creations of the time, including in the process of musical creation.[2]

Lead singer Rob Tyner saw not only Detroit as an influence, but also the realities of living in Lincoln Park, a distinct experience. "Due to the fact that we lived in white suburban America, there were certain things that were your options: You could either go into the military or go into school. Or you could go into the factory. Or you could go into rock 'n' roll, which is what I chose to do. Through meeting Wayne Kramer and Fred Smith, I decided on that" (Sheppard 9). Here, the reality of living in one of Detroit's southern suburbs created a distinct vision of the metropolitan area. Industrial realities connected these communities as they housed workers and participants in the "Arsenal of Democracy," creating both unique community experiences as well as a shared burden or benefit of being connected to Detroit.

The industrial realities of Detroit in the post-war period had a much more far-reaching influence than creating a working class background for its citizens. Drastic population change had direct impacts on the streets and in the neighborhoods of the Detroit area in heightening racial tension and strife among the city's inhabitants. By 1970, the black populace would dominate, with more than 600,428 citizens (45 percent of the total populace of Detroit) (Sugrue 23). The massive shift in population in just a few decades forced Detroiters to deal with an active challenge to established economic and racial lines.

Thomas Sugrue points to a lack of public housing and complete segregation as among the most contentious issues in Detroit. Rental agents, bankers and landlords looked to the black migration as a threat to real estate investments. The result of these racist views was the creation of black enclaves in the inner city (39–44). As of 1947, of the 545,000 open housing units, only 47,000 were available to black tenants (Sugrue 43). Here as well, class and racial conflict would emerge from the territorializing of space, eventually resulting in "white flight" when these racist practices were challenged at local and national levels, in the courts and on the streets. Detroit's enclaves represented the harsh economic realities for blacks in the community, who were disproportionately relegated to the lowest-paying jobs on the economic ladder (99). The continuing discrimination and rising frustration of the community came to the national public eye in the 1967 riot/rebellion. In 1942, *Life Magazine* had featured a headline that stated, "Detroit Is Dynamite," adding, "It can either blow up Hitler or blow up the U.S." This was a reference to the prominent racial tensions present in workplaces, and neighborhoods with numerous strikes because of race and street skirmishes over residential racial lines (Sugrue 29). The greater Detroit area, by the end of 1967, had fulfilled the prophecy in both ways.

By 1967, with this background in tow, the MC5 had been performing in Detroit area venues mostly as a cover band, playing the work of such artists as Chuck Berry, The Yardbirds and other such influential acts of the time. The MC5 had trouble finding a niche in the local music scene. Tyner explains:

> We had done pretty much everything that we could do in terms of playing like the teen scene. And we tried in the bars, and we're like, "this is never going to happen," you know? I mean we knew we had to do something else, so we became involved with people down on the Wayne State University campus, and hanging out down there and partying down there a lot. And we played a couple of important gigs for the movers and shakers in the community and got kind of a little reputation going [Sheppard 9].

Tyner is speaking roughly of a time ranging from 1964 to 1966, when band members had become familiar with local countercultural leader John Sinclair through his Detroit Artists' Workshop (DAW), a meeting place for artists, poets and musicians attracted to the "beat" movement. Near Wayne State University, John and Leni Sinclair (along with others like jazz trumpeter Charles Moore) founded the Detroit Artists Workshop, which functioned as a commune for Detroit area artists from 1964 to 1966. The workshop became a multi-purpose organization: producing concerts, founding and maintaining a printing press, and displaying art (Simmons and Nelson 22–23). Sinclair recalls, "The purpose of the Artist's Workshop was to find a place where we could practice, do our art, poetry, music painting, photography, just with people in the neighborhood around Wayne State. They were more or less on the cutting edge of things culturally, politically, artistically..." (Larabee and Bartkowiak 129). The collective released several manifestos calling not so much for a fevered revolution as for an utopian world based on the joy of creation. Sinclair wrote, "The real revolution that is forthcoming will be a bloodless one.... Armies of artists and students are invading slum neighborhoods.... Should the revolution succeed it will usher in a golden age of arts and letters" (English and Sinclair).

At this point, the small community of artists purposefully avoided becoming a politically charged revolutionary organization and instead focused on artistic communication through music, poetry, art and other mediums, to create a space where members could live outside of the dominant culture. John Sinclair explains in my interview with him, "The Artist Workshop basically was trying to model ourselves on the Beatnik movement." He continues, "The whole Artist Workshop thing was to try to find a place where we could live outside of this [the dominant culture]. Somewhere, where we could do what we wanted and no one would bother us.... So we got our own

Charles Moore, Archie Shepp and David Sempliner (one of the first members of the Detroit Artists Workshop) in Ann Arbor in 1965 (courtesy Leni Sinclair).

place ... there weren't bars or social settings or any kind of thing where what we were doing was welcome in Detroit in '64. So we rented a house and put on our own concerts, readings and we had our own place ... classes ... all aimed at people who felt the way we did pretty much, or wanted to feel that way" (Sinclair 2005).

Band members would often hang around the commune participating in artistic creation and drug use. Tyner says that some of the resistance to the music was, in his eyes, due to the realities of race at the time. "We had extensive experience in playing the blues and extensive experience with black music on a bunch of different levels. Because, don't forget, we grew up in a town that was dominated by Motown, and we know about the racism from the other side because we were the wrong color trying to make it in a town where black music was extremely popular." He continues, "So I think that part of the energy in the MC5 came from our frustration at not having an outlet for our talents that would be on the level that we could relate to" (Sheppard 10). Here, Tyner's perspective is that of a suburban outsider, even though he was a resident of the greater Detroit area. The band members' background would be more immediately challenged as they became part of the Detroit music community, thanks in many ways to their relationship to the DAW. Issues of race and class would become even more intense as they came closer to the city center.

The collective would morph into what would be called the "Trans-Love Energies," (TLE) reflecting less the beatnik/jazz-flavored inspiration of the DAW, and more the growing influence of rock and the rise of LSD use (Simmons and Nelson 25–26). Sinclair observed that the collective began to change when core members began to take acid: "Then we wanted to change the world. It wasn't enough to change it for ourselves. We wanted everyone to see that it could be very different.... So we got this kind of evangelical feel to turn people on to the idea of changing things and making it more beautiful and harmonious." (Sinclair 2005). He says, "We saw the Artist's Workshop as a bohemian embassy, and Trans-Love Energy was more of a psychedelic embassy. We created little service programs for people in our neighborhood" (Larabee and Bartkowiak 130). Some of this initial energy was applied to the struggle for civil rights for African-Americans, a struggle that members of TLE could see on the streets of Detroit in everyday life, as well as in riots. Part of the change in the group was reflected in the growing importance of the MC5, whose developing brand of furiously loud and uproarious rock would allow a connecting point between the artistic aspirations of the group and its growing sense of radicalism, which would lead to the formation of the WPP. Members of the MC5 began to spend time taking in the beatnik culture and aura of the workshop. Within this phase of the community's development, the MC5 would find its revolutionary voice as the TLE continued to formalize into a collective.

The growth in perspective of the Trans-Love Energies collective, including the MC5, can be attributed to the increasing use of LSD and marijuana and the influence of rock, in what was formerly a jazz-loving group. New poetry, music and other arts provided a way for members to confront culturally the realities of Detroit and their nation. This environment fostered the members of the band, who began to hang out at the DAW, increasingly as it morphed into Trans-Love Energies.

The TLE would be marked, according to Leni Sinclair (who would also become official photographer for the band), by the increased presence of John Sinclair and his eventual agreement to manage the MC5. TLE would continue on the heels of the DAW, publishing, encouraging art creation and exhibition, and organizing concerts and light shows. The Grande Ballroom became a hotbed of activity for the group, with the MC5 becoming the Grande's house band. Although starting as a local band covering R&B standards and early Rolling Stones songs, the MC5 became, through an increasing fascination with feedback and amplification, a band regarded for its inimitable brand of sonic distortion and energetic performances. As a central figure in the artistic community, Sinclair would be a valuable connection to the MC5, not only in his centrality within the organization but also as a voice in such publications of the time as the anarchistic *Fifth Estate*.

In Trans-Love Energies, the band and Sinclair forged a mutual partnership. The band sought out Sinclair as a means to enlarge area audiences, and Sinclair looked to the band as a cultural force to enrich his commune. He found the energy and vigor of the band, which by this time had begun to experiment with distortion and noise in the hopes of emulating jazz improvisation, intriguing. The collective's publications, including poems, posters, and newsletters as well as cultural events such as poetry readings and art showings, would take on a decidedly more anti-authoritarian spirit, in the hopes of exacerbating social tensions. Most importantly, its members criticized the government's handling of the civil rights struggle and the Vietnam War, and thus increasingly drew the attention of the police and other authorities.

The power wielded by Detroit authorities created frustration within the commune and band, a frustration that was entrenched when the collective became a target of police harassment. TLE's experience in Detroit in 1967 was shaped by the increased paranoia of a police state that had dealt with significant racial strife and riots. The group, defining itself as subversive of the capitalist-centric social world around it and openly advocating drug use, was a target for police torment. The Belle Isle "Love-In," an event organized by the collective, highlighted this mounting tension between the community and authorities. Tensions spilled over between participants and the watchful local police. This resulted in a violent riot involving a significant number of police, who, according to guitarist Wayne Kramer, "galloped toward the running people and clubbed them like they were playing polo" (Carson 115–16).

Jeff Hale describes the times. "A significant turning point in the history of Detroit was the bloody rioting of July 24–31, 1967, the worst in America's history. Following the riots, the attitudes of Detroit police moved farther to the right, reflecting the growing siege mentality prevalent among many of the city's whites" (Hale). Tyner says that among others, this event was a flashpoint for the White Panther Party:

> All these things are the reasons for the Black Panthers and the White Panthers. The authority [sic] was so arrogant that they would call the National Guard out on our own people. Call out our National Guard on our own people right here in this country. There were so many bad things that happened during the riots, and not just from the rioters' standpoint. The police and the National Guard were just out of control.... The Michigan National Guard, at that point, was issued live ammunition and they had real guns. There were snipers all over the place. And it was like really bad, man — the worst I ever saw. My parents demanded that we leave the city. And we were really worried about trying to get out. So we got in the car and we were driving down the freeway. And you could see on either side of the freeway whole neighborhoods going up, and individual houses burning. It was really, really bad. People got shot and killed [Sheppard 11–12].

Tyner wasn't alone in feeling the impact of the riot. TLE felt the impact of this event immediately, with Kramer tellingly being accosted by the police during the riots, allegedly as a sniper (Kramer 2005). The event pointed out to the collective that the authorities were becoming increasingly repressive in their targeting of TLE and other voices of dissent. Such events as the Love-In, along with increasing police and municipal harassment — especially after the 1967 riot — pushed TLE and the MC5 to move to nearby Ann Arbor.

The highlight of the group's harassment, and the immediate cause for moving to Ann Arbor, was when the TLE was firebombed. Who actually carried out these bombings, according to Kramer, is a bit of a mystery due to a lack of police follow-up. Kramer believes the responsibility could rest with one of the following groups: "The Detroit Police Department (A covert political ops unit). Right wing zealots like the John Birch Society and Breakthrough. The federal government (FBI operation Cointel or White House covert operators)" (Kramer 2006). Whoever the culprit, the immediate threat to their safety pushed Sinclair and commune members to move to the significantly quieter college town forty-some miles down the road.

Here, the band and Sinclair came together to found the White Panther

The MC5 and Social Change

The MC5 and Friends, 1967 (courtesy Leni Sinclair).

Party, issuing the White Panther Statement on November 1, 1968. The group, reacting to the harsh class and racial realities of the riot and of their lives in Detroit advocated complete support of the Black Panther Party, and sought the end of the capitalist state (Sinclair 1972, 105). Like the Black Panther Party, the White Panther Party and its official house band, the MC5, reflected an end of innocence in the civil rights era. Notions of non-violent protest did not seem to match the violent retribution waged upon the African-American community. The party looked to the brooding machismo of the Black Panthers as a model from which to confront the world. "Knowing the power of symbols in the abstract world of Americans we have taken the White Panther as our mark to symbolize our strength and arrogance and to demonstrate the commitment to the program of the Black Panther Party as well as to our own — indeed, the two programs are just part of the same whole" (Sinclair 1972, 105).

From their new base in Ann Arbor, the White Panthers, still focused on the Detroit area and on Michigan, but looked to on a national level in terms of agitation, attempted to bring forth change through their increasing national attention through the press and the music industry. Sinclair points to the band's participation at the Chicago "Festival of Life" during the 1968 Democratic Convention as a turning point when he realized he had to look beyond Detroit. "In order to preserve and develop our culture we couldn't ignore the political aspect of the Revolution anymore" (1972, 44). Detroit and Chicago seemed like microcosms of the national crisis that gripped the United States in the late 1960s to involved members, pointing to a need that extended beyond one or two problematic urban centers.

The American Ruse: National Issues and the Rise of the MC5

As the band developed into a nationally recognized act it was affected by political and social tensions at a national and international level. Drug culture, technological innovation, the Vietnam War, and the civil rights movement all played a role in shaping the White Panther Party and the MC5. The band's voice was unique to its time, and the issues that affected its members in the past were still very much with them, as I discovered in my interviews with Michael Davis, Wayne Kramer and Dennis Thompson, as well in other interviews that give some insight into what the missing voices in this study, like Tyner's, had to say about it.

Michael Davis, bass player for the MC5, argues that "the MC5 was in a sense a victim of circumstance ... a product of a time that is unique ... a time that will never happen again. The situation, the conditions will never happen again, never in a million years." Within these circumstances, he says, "something called dissent came out from under the covers" (Davis 2005). This dissent against the status quo came in numerous forms. Rob Tyner explained in an interview with Doug Sheppard in 1988 the circumstances that Davis spoke of in his interview with me. For Tyner, the influence of this voice of dissent was an immediate one.

> So anyway, we ourselves started playing at the Grande [Ballroom] and stuff, and we began to be like deeper and deeper into the counterculture. All along, when the MC5 was building up their following, there was this tremendous turbulence in the country. I don't think you can really understand what I mean. Culturally speaking, there was a lot of people experimenting with a whole bunch of stuff—like there was a crack-down on drugs, and everybody's

mom was flipped out because there were all these individual family wars going on all over the country. You know, like fathers against kids, and mothers against kids, and kids against their parents — and mix that up with drugs and rock 'n' roll and sex and it was a very, very turbulent time; we came right out of it. We all had our individual wars and we came out of that whole situation not only affected by it, but trying to affect it with our music [Sheppard 10].

The interviewees in this study frequently reflected on their involvement in civil rights and later a concern with Women's Rights. When asked about the influences that led to the band stepping up its anti-authoritarian message, Dennis Thompson said, "One was the minority movement ... which was very powerful at the time. Female rights too ... women still hadn't achieved any kind of equality whatsoever. It was still a pretty chauvinistic society and a pretty racist society and a pretty bigoted society" (2005).

This statement, in regards at least to perspectives on feminism, is a comment of hindsight that developed for band members and Sinclair over time. The band's articulation of support for the black power movement was at times matched by its machismo. As Kramer reflected in our interview, "We were sexist pigs and we masqueraded under the guise of revolution our total hedonism" (Kramer 2005). Although gender equality was something that eventually became a topic of importance for the interviewees, the realities of WPP rhetoric and the MC5's music did not reflect anything close to such recognition of the women's movement.

The WPP showed its support for civil rights and more specifically the black power movement through the MC5's career, such as the band's use of Al White's "Motor City is Burning" on the band's first album, *Kick Out the Jams*. The interviews point to young men who were acutely aware of the realities of the struggle for African-American rights across the nation and who could relate the struggle to their experiences in Detroit. As guitarist Wayne Kramer remembers,

The White Panther became an expression of our frustration with the injustice that we saw in the world around us, that we saw even in our own city in our own police department, in our own neighborhoods. It was a way to get it out to express ourselves where we would use this radical language. Then we identified with the Black Panther Party. They're young, they're brave ... we like to think of ourselves as brave. They've got guns ... so we got guns. They say there needs to be a White Panther party ... we say okay ... so here we are [2005].

Kramer, like Sinclair, saw the civil rights movement as a basis for cultural revolution. In the "White Panther Statement" Sinclair writes that "the actions of the Black Panthers in America have inspired us and given us strength, as has the music of black America" (Sinclair 1972, 105). WPP propaganda maintained that rock, strongly influenced by African and African American musical forms, was the main weapon in cultural warfare. The MC5 was meant to be the musical firepower in this contentious struggle. As Thompson remembers, the cultural revolution was to "help our black brothers be accepted as an equal faction of Americans ... allowing them the opportunity for equal education and employment opportunities" (Thompson 2005). Such lofty ideals were difficult to translate and take responsibility for.

Part of the group's and the party's strategy for changing perceptions towards race and class divisions was the use of drugs, with a focus on LSD and marijuana. According to the White Panther Statement, "Our program of rock and roll, dope and fucking in the streets is a program of total freedom for everyone." It continues, "We are LSD-driven total maniacs in the universe. We will do anything we can to drive people out of their heads into their bodies" (Sinclair 1972, 104). This experimentation with drugs (especially LSD) led to the development of the Detroit Artist Workshop, in which marijuana was the drug of choice, into the Trans-Love Energy group, which depended more on the use of LSD as a consciousness-raising tool. The TLE also had a heavier concentration on rock as a cultural force, especially for Kramer and Rob Tyner and organizational leaders like Sinclair, Plamondon and Leni Sinclair (Sinclair 2005). Eventually, the White Panther Party was born in 1968 from these changing spheres of influence.

The White Panther Party and the MC5 looked to drug use as a method for breaking down social, cultural and political boundaries. "Drugs played a large, large part in people becoming more open and less xenophobic and more open to discussing among themselves the state of their lives and their nation," explains Thompson. Through sharing, drugs could potentially create a bridge for new forms of understanding: "You could sit down with a member of the Black Panther Party, smoke a joint and talk politics" (Thompson 2005). Michael Davis said that although many of the drugs were new to the group, early exposure to these influences heavily affected the band's political and social perspective, and perhaps most importantly, the music which the band made (2005). Thompson said in his interview that the band was heavily under the influence of these substances during the creation of its first album, *Kick Out the Jams*.

Drugs would continue to be a factor through the band's short life, even after it discontinued its relationship with the White Panther Party. The influence of drugs would shape the band in its early days, as well as be perhaps the most influential factor in its demise in the early 1970s. Interviews revealed that soon the band would move beyond marijuana and LSD to what the party labeled as "death drugs," including the widespread use of heroin. Several members of the band would do prison time for this, and remaining members would contend that these ghosts continued to haunt them long after the band's demise.

LSD was a significant influence for the band, beyond its mere consumption. LSD went far beyond the expectations of its developers in medical science laboratories and governmental institutions, which experimented with the drug as a possible interrogation tool. LSD was an example of the central role that developing technological innovations had on the rise of the dissident environment of in the late 1960s and early 1970s. For the band, the realities of technology reached beyond the realm of drugs. The band valued massive technological innovation in society. Prior work on the MC5 often ignores technology as a contributing factor towards the formation of the band's aesthetic. This influence would have been easily overlooked if it had not been for this series of interviews with band members, especially with Michael Davis. To him, the focus on technological innovation is a key influence that shaped the perspectives of his generation. "The key main element is this technology ... basically the number one factor. We all grew up in post World War II" (Davis 2005).

Psychotropic drugs were representative of a larger scene of potentially destructive technological innovation. The dawn of the atomic age created a measure from which the future was calculated. "The creation of the nuclear warhead ... it was a breakthrough in what human beings could do with the phenomena in which we live" (Davis 2005). This connection would be a constant reminder for Davis of the destructive potential of technological advancement in society, a factor that would come directly to the public's eye through such events as the Cuban Missile Crisis and, perhaps most importantly in terms of determining the band's and WPP's message, the Vietnam War.

Other technological advancements occurred in communications, including those that shaped the modern face of rock and the baby-boomer generation en masse. Davis comments that the transistor fundamentally "changed society." It allowed for music to become a portable electronic form not only transported by people, but by automobiles in the '50s and '60s. Another communications innovation breaking down space and time was television. "We grew up with that ... TV brought commercialization of everything! It was displayed ... we kind of became victims of media" (Davis 2005). This exposure allowed a view into the power of media and its framing abilities in terms of shaping issues of politics, commercialization and music. The new mass media technologies, as Gitlin states, "have become systems for the distribution of ideology" (2). The WPP along with other groups like the Yippies would harness this energy to develop a voice in American society. This same energy would also eventually play a part in their downfall.

This channeling into media would bring the sound of rock to homes and cars and therefore to a newly defined segment of the population, teenagers. Images and sounds of performers like Chuck Berry could be consumed daily by youth across the nation. In turn, new technologies of amplification and electric instruments could be bought by those same youth that were exposed to these products through television, radio and records. They could emulate musicians seen in the media. "You could buy an electric guitar for $125 at Sears. The better stuff like Fenders and Gibsons, were way up to about $300, but all within the reach of kids like us," said Kramer (Simmons and Nelson, 15). The widespread purchasing of electronic instruments and amplifiers among this demographic could especially be seen after the worldwide success of the Beatles and the subsequent "British Invasion" in rock and roll. To return to a theme of the first chapter, technological innovation coupled with upturns in consumption habits helped create a personal, local space of usable rebellion where rock music was performed and literally amplified.

Such diverse influences as technological development, civil rights struggles, drugs and nuclear proliferation are hard to bring under one comprehensive umbrella. Yet the interviews revealed that these diverse factors all need to be understood under the growing influence of the Vietnam War in the 1960s. Vietnam overshadowed and at the same time brought together these concerns. "The essential ... the umbrella under which all of these dynamics fell was the Vietnam War. If you dropped out of school ... you were drafted. There was definitely a personal liability. Their ass could be on the line.... They could go to some foreign jungle and die" (Thompson 2005). Drugs, anger about domestic social issues, advancements in technology both in the home and on the battlefield were channeled into the MC5's and WPP's anti-war stance, which examined the effects of the war on social, political and cultural life.

Media ensured a constant barrage of coverage and exposure to the war and these attendant issues.

> We had drugs, we had rock and roll, we had social issues that were dissatisfying, we had an emerging culture of people who were aware that things weren't quite kosher in normal life ... that the government was feeding us a crock of shit. The guys who were supposed to be our leaders, the guys we were supposed to respect were just ramming us. We knew better. All these factors came together at once ... then I met the MC5 [Davis 2005].

The White Panther Party was a way of concretely expressing resentment towards the government and powers-that-be, who were viewed as perverted monsters of enlightened thinking. The White Panthers' 10 Point Program provided a plan for the breakdown of these powers. "Number 9, Free all soldiers at once — no more conscripted armies!" and, "Number 10, Free the people from their phony 'leaders'— everyone must be a leader — freedom means free every one! All Power to the People!" (Sinclair 1972, 105).

Such reflections showcase a focus on and a relation to the rise of the New Left to varying extents by members of the group. The notion of the New Left is problematic in academic and lay circles, especially with a generation now facing questions about what its legacies will be. As Chapter Six will show, individuals within the WPP and MC5 and critics outside of the groups questioned whether such entities were part of the New Left. Much of this is focused on the debate over "cultural products" and practices versus politics as the true agents of lasting social change. For that reason, it is important to see how the New Left came into being, and examine its spectrum of usages and the parameters of debate that this book will consider when discussing the possibilities of music in social change. Reaction to Vietnam for the New Left became the de facto organizing issue, no matter how much the movement's leaders were attempting to effect a more holistic program of social change. As the comments above show, the members of the MC5/WPP were inspired for action (whatever that might be) through this umbrella issue, as were many of the participants in the New Left. The MC5 and WPP reflect the language and ethos of the New Left, no matter how unwelcome they were at the table by those trying to steer the movement. It was a movement that many in the MC5 and WPP identified with. Many would see their participation as playing a part in the New Left.

The origins of the New Left are seen in numerous lights by those making sense of the phenomenon, both inside and outside academia. Van Gosse's *Rethinking the New Left* sees the civil rights movement as the single most important spark igniting the New Left. He also sees "deep continuity between the movements of the New Left and the diverse Marxist, radical, and pacifist organizations that managed to survive during the Cold War, despite considerable repression" (6). Gosse believes that prior programs of theory and practice maintained a central role in the New Left's development and had a lasting impact.

In much the same fashion, Andrew Hunt in *The New Left Revisited* agrees that civil rights was a flashpoint for the creation of the New Left. Like Gosse, he sees a larger structure of participatory democracy being handed down to the baby boomers. "Whether or not the draftees of the *Port Huron Statement* knew it, their ideal of participatory democracy was indebted to the writings of utopian socialists such as St. Simon and Fourier, early-twentieth-century British socialists Sidney and Beatrice Webb, French syndicalist Georges Sorel, anarchist Emma Goldman, and more contemporary political thinkers such as Saul Alinsky, Dave Dellinger and Dwight McDonald" (145).

Such studies do possess the gift of hindsight. Many studies since the New Left's inception have looked at the primary causes for its rise and questioned the role of ideology. Contrary to Hunt, books about the New Left written *during* its height and downfall present a different perspective on the influence of the Old Left and ideology. In 1973, John P. Diggins wrote in his *The American Left in the Twentieth Century*, "When the Old Left intellectuals abandoned all hope of radical transformation, they tended to accept what existed as the true reality to which all human ideals must conform if they are to be realized. The New Left, innocent of the burden of historical experience, rejected this definition of reality and defiantly invoked a new sense of the possible" (18). Yet a historical linkage occurs in Diggins's mind that the Old Left, Lyrical Left, and the New Left "articulated a new historical vision, a new sense of reality and possibility that transcended the given state of things, a new consciousness of the negating ideal — that which *ought* to exist, but does not" (18). Revolution thus was fodder for the young. Never trust anyone over thirty, as they inevitably will have sold out. The 1967 edition of *The New Student Left* by Mitchell Cohen and Dennis Hale (both at the time publishers of *The Activist*) saw the New Left as "at once fluid and anarchic" (xv). Generational divide was prevalent and the old order obscured.

> We felt the time had come for students to attempt a systematic analysis of their own movement, in the words of its own partisans. Others have tried, using the values and experiences of another generation. Comparisons have been made to the thirties which tend to obscure the radically different nature of the sixties.... "Men when they age," Machiavelli reminds us, "lose their strength and energy, whilst their prudence and judgment improve; so the same things that in you appeared to them supportable and good, will of necessity, when they have grown old, seem to them insupportable and evil; and when they should blame their own judgment, they find fault with the times" [xvi].

The WPP/MC5 relationship echoed such sentiments. They looked to youthful passion as the fuel for their rock-induced insurgence. Much like the case with the band, there appears to be a vast spectrum of uses for the "New Left" as a text. Such interpretational differences continue in the literature that looks to isolate and make sense of the New Left.

For instance, Gosse isolates the rise of the New Left through a complicated intertwining of historical circumstances and influences. Gosse declares that a fundamental shift occurred from the "Old" to the "New" Left. "Crucial to our understanding of how American radicalism changed in the Cold War era is how the Old Left's central concern for the working class was replaced by a focus on ending racial oppression, militarism, and male supremacy or patriarchy. This shift away from the politics of class to a broader, more diffuse set of ideological concerns marks the distinction between Old and New Lefts" (29). He asserts that the New Left, instead of being defined by a certain identity (namely young white students), should be considered a "movement of movements" (5). Gosse sees a vast spectrum of groups that could legitimately claim membership. The further you break this down, the further it becomes problematic. "In fact, there were many countercultures overlapping with many radical movements, and when one looks at Women's and Gay Liberation, or Black, Brown, Red, and Yellow Power, it is hard to say where politics ends and culture begins" (7).

To point out the difficulties of an absolute definition of the movement, take Gosse's definition of a "movement of movements" and measure it against

John McMillian's work in *The New Left Revisited*. Here, McMillian carefully qualifies that indeed, there was an "astonishing level of fluidity between the civil rights movement and the college-based protestors of SDS, between New Left 'politicos' and countercultural hippie types, and even between the New Left and the Old Left." Still, he cautions, "It is important to draw a distinction — for the sake of both clarity and accuracy — between the New Left and what is sometimes called 'the movement'" (5).

McMillian then says that the New Left "can be defined as a loosely organized, mostly white student movement that promoted participatory democracy, crusaded for civil rights and various types of university reforms, and protested against the Vietnam War" (5). On the other side of the divide was "the movement." He says this was "a much larger constellation of social protest activity that either grew out of the New Left (e.g. gay liberation, radical feminism, and the hippie counterculture), or influenced and inspired the New Left (e.g. the civil rights and black power movements)" (McMillian 6). He cites the fact that many student groups were actively making this distinction in the time period itself.

In regard to the interviews used in this book, such a separation was not something that was ever expressed or thought of at the time. Whether they wanted to be considered part of the New Left or not, White Panther Party members did not see such dividing lines (ideological or otherwise). All were concerned and to some extent were influenced by a "movement of movements." As time went on, individual members would see themselves as part of or as distanced from the New Left. Further complicating the confusion was the critical reception outside the group. In Chapter Six we will see how the band could be viewed as the vanguard of the revolution, or as exploitative imposters. The latter fits better with McMillian's notion of a differential from the start. It seems, though, that many then and today through the eyes of history have pragmatically blurred these lines.

The extent of WPP members' loyalty to this larger vision of social change and whether they saw themselves as part of the New Left would be a point of confusion for the band, its audience, and its circle of influence. After the initial period of the party's formation, the band felt that politics and the media's representation of the band as the "vanguard of the revolution" was actively working against its success as a band.

This mirrored the experience of other groups identified with the New Left where the media were active in shaping groups into palatable, essentialized forms that for Gitlin and SDS stripped them of the original intent. Gitlin states that this media framing process had real ramifications, robbing the SDS, for example, of its meaning and representation. "I worked in a movement and watched it construed as something quite other than what I thought it was" (17). It is important, though, to keep in mind that many groups in the New Left helped to shape their own legacies, via the sometimes overzealous use of the media. The MC5 and WPP shaped their image in many ways themselves. While they realized they were partly to blame, they were still shocked at the power of the media and the various interpretations of their messages. The creation of the band's image by band members and the media is the focus of the following chapters.

The Music Is What It Was About: Assembling the Sound

Interviews with the band and with WPP leaders reveal that the musical life of the group is hard to reconstruct amid the political reputation the band has collected over the past 40 years. Although interviews today express a certain frustration with the politics overshadowing the music, for some of those involved, like Kramer, music was politics. Music was the means by which one could make sense of and comment on the world. Yet simply listening to the band's catalog demonstrates that lyrically, this did not result in an overwhelming amount of revolutionary rhetoric. But in context of the musical world of the time, revolution could be more a sonic than a lyrical undertaking. This section examines the musical background of the group, and to start to discern its lasting musical influence. The MC5 sound, as many critics would attest, has heavily influenced punk, metal and beyond, through such things as the use of distortion and dissonance, and through the attitude the band projected.

The diversity of influences cited by the band crisscrosses genre boundaries and sounds. The MC5 seems to have been a sponge for countless influences that ranged from the Motown sound of its members' adolescence to such legendary names in experimental jazz as Sun Ra. One of these early influences was the socially challenging, yet sonically non-threatening sound of the '50s and '60s folk revival, "White guys got a hold of that stuff [Alan Lomax collections of 'folk' music] and they said we can do this too but our guitars are made by Gibson and Harmony! You started having this folk music that was talking shit. You had lame kind of pop folk music people like Peter, Paul and Mary, which I happen to like, and the Kingston Trio. Even to us straight guys, and I was a straight guy back then, that was radical, that was like you were hip. It was intellectual at some level, it wasn't little Pretty Peggy March ... it was Pete Seeger" (Michael Davis 2005). The artists that Davis speaks of here were sonically simple in terms of instruments and musical tools (like chord progressions), and instead utilized lyrics as the political delivery system. The MC5 set itself in opposition to this softer sound in music. Yet the notion of rebellion through musical forms was one that identified the band, even if it was not through lyrics. In essence, the MC5 was more known for its sense of sonic rebellion and anarchy, which came through heavy use of distortion, pulsating rhythms and improvisation, called by members "High Energy" music. This sound and this carefully constructed rebellious *music* was more important than the modest use of political rhetoric on the MC5's three albums, *Kick Out the Jams, Back in the U.S.A.,* and *High Time.*

These early influences make sense in terms of the rise of dissent that Davis spoke of. These children of the Detroit area heard the challenge to the status quo lifestyle in these supposedly "traditional" forms. From this folk revival came an icon to the MC5, and, one could say, to a generation, Bob Dylan. "Then he came along, Bob. Bob spoke to us like no one had ever spoken ... he spoke for us. He sang these same songs, traditional songs, only the way he sang 'em ... it was like he was there. Like you were there, like it was you singing it ... because he couldn't sing!" recalls Davis (2005). Absorbing the poignancy of Dylan's message and delivery, Davis developed a broader perspective on the power and viability of music in uniting large and diverse audiences.

However, a more important influence on the MC5 was the British Invasion, a musical movement that looked to American R&B and blues performers for its sound. The MC5 had encountered the music of some of the artists that inspired the invasion, like Muddy Waters, John Lee Hooker and Chuck Berry. Groups like the Beatles, the Rolling Stones, the Who, and the Yardbirds furthered these influences on the band through their reinterpretation of these artists. Davis recollects that at the invitation of Tyner, he checked out the MC5 in its early stages before deciding that he would join it. "Well, when I got there, I saw a small group of musicians on a small stage, dressed in similar clothes [band outfits], playing an assortment of classic R&B tunes, mixed with pop hits of the day" (Davis "Diary of a Mad Dog"). Soon Davis would join the MC5, as its members began to broaden their repertoire with more British interpretations of an American R&B aesthetic. In an interview with John Sinclair in *Jazz & Pop*, this marriage of American R&B and the British Invasion is laid out.

> JOHN SINCLAIR: That seems to be the difference, actually, with the new rock & roll, and that's the thing that seems to me to be the most exciting thing about the new rock, outside of the music itself—that the rock players are becoming musicians now, not just plastic guitar-strummers, bouncers up and downers....
> ROBIN TYNER: Well, yeah, I mean what else are you gonna do? I'm sure everybody who digs rock and roll will thank the British cats very much, because they're the ones who started the whole thing, they made us into musicians....
> JOHN SINCLAIR: Right. And the British got theirs from the R&B people over here.
> ROBIN TYNER: They just turned it around, they just gave it the emphasis ... I think they ought to be rewarded for that.
> JOHN SINCLAIR: Well, they have been ... (Laughter) [Sinclair "Rob Tyner Interview"].

Tyner recalls in a later interview, "I liked a lot of the obscure early English stuff. I liked the Pretty Things and the early Kinks and early Who and early Beatles, you know? I wasn't really much of a real heavy-duty Beatles fan, but I could appreciate what they were all about. I liked the Stones probably a lot better. The actual influences of the MC5 were probably mostly based on the Rolling Stones" (Sheppard 9). Influence on the band by the British invasion artists was a central theme in such vintage interviews as well as later ones (including my own). But who most influenced the band was up for grabs among those involved.

According to Thompson, the Yardbirds were of special interest because "they were an experimental band" (Thompson 2005). This fascination with Yardbirds-like experimentation was mentioned in some of the earliest press about the MC5. In a February 1967 feature in the *Detroit Free Press* "Teen Beat" column, the group called it "the new music." Kramer said in the piece, "Now we are taking rock and roll further than it's been taken before. We're into playing sound as a method of expression." The article later refers to the Yardbirds and The Who as "leading exponents of the new sound" (Alterman 3B).

For the MC5's inspiration, Thompson indicates that the British Invasion was balanced by domestic talents including artists from Detroit. "From that point and time you could add James Brown, Otis Redding Wilson Pickett, and the Motown influence because we lived here in Detroit ... so we had a lot of great music on the radio all of the time"(Thompson 2005). One can hear many borrowings on the band's first album, *Kick Out the Jams*, where heavy guitar distortion meets pulsating rhythms, hype men, lasting grooves, shuffle rhythms and Rob Tyner's pleading and emotive vocal delivery. Music, like politics and social issues, was a mix of international, national and local forms. This combination of musical forms would be further complicated as the band established a relationship with John Sinclair.

Because of his affiliations with publications like *The Fifth Estate*, and *Downbeat Magazine*, Sinclair was known in the musical community as an authority on jazz and its appreciation in the Detroit area.[3] Through the DAW and Sinclair's record collection, the MC5 was exposed to jazz that would provide new fuel for its musical fire. Such names as Archie Shepp, Pharoah Sanders, Sun Ra and John Coltrane further diversified the band's approach to music and to the possibility of experimentation with dissonance, feedback and improvisation. Davis recollects an initial kinship with Tyner that was formed through the appreciation of jazz and the beat movement as well. "He grew up around the same era as me, and so was also impressed by the world of bebop, jazz, poetry, and the forms of intellectual beatism that marked the beginning of rebellious popular culture." He says that later the band expanded its appreciation of jazz when working with Sinclair. "Within a year, we were all living together, doing our version of communal life, and being absorbed into the world of jazz and political upheaval of the late '60s" (Davis "Diary of a Mad Dog").

Soon, through their association with Sinclair, band members became regulars at Detroit's Grande Ballroom. Owned by a former schoolteacher, Russ Gibb, the Grande Ballroom was the center of the Detroit music scene, with rock acts trying to find a presence in a town that was dominated by Berry Gordy Jr.'s internationally celebrated Motown label. The MC5 would share the stage with nationally known acts like the Grateful Dead and Big Brother and the Holding Company as well as up-and-coming local acts like Bob Seger, Iggy and the Stooges (from Ann Arbor) and Ted Nugent's Amboy Dukes. Thompson reflects, "We had a concept and that concept was called High Energy. We looked at it as music that had a lot of strength, music that had a depth of emotion, music that was powerful not just in terms of volume, but it was powerful emotionally and powerful dynamically. Once exposed to the free jazz movement, then we understood that sound itself was the palette" (Thompson 2005). Thompson says that most of the groups playing the Grande were "keyed into" this concept of High Energy music. He attributes this to the working class realities of Detroit (Thompson 2005). Tyner explains the aesthetic:

> I mean people should be at ease so that they don't have any body hang-ups, so they can sit down and just let their bodies disintegrate and just be a mind and an ear, you know, just listen to the music. Feel the music and watch it. But any more man, I ... if the audience doesn't vibrate back, if you don't play for an audience that vibrate strongly, then it'll either do one of two things to us; it'll either turn us off completely, or it'll shoot us to heights to try and make the audience vibrate back — because we know they can vibrate, we felt them vibrate before [Sinclair "Rob Tyner interview"].

The scene and this attributed High Energy aesthetic eventually commanded some attention from the major record companies. The MC5 was one of the first bands from the area signed to major record labels from this period, along with Iggy and the Stooges. Numerous other performers like Alice Cooper, Ted Nugent, Bob Seger and The Rationals would all eventually find a national audience, thanks to being part of the vibrant Detroit scene of the late '60s.

The popularity of these Detroit acts would challenge the dominance of the San Francisco and Los Angeles psychedelic scenes of the same period; with acts like the Jefferson Airplane, the Grateful Dead, Santana and the Byrds becoming major forces in popular music. Thompson believes that the two scenes possessed many similarities like the psychedelic drug use and anti-war activity, but Detroit was fundamentally different. He points out that the West Coast scene was heavily influenced by Timothy Leary's mantra of "Tune in, turn on, drop out" and pacifism to create an alternative way of life. "Mommy and daddy were paying their way through school while they were developing these ideas, this alternative reality" (Thompson 2005).

The youth in the Detroit scene, due to economic realities, faced a more immediate threat of forced conscription, because they were unlikely to be able to pay for college and receive a draft deferment. As John Willis has found, more affluent men were able to obtain deferments during the Vietnam War (564). The annual per capita incomes of Detroit and San Francisco during this time period show significant differences in wages and earnings potentials (U.S. Census).

The MC5's particular local context and gritty hostility created problems for companies trying to make the band an attractive commodity, especially compared to San Francisco acts. For instance, Elektra Records dropped the band after its first album for "unprofessional conduct" when the band used the company's trademark on an ad that read "Fuck Hudson's." Hudson's had refused to sell the album because of the profanities used in the song, "Kick Out the Jams Motherfuckers" (Holzman). Elektra found the band difficult to control and the WPP disheartening when viewed as more than a gimmick, a Midwestern oddity suited only to sell records.

Such realities of geographical placement closely mirror the experience of the so-called "prairie radicals" in the New Left who represented a "broadening of SDS to include more students from working class backgrounds." The economic reality of Midwestern labor and life, according to activist Robert Pardun, "gave us reason to hope that we could build a broad-based movement that would change America" (Pardun 2). Prairie radicals were offering another narrative of the anti-war movement and interpretation of the New Left that extended beyond the campuses of Columbia or Berkeley. Pardun identifies these prairie radicals as possessing a unique geographical and hence different ideological construction of America. Here, "no one read the *New York Times*" and "conformity was the norm" (113). A sense of moral outrage over racism and the Vietnam War pulled these individuals from their Midwestern sensibilities, a new stance that could alienate them from their communities and families (113). This was also true for the MC5. As a product of the Midwest, the band also seemed an oddity in the larger scene of music and politics.

Conclusion

Michael Davis's comment that the MC5 was "a victim of circumstance and a product of a time that is unique" astutely points out the necessity of understanding the forces that shape cultural forms. It is within these forces that one can begin to understand voices that have an immense potential power to reach audiences through their creations and provide a space to express social location and dislocation. The cultural force that has been most studied in relation to Detroit, Motown Records, can perhaps teach us a valuable lesson about the rise of the Detroit rock scene of the late 1960s. Smith states, "Motown's relationship to the cultural politics of Detroit teaches that place matters — the productive social, cultural, economic, and political change emerges from distinct communities" (259). Because of the political history and myths that grew from the MC5's short career, the complex intersection between politics and popular culture must be understood. The realities of band members' lives in the Detroit area, their affiliation with Trans-Love Energies and the White Panther Party, and their engagement with national and international issues allows a glimpse into an experiment that, as Davis states, "is its own entity now." Because the music and image of the band have survived nearly four decades, influencing acts as diverse as the Sex Pistols to Rage Against the Machine, the process of understanding can be confusing.[4] The following chapters will demonstrate the historical influence of media frames that have reified the WPP and the MC5 as political radicals. The band members have expressed disappointment and frustration with the media, repressive state apparatuses, and the music industry, which they see diverting and marginalizing their musical legacy.

The history of the band allows some contextual insight into a product of popular culture that still generates debate among fans, critics and even band members themselves. Cultural creations cannot escape the cultures from which they were formed. To discern the legacy and influence of a band such as the MC5, a legacy invested in by generations of fans and musicians, is to discover not a specific, linear history, but instead to open a forum for discussion of meaning and investment in a band that was musically and politically larger than the sum of its parts. Public memory has played a key role in the maintenance of this legacy. The MC5's past is rife with polysemic messages for its audiences and for band members themselves. This chapter has laid the ground work for understanding of the MC5's career and legacy within popular culture and within the political history of this country. This complicated legacy will be further explored in the coming chapters.

CHAPTER THREE

Motor City Burning: Rock and Rebellion in the WPP and the MC5

In the late 1960s, the United States was a country in turmoil. The Vietnam War and the movement for civil rights had generated numerous voices of discontent against the status quo. This fight found its way onto the streets, as organizations like the Students for a Democratic Society and the Black Panthers advocated various programs for social change, some peaceful, some more direct. In Detroit, amidst race riots and startling discrepancies in wealth between those who worked in industry and those who owned it, the seeds were sown for the eventual rise of the White Panther Party and its official house band and propaganda machine to the masses, the MC5.

Calling for the complete dismantling of the forms of power and control in the United States, the White Panther Party focused its efforts on and through the power of popular culture and media. John Sinclair, his wife Leni, members of the MC5 and other local revolutionary figures in Detroit and Ann Arbor founded the organization to antagonize the dominant U.S. culture and to generate social change. The *White Panther Statement,* which was issued by the fledgling group in November 1968, states, "Our program is cultural revolution through a total assault on the culture, which makes us use every tool, every energy and any media we can get our collective hands on. We take our program with us everywhere we go and use any means necessary to expose people to it" (1968, 1). This musically led ambush of noise and rhetoric looked to exploit media forms, and situate the message of the White Panthers into every home, primarily through young people.

This chapter will begin with the perspectives of organization leaders and members apart from members of the MC5, such as John Sinclair, Pun Plamondon and Leni Sinclair on the WPP and the MC5's role in the group. These organizational voices have been the de facto sources of interest in regards to the political life of the MC5 since the band began to garner notoriety. With a heavy focus in the popular press directed towards John Sinclair, as *the* determinate political power, the voices of the band members are often pushed to the margins by the press as belonging to secondary actors along for the ride. This is actually a frustration of John Sinclair — notions of Sinclair acting as the svengali, taking the band members on a ride. Perspectives of the band members themselves will be the focus of chapters following, demonstrating that this notion is false. To understand how usable rebellion played into the image of the MC5, we need to hear from all the stakeholders involved in creating that image.

Rebellion and its ties to market success and audience engagement has become a gauge for authenticity and for understanding the possibilities of rock as an effective, socially subversive practice. Can music foster radicalism? Can music foster change? The MC5 represents a rich intersection of musical, political and social identities through which one can explore these questions. Here a group and an organization that sought an array of goals depended on and pushed one of rock's cornerstones — rebellion. The following conversations with John and Leni Sinclair, and WPP Minister of Defense Pun Plamondon provide perspectives on an experiment that became too big for any of the individuals involved and which has often evoked emotionally charged disagreements over how and where music and politics intersect. From Jeff Hale's use of the WPP to understand "why some segments of the counterculture progressed from strictly non-political ideologies to positions of radical extremism" to John Strausbaugh's view of the MC5 and WPP "as simply making the media look and sound more cool, the better to market their products and their advertisers," the perspectives on the band itself center on issues of an either\or idea of purity and intent (Hale 125, Strausbaugh 91).

The band garnered both affection and dismissal because of its association with the WPP, which stood as its connection to an authentic rebellion. While many bands communicate social and political messages through their music, the MC5 phenomenon was different in that there was, as Sinclair describes, "an extra vision" of helping fund TLE and WPP projects. This relationship would allow the band to "explore the possibilities of subverting

Three. Motor City Burning: Rock and Rebellion

the music industry and using its resources against it" with an overall aim to tear down the American capitalist state (Sinclair 2005).

Interplay between the mass media and seditious groups in the 1960s and early '70s has been the focus of numerous scholars. Dissident groups like the WPP, Black Panther Party, SDS, and the Yippies were both exploiters and victims of media. The WPP, like SDS, looked to the media as a tool for promoting its ideas. WPP members would soon learn that the media was something entirely beyond their control, and in their eyes the media would often compromise or sensationalize their efforts. The ways in which these groups were reduced into palatable media forms is of concern to media critics such as Todd Gitlin, who sees a danger in such representations. This is because information, "must be timely, unambiguous, intense, predictable, culturally familiar — and precedented" (45). Hence, the intricacies of a group, movement or party are often left by the wayside. "Some of this framing can be attributed to traditional assumptions in news treatment: news concerns the *event*, not the underlying condition; the *person*, not the group; *conflict*, not consensus; the fact that '*advances the story*,' not the one that explains it" (28). In the case of the New Left, "media treatment helped polarize the society, mobilizing a repressive Right and a controlling administration against a caricatured New Left" (127). The difficulties encountered by SDS in terms of its relationship with and dependence on the media are also featured prominently in other scholarly works that include Kirkpatrick Sales's *SDS* and Jim Miller's *Democracy Is in the Streets*.

Other groups were susceptible to this misrepresentation and the loss of attempted self-representation as an organizing tool, including such prominent groups as the Black Panther Party. Jane Rhodes contends that these distortions not only come from above but also come from within. In the case of the Black Panthers, members "consciously relied on the press for salience and visibility, and they carefully crafted visual and rhetorical material to be disseminated for public consumption. The press shaped stories about the Black Panthers to fit the organization, practices, and constraints of media institutions and the ideologies of government and law enforcement" (97). Hence, all of these interests found some benefit in media exposure, which carried the risk of making them look less genuine. Rhodes explains that multiple usages of media created "contradictions of the national response to the Panthers' self-representations" and three thematic frames that "dictated the coverage of the Black Panthers as the group moved from obscurity to national icons" (104). These frames included: a fear of the Black Panthers, condemnation of the group, and the creation of celebrity for group leaders. As we will see, the WPP found itself susceptible to these same three interpretations, including the elevation of John Sinclair to celebrity status as his legal woes continued.

Such media frames/caricatures, according to Aniko Bodroghkozy, were present not only in the news media but also in television entertainment. Television shows of the time including *Dragnet* and *The Monkees* provided dual interpretations for audiences not sure what to make of concepts like "counterculture," "New Left" and "hippie." Presentations of drug-crazed youth on shows like *Dragnet* pushed the idea that generational disconnect was beyond control when drugs entered the picture. According to Bodroghkozy, "many shows labored to find ways to portray the flower children sympathetically. The extent to which representations of the hippie counterculture could be separated from mind-altering substances determined the degree of favor or approval attached to those representations" (86). The counterculture could either find itself feared, condemned, (this was especially the case on law and order programs) or, in the case of the Monkees, heralded, depending on how the media framed it (81, 75).

The reductive practices of the media of which Gitlin complains helped to propel numerous individuals within these groups into celebrity status. Huey Newton, Stokely Carmichael, Angela Davis, Tom Hayden, Jerry Rubin, Abbie Hoffman, and, of course, John Sinclair, became celebrities through their own propaganda funneled through the media. These individuals were often deconstructed and debated instead of the groups themselves by cultural critics and news organizations seeking to package complex political and cultural entities nightly into consumable frames for middle America. They were keys to fearing or celebrating the New Left. According to Gitlin, "The leaders elevated to celebrity were flamboyant, or knew how to impersonate flamboyance: they knew what the media would define as news, what rhetoric they would amplify" (153). For leaders of radical movements, McLuhan's promise that "the medium is the message" meant they had a powerful weapon at their disposal (Bodroghkozy 39). And according to Bodroghkozy, the possibilities were especially ripe in two certain media. "For members of the counterculture, art films and rock music were the preeminent arenas of cultural consumption" (48).

Sinclair looked to rock as a part of the everyday lives of youth that could potentially get them excited and ready for drastic social change. Popular culture and the use of the media provided direct access to youth across the nation despite any racial, gender, or economic lines. He discusses the excitement he felt when encountering rock for the first time. "It was incredible! These dudes opened their mouths to sing and a whole new race of mutants leaped out dancing and screaming into the future, driving fast cars and drinking beer and bouncing half-naked in the back seats, getting ready to march through the '60s and soar into the '70s like nothing else had ever existed before" (Sinclair 1972, 9). He continues that the energy of this music shot out "through the radio into every corner of Amerika [common spelling in the related materials] to retribalize its children and transform them into something essentially and substantially *different from* the race which had brought them into the world" (9). Rock allowed for the liberating impulse to go forth into the masses. Music would also allow a bridge between popular culture and the political and social underground of Detroit and Ann Arbor. "What we must understand more than anything else is that our music and our culture constitute a political force that the cultural revolution is inseparable from the political revolution, and the revolutionary potential of our culture cannot possibly be fully realized as long as the capitalist social order continues to exist" (35). Sinclair, as well as some members of the MC5 and associated groups, saw no disconnect between cultural revolution and political life. In effect, the group and the community built around these ideals benefited communally from the spread of music like the MC5's in both monetary and culturally revolutionary ways.

Until this time, Sinclair's has been the dominating celebrity voice in terms of the WPP through his writings and propaganda. This study corrects the concerns of scholars like Gitlin and Rhodes in terms of essentializing reductions. Interviews with John and Leni Sinclair, Pun Plamondon and band members provide a multi-tiered conversation that unlocks the complexity of interactions and realities of the WPP. Addressing Rhodes's point that these groups took part in the framing themselves, these voices also provide insight into the WPP's propaganda and how its members saw it determining their life in the media. The WPP and the MC5 proved to be more an organic and communal undertaking made up on the spot than the organized political force portrayed in the media and many studies. The collection of these voices fundamentally breaks down the continuing, essentialized visions that these frames have ensured.

A Total Assault on Culture

In terms of the Sinclairs' and Plamondon's perspectives, the White Panther Party saw the United States as an international superpower and bastion of capitalism, a subsuming system that sought to hold its subjects within its clutches. They saw their role as using music to recruit and harness the viable, intense passions of youth. These harnessed energies would be used to tear down the status quo in everyday life. The group thus advocated an all-encompassing program that would show itself on local stages, also in a more public manner. According to Sinclair, "The White Panther Party was the same people that were Trans-Love Energy, people who had moved to Ann Arbor to get away from the Detroit police. And we were increasingly radicalized as individuals by the events going on, people opposing the war, the Black Panther Party organizing itself and presenting its program to people — to monitor the police through self-defense actions" (Larabee and Bartkowiak 131). Plamondon asserts that the Black Panther influence, for

Black Panthers demonstrating for the freedom of Huey P. Newton at Detroit's federal courthouse in 1969 (courtesy Leni Sinclair).

him, much like for Sinclair, provided one of the flashpoints for organization. "They took it to the next level of saying, 'We're willing to lay down our lives for some basic rights. We have a right to defend ourselves against these racist police.' And of course, the Black Panther Party put forward the concept of the domestic colonies" (Larabee 114). In the hopes of leading "tens of thousands of alienated and disenfranchised young people into a movement that could create a revolution," the WPP based itself on the Black Panther Party. Plamondon, in his *Lost from the Ottawa*, says that like the Black Panthers, it utilized "collective input and [a] decision-making process known as 'democratic centralism,' in which power, like a spoked wheel, moves to and from the center, rather than in the top down pyramid of western politics" (120). As we will see, such a distribution of power in a hypothetically democratic system proved to be increasingly problematic for many involved.

The plan was now for an all-out rejection of every facet of the dominant society, as demonstrated in the manifesto's claim that "our program of rock, dope and fucking in the streets is a program of total freedom for everyone. We are totally committed to carrying out our program. We breathe revolution" (Sinclair, 1968). The MC5 would be the WPP's greatest asset, as their increasing popularity garnered them national interest with a record contract and countless concert appearances. The colony made its presence known with the release of the *White Panther Manifesto*.

The manifesto contends that youth are the key to mobilizing social change. Sinclair preached that young people were the energizing bridge to the revolution he hoped for. "THESE KIDS ARE READY! They are ready to move but they don't know how, and all we do is show them that they can get away with it. BE FREE goddamn it, and fuck them old dudes, is what we tell them, and they can see that we mean it"(1). *The White Panther Manifesto* states that the energy encompassed within the potentialities of rock and roll and its audiences can tear down "the machine": "ROCK music is the spearhead of our attack because it is so effective and so much fun. We have developed organic high-energy guerrilla bands who are infiltrating the popular culture and destroying millions of minds in the process. With our music and economic genius we plunder the unsuspecting straight world for money and the means to carry out our program, and revolutionize its children at the same time" (Sinclair 1968). The White Panthers sought to exploit the system in this regard: they would create, promote, manage and develop artists like the MC5 to take their dreams of revolution to the masses. While working within the capitalist establishment, the group's main goal, according to Sinclair and some others, was to exploit that system until it could be overthrown.

Their plan for the development and outcome of the revolution was laid out in the accompanying White Panther 10-Point Program. Besides advocating for the complete support of the Black Panthers' 10 Point Program and the release of all prisoners in the United States, the White Panthers sought the complete breakdown of the capitalist system. The group sought to eliminate money, to open access to information media, to dissolve all "unnatural boundaries," to allow for free schooling for all, to end armies, to free people from leaders and wanted a continuous, "Total assault on the culture by any means necessary" (Sinclair 1968). In their openly dissident nature, these plans differed from those of the DAW or TLE, which sought broad social change through less aggressive approaches. Sinclair and the Party, especially in their admiration of the Black Panthers (mostly because of their encounters with police forces), were looking for communal life in a completely different world. The Party was now no longer content with its own small community; the media and the music of the MC5 was meant to take this message around the globe.

Come Together

The interviews with both John and Leni Sinclair reveal that the group was less an orchestrated plot and more a collective creation that occurred between band members, John Sinclair and community members involved in the DAW and TLE. Levels of ideology and commitment would vary greatly. The band was also no longer merely a musical vehicle meant to further a political message; instead, politics and music were woven into the very lives of TLE, the WPP, and the MC5. The MC5's early career through its first album should be seen as indicative of a complete lifestyle, in which politics and culture demanded equal attention because they were ideally a part of everyday life for those participating in the various incarnations of the communes.

The MC5 was not a tool completely manipulated by the WPP and TLE, as the band and the community came up with any ideological discussions communally, usually sitting around a table, smoking joints. Sinclair observes,

> The WPP *was* the MC5. They weren't some kids conscripted into this evil scheme. It was them and their manager and their road manager, the roadies and other people who lived in the same communes. We came to this together. Rob Tyner [lead singer of the MC5] and I spent most of a year just being best friends and hanging around ... ranting and raving, taking acid, smoking a lot of joints. He influenced me as I conversely influenced him. He was a brilliant kid! [Sinclair 2005].

The band proved to be the nucleus for TLE and the WPP. Its increasing success as a local, then regional, and then national act, according to Leni Sinclair, actually became the driving force in the transition into the WPP. The increasing success of the band regionally would lead to its first national record deal with Elektra Records.

The MC5's first album, *Kick Out the Jams*, taken from the title of its most successful song as a band, "Kick Out the Jams Motherfuckers," reflected this artistic and revolutionary assault on culture. John Sinclair wrote the liner notes introducing the group to the nation. The record sleeve reads, "We are a lonely desperate people, pulled apart by the killer forces of capitalism and competition, and we need the music to hold us together. Separation is doom. We are free men, and we demand a free music, a free high-energy source that will drive us wild into the streets of America yelling and screaming and tearing down everything that would keep people slaves" (Sinclair 1969). The ferocious and amplified sound of the band was a call to order for Sinclair's vision for the White Panthers. Besides the call to "Kick Out the Jams" (Sinclair would use this language in the White Panther Statement saying, "There is a generation of visionary maniac white motherfucker country dope fiend rock freaks who are ready to get down and kick out the jams — ALL THE JAMS — break everything loose and free everybody from their very real imaginary prisons") the group sought numerous means to enact its program for change (Sinclair 1968, 1). Music and drugs would provide the impetus for the revolution; the rest would naturally follow in the minds of Sinclair and some of the band members. The contract with Elektra offered the group a much larger potential for financial success and also for realization of its political and cultural aims.

The relationship between the label and the band appears to have been symbiotic. "They thought it was an act. It was an interesting thing and a lot of people liked it," Sinclair said about Elektra's reaction. No matter Elektra's views towards the band, the WPP was able to further its goals through the contract with the band. "Our idea was that this gave us a bigger stage for what we were doing. We could be a popular band and still propagate our ideas about the ways things should be ... anti-authoritarian, anti-government, anti-war, and pro-civil rights." The contract with a national label was embraced because it could support the communes as well as further the music and message of the band. "My goal was to work within that format of a band and audience, records.... The money earning part of it was important. I thought this is the way you support a revolutionary force, people that put out underground papers, etc. We were a single economic unit in Trans-Love Energies, White Panthers Party, and the Rainbow People's Party.[1] We devised a format where everybody lived together and nobody had an individual economic identity" (Sinclair 2005). The message was not, in either John or Leni Sinclair's eyes, something formalized. The music itself and the live shows were the message. Leni Sinclair claims, "With the MC5 they didn't go out organizing people ... they played music and organized when they channeled that energy" (2005). John Sinclair adds,

> One thing we were trying to do was exacerbate the tensions between kids and the authorities. That was our main organizing tactic was to kick up the tensions between the youths and the authorities and parents. And it worked like a charm. There was no calculation. I mean calculation was sitting around a table like this with three or four other guys, smoking joints, 3 o'clock in the morning, laughing, talking about how fucked up everything is [Sinclair, 2005].

It was through the music that WPP made its aims public. But the band, for the most part, did not sing of social revolution, instead focusing on "high-energy" rock as a means for harnessing the energy of the youth. Sinclair makes this very clear: "They don't have no songs Ho Chi Minh you got to win. They were about fucking, getting high; they were about playing high-energy music. All of that was outrageous ... it wasn't like SDS! We didn't engage in debates with people from the other side. We just tried to get as many people as we could to come to our events and enjoy our presentation from our hearts with them from their hearts ... really" (2005). The "jams" in essence were the force that could break down the initial impenetrable outer shell of the machine, which included societal apathy. The energy and ferocity of the MC5 was meant to demand investment and vigor from its audience. Political philosophies or communicated, manifesto-like programs of action are not addressed in most of the band's lyrics (which comment primarily on themes of sex and youthful rebellion), and instead are left to the propaganda machine put together by visuals, performance, and Sinclair's writings. Inherent in the audience's experience of the MC5 was the rejection of mainstream social values, replaced by "fucking, getting high, and playing high-energy music." The music of the MC5, rather than an overt lyrical barrage of ideologies, seems to rely more on the noise and the energy it produces to harness social upheaval. Leni Sinclair shared in her interview that "there was an attempt on part of the band, and John and Pun Plamondon and the rest of us, to try to harness this gathered energy. ...that kids wanted to do something. They wanted to implement ideas ... but there had to be a vehicle. So the White Panthers tried to pull them together so that they could start organizing in their own communities to make things better. The whole thing was based on the Black Panther Party model of organization" (2005). That model of organization was one in which local communities would organize their own people for programs of social change. The band, in lead singer Rob Tyner's view, harnessed this potential energy through a symbiotic relationship in which the band aroused and released energy from town to town. Tyner comments that the MC5's stage show "was a beautiful demonstration of the principles of high-energy performance: as the performer puts out more, the energy level of the audience is raised and they give back more energy to the performers, who are moved into a higher energy level which is transmitted to the audience and sent back, etc., until everything is totally frenzied. This process makes changes in the people's bodies that are molecular and cellular and which transform them irrevocably just as LSD or any other strong, high-energy agents does" (quoted in Waksman 229). He adds in an interview with John Sinclair for *The Sun*, "People of the world, the next time you see a live band, and they go up there and do top ten material, or shuck around material, you oughta turn on them and say PLAY THE MUSIC — either play the music or GET OFF THE STAND. Tell them that..." (Sinclair, "Rob Tyner Interview"). This was, in essence, the practice of "kicking out the jams:" bringing and participating in an invested and total experience.

This notion of the non-separation of the music and politics by some band members and WPP community members, especially in the sonic organizing potential to be "turned on" as Tyner describes above, parallels concisely the theoretical framework Jacques Attali describes in *Noise*. Attali sees the potentiality for energy, and its organization tied to the life of music. In essence, music conducts and directs the chaos of noise in the world into ordered forms. "First, music — a channelizer of violence, a creator of differences, a sublimation of noise, an attribute of power — creates in festival and ritual an ordering of noises in the world" (Attali 23). Noise, in Attali's mind, is the key to power in society in that one form of noise can subsume other forms. Attali explains, "Everywhere we look, the monopolization of the broadcast of messages, the control of noise, and the institutionalization of the silence of others assure the durability of power" (8). John Sinclair and the MC5 saw in their "extra vision" that a band bridging the underground and the popular could be a massively powerful organizing force by harnessing potential audience energies for revolutionary purposes. By producing and ordering noise into a stimulating flashpoint, the potential violence in noise could be exhumed and ordered through the music of the MC5 and through the continued mythos of rock's relationship to a sense of usable rebellion for artists, audiences and the industry, which depends on this mythos to sell it.

In *Instruments of Desire*, Steve Waksman examines the connection between the MC5 and Attali's perspectives on noise. Waksman observes that the context of working class Detroit gave the band and those associated with it a unique perspective on the potentialities of noise that sought to subvert Fordist notions of standardization:

> The production of a disorderly electronic noise in this context indicated a contradictory stance toward technology, a willful move to master the tools of standardization which at the same moment threatened to drown out the human presence with the force of the machine. The repetitive sounds and lyrics in the Five's music signified the boredom and sameness of everyday life, but also counteracted this boredom by producing a disorientating noise that brought listeners to an ecstatic pitch [216].

But this combination of boredom and its ecstatic transcendence communicated through sound and lyrics is not the whole story. If one considers the MC5's creation of music both lyrically and instrumentally, the band, in the context of the history of rock to this point, was actively finding a voice in the public sphere of rock as a rebellious force. John Sinclair's comments on the band's interest in "fucking, getting high and playing high-energy music" was not too distant from archivist Michael Ochs's earlier statement that "if rock was the soundtrack to our lives, then these soundtrack albums had to encapsulate any of the teen topics of interest—automobiles, assorted fads, sexuality, rebellion, escape, energy, life, death, loneliness, dancing and dating" (Ochs 10). The MC5 did this in a contextually new fashion. The same notions of basic rebellion and questioning through the power of music that came in early rock were alive and well in the MC5. The group took the initial energy of the rock music that the group and Sinclair had found so much value in, and put it into a plan for social action.

This sonic dimension, based on amplification and distortion, meant that the band went further and further in seeking to realize Tyner's vision of music and response. Waksman states that "it was not technology as a thing itself, but technology in its capacity to generate noise that the MC5 found so full of possibilities" (232). By embracing technology (that is, developments in amplification, the electric guitar, electric bass, and so forth) and rock's continuing, inherent rebellious ethos, the MC5 sought not only to create noise, but to use noise to reach for new possibilities in the world of music. Attali claims that the ordering of noise that occurs within music "has as its function the creation, legitimation, and maintenance of order" (Attali 30). He maintains that "its [music's] fundamental functionality is to be pure order. Primordially, and not incidentally, music always serves to affirm that society is possible" (31).

To some extent this is both true and untrue when applied to the MC5. The use of noise through the channeling of music was a tool to harness energy and to subvert existing systems. The guerrilla reputation of the band took rock to new levels of usable rebellion and encouraged hope for social change. Yet the group and the WPP in their focus on their program of "rock, dope and fucking in the streets" utilized the creation of noise, of music, of the rebellious nature of rock also as a promise that indeed a new "society was possible" as Attali says. The society was one in which the creation of art, music, poetry, and communal living could challenge and ultimately take down, they believed, the capitalist, imperialist United States of the time. As Attali hoped, some found within the MC5 a new level of musical composition that reclaimed music as a form of communal enjoyment and societal use. Here, "the listener is the operator. Composition, then, beyond the realm of music, calls into question the distinction between worker and consumer, between doing and destroying, a fundamental division of roles in all societies in which usage is defined by a code: to compose is to take pleasure in the instruments, the tools of communication, in use-time and exchange-time as lived and no longer as stockpiled" (135). Music is then a mode of communication and commonality meant to be actively used, whose authorship rested with each individual and the use he made of it in everyday life. Such conceptions of organic purity when applied to the band were of course complicated in the dependence of the band on its recording contract to spread the WPP message. Those investing such notions of purity into the band were to be quickly disappointed when political and revolutionary hopes for the band were not met.

Comparative Rebellion

At this point, we should consider the socio-political dimensions of the MC5 in relation to other contemporary radical groups. After all, John Sinclair did not see the DAW, TLE, WPP, or later the Rainbow People's Party as mirroring groups like the Students for a Democratic Society, or SDS. Rather, in *Guitar Army,* Sinclair postulates: "We are given to feel that in order to be "political" we have to take part in demonstrations and rallies and confrontations with the established political system, that we have to make the choice between getting high and digging the music and getting down with each other on the one hand, and "taking part in the struggle" on the other....

> We *are* making the revolution by living and carrying on the way we do, that our cultural revolution *is* an integral component of the worldwide struggle against imperialism, and that the way we can best contribute to the liberation struggles of other oppressed peoples is to deepen our commitment to our own alternative culture, to develop that culture along its highest and purest lines, and to bring it consciously within the context of the political revolution of which it is naturally a part [Sinclair, 1972, 37].

Sinclair saw the actions of groups like the SDS or their more radical breakaway group, the Weathermen, as merely reacting to what he called the prevailing "death culture." Pun Plamondon saw such groups, now considered cornerstone members of the New Left as too static.

> At the early stages of the organization we focused more on the "party" part: the "whoopee! Party!" As we surveyed the political scene at the time, to see

what the model for the organization would be, we looked at the Students for a Democratic Society. Though many of those people who were involved with Students for a Democratic Society were close personal friends and even neighbors, the few meetings that I went to seemed to be just dull, debating society meetings. It was endless position papers, endless debate, and that's not to say that SDS didn't do some good work. They mobilized a lot of people and educated a lot of people, which was certainly important to do [quoted in Larabee 113].

By contrast, the idea of the WPP was to create, through the power of artistic communication and expression, and especially through the MC5, the energy for young people to create local communities that shared communal styles of living and that could effectively subvert the capitalist, imperialist worldview that Sinclair, Plamondon and others deplored. Again, this development of the WPP was based on models that the Black Panthers were practicing, including the aim to establish numerous colonies across the nation that would be able to reach local populaces.[2]

John Sinclair comments that in terms of what the Weathermen were doing (clandestinely bombing government buildings, including the Pentagon), "We were sympathetic to anybody radical." Yet the violent approach was not something that the WPP thought would be as effective as creating organic communities to combat the "death culture." He points out that "all the things that they were developing to embrace ideologically ... we were already practicing. We were an affinity group, we were a commune, our lives were integrated with our thoughts ... we had been to prison" (Sinclair 2005). Sinclair believed that there was no separation between practice and ideology. Instead of being caught up in commenting on or protesting (as SDS did) the "death culture" a complete practice was needed to allow for the continued growth of the revolutionary movement. The ideological impetus for this cultural practice came primarily through music. "'Tutti-Frutti' by Little Richard, 'School Days' by Chuck Berry, blues records, that was my first inspiration. That's what inspired me to find a life out of white cultural America.... It was young people making the records, so yeah; it was an expression of a zeitgeist." Sinclair continues, "Everything I ever did is founded on that." Sinclair also described his development of ideology also being closely tied to beat writers like Allen Ginsberg and Lawrence Ferlinghetti. Although in Sinclair's view, Mao, Che, and Castro provided beacons for people to liberate themselves from oppression (Sinclair 2006), music was to remain central to his notions of social change and would continue to do so even after his eventual break with the MC5. For Plamondon, the path was similar: "For me, this high-school dropout, this budding alcoholic who was into LSD and marijuana and rock 'n' roll music and all, this wasn't how I wanted to spend my time [SDS meetings]. I could grasp, and understand completely, what they were saying about imperialism, racism, exploitation, and oppression. But it wasn't articulated in any way that I wanted to be part of" [quoted in Larabee 113].

One organization that was more pragmatic in its call to revolution for Sinclair and Plamondon was the Youth International Party or the "Yippies." Sinclair in his interviews and Minister of Defense Pun Plamondon in his autobiography pay homage to the Yippie movement.[3] Like the Yippie movement, the White Panther Party would uphold a central reverence for spectacle and usage of the media as a tool of empowerment. Sinclair's call to use "every tool, every energy and every media we can get our collective hands on" (Sinclair 1968) bears a striking resemblance to Abbie Hoffman's con-

Abbie Hoffman and Bob Rudnik (a TLE/WPP member), taken in 1971 in Chicago (courtesy Leni Sinclair).

tention that "advertisements for revolution are important in helping to educate and mold the milieu of people you wish to win over" (Hoffman 67). The ability to utilize media outlets as well as create alternative outlets became a central tenant of WPP life. Sinclair states that "we were the same people!" He continues, "At the Chicago convention ... we're down; we're there ... we're the Detroit chapter and that was a full ten months before we became the White Panther Party." He adds,

> See the difference between us was that we did things. We had a program in real life. They [Abbie Hoffman, Jerry Rubin and other key Yippie figures] gave talks and speeches and symbolic gestures and actions. It was extremely valuable in advancing the movement, but it wasn't what we did. We didn't do protests ... we didn't call press conferences. We didn't care about being on television; our world wasn't on television, it was on the radio. We put out records and did dances. We could organize people to come out and not only make a statement and have a dance but also get some money to print some leaflets with to get people out of jail [Sinclair 2006].

For Plamondon, individuals like Jerry Rubin and Hoffman were able to, without formal appointment, "express the attitude and aspirations of millions of progressive young people" (Plamondon 116). In a 2007 interview he saw the possibilities of performance in the Yippies. "They had a sense of theater, calling attention through outrageous, nonviolent actions. But what's most significant about them was their understanding of how to use the media to put our message out. People in Fargo, North Dakota, the Upper Peninsula of Michigan, and Atlanta, Georgia, who had no way of being indoctrinated or even exposed to these antiauthoritarian ideas, watched CBS news and Walter Cronkite reporting about these weirdo activities" (Larabee 114). Here we see the reality of media frames in shaping reception for dissident groups. Plamondon, in the same interview, goes on to discuss how friends in the "Netherlands of Michigan" were able to see the possibility of a movement (114). But such frames, as this study shows with the MC5 and WPP, can be problematic. For Plamondon, the downfall of the Yippies' media practice was a lack of staying power and lasting social change. Their specific media events did not necessarily ensure further specific actions from their audiences towards the cause. The lack of formal organization pushed Plamondon increasingly toward the community-focused actions of groups like the Black Panthers. "The YIPPIE! model had a certain attraction, but it also had its obvious drawbacks. As a non-organization, it was difficult to organize anything practical or long lasting, like a food co-op or medical clinic or free music in the parks. It's 'members' were limited to calling for demonstrations, promoting pranks, and performing street theater — valuable activities, to be sure, but not enough to sustain a movement over the long haul" (Plamondon 116). For Plamondon, the Yippie penchant for media exploitation combined well with more solidly ideological boundaries in the writings of the Panthers as well as within texts by "Mao, Lenin, Ho Chi Minh, Fidel, Nkrumah, and Fanon, as well as anything I could get my hands on regarding the American left" (120). In Larabee's 2007 interview, when asked about the human toll of Mao's leadership, Plamondon said, "What I take mostly from all these revolutionaries from around the world — Fidel, Ho Chi Minh, Mao Tsetung, Lenin — is their struggle for power. Once they get power, they become governors, they become restrictors, they become what I fight against" (Larabee 121). Many involved within the MC5 and WPP found the same thematic qualities in these revolutionaries. However, at the time, the formalization of ideology and practice within the WPP and the incoming influences would exacerbate contention among community and band members. In fact, some saw this "restrictor" mentality penetrating the group through the more politically involved members. This debate was heightened as outside pressures and attention from governmental and music industry sources mounted.

Whatever the internal differences, the authorities saw the WPP as a serious threat. John Sinclair and Pun Plamondon were targeted by police as subversive forces. Sinclair would eventually be sentenced to ten years in prison for the possession of two marijuana cigarettes (in Michigan). This conviction was fought by Sinclair's cohorts, leading to a "Free John Now" concert featuring such names as John Lennon, Yoko Ono, Bobby Seale, Jerry Rubin, Allen Ginsberg and others in Ann Arbor in 1972 (Simmons and Nelson 82). Sinclair was released three days after the event. Sinclair felt that the rise of the MC5 was the main cause for his incarceration. "I went to prison, because basically I was manager of the MC5! That was what really cheesed me off! I was an underground figure. I was big in the underground, I wrote for the *Fifth Estate*, I was a poet ... nobody knew anything about that in the outside world. Where we went with the MC5 ... we intersected with the popular world, because they were a rock band. That's where they operated, within the popular arena. That was what made me a notorious figure that they had to lock up" (Sinclair 2005). Although he had been locked up earlier for marijuana-related charges, Sinclair's later sentence was viewed by many as excessive. The Supreme Court eventually overturned the conviction on its own motion.

Police and prosecutors also targeted Pun Plamondon in the "Keith Case" with John Sinclair. Leni Sinclair claims that Plamondon was a fall guy for the bombing of a CIA office in Ann Arbor in September 1968. Plamondon was also vulnerable to drug charges. Sinclair says:

> The government had a plan all along I think to use us as a testing grounds for the constitutional power grab by the Nixon administration. They thought we were universally reviled and that no one would come to our defense because we were not part of the New Left. We were not like the people at the Chicago 8 trial, we were not lefty radicals and they thought people would just think, "Oh ... they're weirdoes" and we wouldn't have any support and they could get away with doing what they did ... and it didn't work. The same lawyers that defended the Chicago 8 also defended us! [2005].

The "Keith Case" wound up being about much more than the individuals on trial, and would become a cornerstone case on government surveillance that continues to be discussed in the post–9/11 United States. A sealed indictment by a grand jury indicted Sinclair, Plamondon, and John "Jack" Waterhouse Forest (Damren 1). Essentially the case became a test of the Mitchell Doctrine, which asserted that "the Executive Branch had the inherent right to conduct warrantless electronic surveillance on domestic groups that posed a threat to national security" (Damren 1).

The trial took an unexpected turn after the defense filed a motion to disclose any electronic surveillance. Here the bottom fell out for the government and the prosecution. As Samuel C. Damren in *The Court Legacy* states, "In his decision granting the defendant's motion to disclose government surveillance, Judge Keith rejected the government's position, known as the 'Mitchell Doctrine.'" In appeal, "the government sought a writ of mandamus against Judge Keith to require him to release the surveillance tapes of the Sinclair defendants that he had impounded" (5). Keith did not and eventually found himself in front of the Supreme Court. The court ruled in favor of Keith in 1972. The court said, "We cannot accept the Government's argument that internal security matters are too subtle and complex for judicial evaluation" (quoted in Damren, 6). Charges against the defendants were dropped. The case was a lesson for those involved about how far the government would go to keep track of activities of those considered part of the New Left. Even though Leni Sinclair, as a participant, didn't see an association with the New Left, it will be apparent in upcoming chapters that many others did. Unwittingly, these actions by the government exposed the excesses of the Executive Branch in this intelligence gathering.

It didn't take the Supreme Court ruling for the WPP to realize the level of interest by the government in its affairs. The WPP, several years before the ruling, began arming itself, but said it was only for defensive purposes. Leni Sinclair explained: "As things got more overtly political, we also tried to follow the Black Panther Party example in self-defense. We figured if we were ever attacked by right-wingers or police ... we should be able to exercise our Constitutional right and defend our homes and our families with legal guns" (2005). It seems as if this move was less preemptive and more a reaction to the changing nature of resistance in the United States as described by Plamondon in *Lost from the Ottawa*. He asserts, "With the recent beatings and arrests of antiwar demonstrators across the country, it was clear to me that the power structure would do whatever it took, including beating, arresting, and even killing its own children, to maintain the status quo" (115). He continues, "The Black Panther Party for Self-Defense seemed to be effective in organizing and instilling discipline in street toughs and ex-cons. Their platform called for black citizens to defend themselves with arms against racist police acting in an unlawful manner" (115). In short, the WPP did assert its own right to armed self-defense, but armament does not seem to have played a central role in the organization.

The Last Jams to Be Kicked

Ultimately the band would dissociate itself from Sinclair and the Party, releasing two more albums that failed commercially, leading to the demise of the group in the early '70s. Pressure from authorities, a reputation for drawing unruly crowds and associated antics (obscene language, performances, etc.)[4] limited their ability to produce capital and reach an audience. This pushed the band into dropping all associations with Sinclair and the WPP. Still, the notion of rebellion has stayed strong in the history of the MC5. This is true for other groups that would find their voice through the doors opened by the MC5, including the Sex Pistols, Fear, and Rage Against the Machine. The MC5's music provides insight into how rock can become a space for the commodification of rebellion, as demonstrated by Elektra's perception of the MC5 as a great gimmick. Critics denigrated the band for this reason at the time and for decades. But implicit and often explicit in the band's music and in related projects was the desire to subvert dominant power structures and to allow a public place for audiences to challenge the status quo in ideology and in sound. These groups represent a foundational ethos and promise for rock. They are texts through which identity can be asserted or challenged in a common space of rebellion.

This was the inherent promise of potential for the band, Sinclair and members of the respective collectives. Instead of picking up a weapon and/or fighting in the streets, audiences could assume and follow a rebellious spirit, just for the price of admission. The seriousness of this commitment varied significantly among those involved. Whatever the case, construing the experiment as either authentic or as a capitalist ruse misses a perspective on power and the potentiality of media that warrants further discussion and that can assist in understanding the relationship between music, social change, and potential political subversion.

Ultimately, music did not provide the impetus for revolution that some WPP community members sought. However, Sinclair's admiration for music's power and its potential to offer people a usable sense of rebellious space is alive and well, not only in audiences but also in the industry that counts on this promise to sell. The MC5 and key organizers like John Sinclair, Leni Sinclair, and Pun Plamondon momentarily found and used the potential energies that they saw in rock, in their opinions an organically rebellious music. Rock has not left this reputation behind; it continues — in the industry, in artists, and in audiences — to allow subversion and/or commodification within its borders.

Organizational perspective and thought only demonstrate part of this experiment in power and in the inherent capabilities of usable rebellion and the potential for social change through music and the WPP. The individuals who would become the spearhead and (for some) unwilling organizers of the WPP were the members of the MC5. The MC5 would garner the most attention and funds for the ongoing WPP project. In essence the project was the band, and gathering these perspectives is required to understand the parameters and possibilities of power in this many-headed creature. We began by looking at the fundamental social locations that these individuals would bring and the visions they would have for their careers as a band and as an ideological force, but much more needs to be said. Sinclair was far from alone in building the MC5 mythos and other voices demand attention for a complete picture of the band's life and its relationship to the WPP.

CHAPTER FOUR

Sonic Anarchy: The Making of the MC5

Within the context of late 1960s Detroit, a rock band called the MC5 found its musical style and ideological voice. A Motor City–based outfit, the MC5 exploded onto the national music scene after achieving regional and local success. The exposure came as a result of both the band's music and its political aims and associations, thanks to its affiliation with the WPP. The band harnessed this energy and shaped it into a mobilizing force. Therefore it was seen by some, including federal and state authorities, as a politically subversive threat. Through individual band members' voices, we can better understand their intentions and their collective memory not only in regards to music but also in regards to political and social change. These perspectives counterbalance the views of party leaders like Sinclair and Plamondon, which for individual members could be a blessing or a curse depending on the individual and the band's career timeline. The blessings came through increased attention to the band thanks to the media storm of often-revolutionary rhetoric that accompanied the band throughout its career with the WPP. But this same attention also brought with it critical reception in the music press and scrutiny from increasingly concerned police and federal forces.

This micro-level investigation into the MC5 hopes to reveal what members intended in their call to a "total assault on culture" through their association with the White Panther Party. We will explore how rebellion as a theme and practice was used in the band's career. The interviews reveal multiple perspectives on the popularity of the group at local and national levels and the emotional investment in the success of the band. Disagreements about the experience at the time and in hindsight abound. The realities of

Detroit helped to shape these perspectives, framing them through the usability of rock and its role in expressing grievances about race and class that had literally been taken to the streets. As local events like the Detroit riot made national news and intersected with larger concerns about a fractured and unequal society, the charged atmosphere launched the MC5's career and helped make it the voice of its members' youth, time and place.

All in all, as the interviews reveal, the band and its manager, Sinclair, were not ready for the reaction that their creation solicited, especially from increasingly repressive government interests and from their perceived brethren in the New Left and in the music press. As Dennis Thompson notes, a public myth of the band was created through an interweaving of self-generated propaganda, dominant media frames, and musical style. Thanks to the MC5's continued influence on popular music, especially in punk and heavy metal, as well as occasional coverage of band in the popular music press, its vigor and the sound are still alive. Along with the musical legacy, the question of how far were they willing to go politically and culturally occupies a place of infamy among fans and critics, testing where fact and myth met in the political life of this band.

Perspectives on the White Panther Party and Its Intent

The White Panther Party was a reaction of young Americans to the realities of life in Detroit, as well as to national concerns like the war in Vietnam and the rise of psychedelic drug use. Guitarist Wayne Kramer expresses the sense of frustration that led to the WPP's formation. But he points out that the organization did not have a coherent strategy for political change, even as it adopted the image of revolution.

> It was never thought through far enough to become say the Green Party ... an actual political entity in national and international politics. It was only intended to be a voice, an expression of these young people's frustration. It's a way to say "Goddamn will someone listen to us?" That's all we're asking is for someone to listen to us. You keep saying it and saying it and it falls on deaf ears. Your natural instinct is to raise the volume, raise the level of the rhetoric. Start talking about by any means necessary, start posing for pictures with guns in your hands. That will get their attention and it did! [Kramer 2005]

Four. Sonic Anarchy: The Making of the MC5

The White Panther Party was a meeting of minds inside and outside the band, namely those of singer Rob Tyner, Kramer and Sinclair. The frustration that Kramer speaks of is demonstrated in the White Panther Statement issued in 1968: "The white honkie culture that has been handed to us on a silver platter is meaningless to us! We don't want it! All we want is our freedom, and we know we can't be free until *everybody* is free! (Sinclair 1972, 104). A release put out by the party a short time later says: "We are responding to the increased pressure of the power structure by building a dangerous power structure of our own!" The main delivery point of that attack was the MC5, which would "get the Panther message to the people" allowing them to "meet with militant brothers and sisters wherever we go. All Power to the People" (108).

For Tyner, the challenge was to the band's freedom of speech and ability to perform the way it wanted. Like Kramer, Tyner reflects a sense of frustration with the powers-that-be in being recognized and heard. In Sheppard's 1988 interview, he said:

> You can't change the truth by just shutting somebody up. You can't change the situation just by making somebody stop talking. So these people began to like play with us a little bit. In other words, they would actually be waiting for us with this whole thing. They'd come to us and go: "You can't do 'Kick Out the Jams' the right way." They would say, "Okay, well you're not going to get paid if you do this." So we'd have to cook up some way of gettin' around it, and it really became a pain, you know? And you get to the point where you go: "Jeez, man, what is this?" .... And then the White Panthers started to make sense to me. You know, it's kind of like: Where do these guys get off on this stuff. It says so in the Constitution that you can do this, and that you're free to do this, and then you go ahead and do it, and they come up with some kind of way to bust you and get the money [Sheppard 11].

Embracing media forms to spread the WPP message drew a great deal of interest from fans, critics and the authorities. The WPP's avocation of the Black Panther 10-point program and platform, and call for a program of "rock and roll, dope and fucking in the streets" made the group a serious force to be reckoned with (Sinclair 104). For Kramer and other members of the band the message held many possibilities, some more serious than others. Such thoughts emanated from life in Detroit and from the state of social and cultural strife at a national level. This consciousness was balanced with an unapologetic desire to become a popular rock band. Thompson states that this brew resulted in violent gestures that were mostly theater:

> The notion of change, societal change and pushing them [the youth audience] into the fight ... we didn't really want to push them into any kind of fight. What we became was a representational model of a group of people who were willing to fight, especially when there were photographs of us holding machine guns. That sent out a message to the establishment. Now we got these MC5 guys who we already don't like because of their obscenity, because of the crowds they were drawing, the anti-establishment hysteria that they did not know how to deal with. [Thompson 2005].

Critics of the band have, according its members, perhaps misunderstood their meaning and intention. In his review of their first album in a 1969 issue of *Rolling Stone*, Lester Bangs said, "The difference here, the difference which will sell several hundred thousand copies of this album, is in the hype, the thick overlay of teenage revolution and total-energy-thing," which he said actually masked a less-than-desirable musical product (Bangs 34). Even recently, a 2005 *Uncut* review complains, "Shorn of their political context, they sound like a third-rate pub band." In this review, authenticity comes into play, questioning how far the band was willing to go and how commercialism could potentially strip it of any real daring. (*Uncut* 148).

Davis seems to concur that at least at first, the desire to become a major force in rock was what propelled the MC5, not any political context. "I thought we were out to show the world what we had. It was all about making a record and being a big time rock and roll band. By that time I didn't give a fuck who was running the government ... that bullshit. I just wanted to be a star ... to take our rightful place in the rock world. I wanted us to be a rock and roll band not a political party" (Davis 2005).

Kramer agrees that fame and profit outweighed any political ideology as he came into his teenage years and early twenties. The band was not an organic creation of guns and revolution from the start. Kramer discusses how he became more politically awakened as the struggles of the late 1960s continued to take shape.

> The band as teenagers were fundamentally most interested in becoming a successful band, a popular band, to be stars. We looked at the kinds of thinking that John Sinclair brought to the table as a stepping-stone to our stardom. It wasn't for me personally until I had been polarized by outside events, police violence, the war in Vietnam, things that touched me personally, that I developed a personal stake in political action or rhetoric. Literally the plan was to win over Sinclair then we'll win over the hippies and then we will be big stars! It was all about stardom as the motivating force. It wasn't until, as I said, some

Four. Sonic Anarchy: The Making of the MC5

point when events unfolded as members of a generation that I became personally politicized or radicalized. Then it became real for me [Kramer 2005].

Like other members of the group, Fred "Sonic" Smith had lofty goals in the early stages of the band's career. Much of this was based upon the promise of "high energy" performance. "The extent of our relation to politics was the high-energy intensity of it. And when we were 18 or 19, we wanted to take over the world. We wanted the world to be the way we saw it. We didn't relate to convention. We just wanted to take over the world" (Baker 30).

As with Sinclair, band members who were active agents in shaping the WPP primarily had a musical focus that did not rise to the level of strict political conceptions. Kramer says,

Fred "Sonic" Smith (courtesy Leni Sinclair).

My introduction to the concept of revolution was cultural ... it was through the music itself. It was visceral, it wasn't intellectual, it wasn't studied. It was a gut feeling, an intuitive sense that something was wrong. That something was out of kilter in America, in my country, in my neighborhood.... That questioning was really the source where everything started. Then I began to fill in the blanks when I could say geez, this war that we're involved in some country far away, in some culture that has nothing to do with me and my culture with my neighborhood and my city and my country ... doesn't make sense to me [Kramer 2006].

Music provided a place for

like-minded individuals to come together. Davis, in reference to The Beatles and the Rolling Stones, says, "First it was just a sound ... it was just fucking-a, that's great ... wow ... keep it in your head and go through your day with that tune ... thinking of that tune and everything would be better. As soon as I found other people who were feeling that vibe, these were the people that I wanted to hang with because we were on the same plain" (Davis 2006). This shared musical community that was building among those in the group included the cultural and racial challenges issued by the modern jazz movement, from artists like John Coltrane, Archie Shepp, Sun Ra and Pharoah Sanders. The band familiarized itself with these artists, primarily through John Sinclair, a jazz aficionado and critic. "Ideologically speaking, I think we got more information from the music, and from the jazz music that we studied. The philosophy of the thinking of the jazz players was of freedom in music. You could change music; you could do whatever you wanted to if you used your imagination. I think that was the real message" (Thompson 2006). Kramer, in an interview with *Uncut*, described the sonic rebellion the group put forth in this space of free musical expression. "The militancy and anger of the black Free Jazz movement was the same anger we felt. That was one of the levels that we connected to them, that they were pissed off about things, and were trying to find a new way to say it in music" (Hasted 83).

Thompson says that the intrinsic link between the enjoyment of rock and jazz was the promise of a collective energy, one that the MC5 would label as High-Energy music — an energy that could allow for youthful explosion of thought, emotion and hedonism. "What we found in that music was energy. The MC5 were interested in drive. We got that from the drag strips, fast cars, acceleration. We got it from The Who. They understood what drive was all about" (2006). Such a notion of High-Energy music was nothing new to the group. Through a meandering page or so, the band talked about the concept to David Walley in *Jazz & Pop* in 1969. "So we met John Sinclair, and he helped us to the whole concept of energy which is essentially, man, if you take everything in the universe, take everything that the mind can conceive of, anything, everything, and break it down, you can only go so far as energy," said Kramer. "In other words, energy is freedom. Energy is real, as opposed to a fantasy that exists only in somebody's head." Fred "Sonic" Smith added, "Because everybody knows that if we take as much energy as we can and put [sic] towards doing one thing, then it'll get done.

Four. Sonic Anarchy: The Making of the MC5

The more energy you put towards it, the more you get done" (Walley "Interview"). Although an incredibly generic notion, as we will see, this was the only unified ideology among all band members. Other ideological paths would prove to be more problematic.

The ideological formation of the band and the WPP reflected musical forms as well as other cultural fare such as beat poetry. Davis was influenced by revolutionary models of the time other than those provided by Castro or Ho Chi Minh. Growing up in the '50s and early '60s "was a really hopeful time, the beatniks were happening, poets, Kerouac, Ginsberg were writing. There was this tremendous explosion of intellectualism. Whereas my parents' generation ... the post war generation was 'I like Ike.' It was all very red, white and blue and stupid. It didn't account that there were other cultures in the world." These models did not provide a direct revolutionary focus but instead allowed for youthful rebellion. "We were just kind of coasting ... going from day to day. When some stupid shit would come up and you would be looking at it ... you would just be get that out of my way ... that's how this all started" (Davis 2006).

For individuals like Kramer, political consciousness was being shaped by a process of immersion that was affixed to their quest for fame. This consciousness developed as the five young men increasingly encountered discontent and upheaval on the streets of late '60s Detroit and Ann Arbor, as well as through the radically savvy minds surrounding them in the WPP. For the WPP, as outlined in *The White Panther Statement*, the revolution was to be cultural. "Our program is cultural revolution through a total assault on the culture which makes use of every tool, every energy and every media we can get our collective hands on" (Sinclair, 103). Kramer, in the process of the interview, clarified that the idea of a band "being" the revolution was a fallacy. The true power of a band like the MC5, whatever its motivations, was the very possibility of organizing and providing a place for dissent in society. "We've created a sense of community ... there is a power to that ... there is a place for that within the political movement, but it is not in my humble opinion the political movement. The political movement is one in which the French Revolution or the American Revolution was an armed revolution of the government, was never the revolution we were talking about. We used those words and those symbols, but it was a representation" (Kramer 2005). Thompson echoes these sentiments when he discusses how the band and the WPP have taken on mythical proportions, with some fans and critics waxing nostalgic about the '60s, searching for meaning in the 1960s counterculture:

> The myth grows because we embraced a lot of revolutionary ideas, and that is a good thing. The idea that you can be different, that you can wear colorful clothes, that you don't have to marry the first girl ... court her for 6 months before you have sex, the fact that you could experiment with recreational drugs like pot and not be a killer. The fact that you can think differently than the establishment and the fact that there were thinkers where the thinking was maybe if we could all talk to each other, maybe we could end up with some different solutions, maybe we could change the way that people think about life. I think that is the true power, the ongoing power of the MC5 ... it's in the music, it's in the three albums we created, it's in the lyric ... the feel of the band. It is propulsive, it's dynamic, it's different, and there are elements of risk. "Black to Comm," that's the platform for freedom ... in that moment in time ... where can we go, what can we do. That kind of philosophy is rebellious in nature because the status quo wants you to be a consumer, to go to work [Thompson 2005].

"Black to Comm" was a usual closer for the band, where its members would partake in a jazz-influenced improvisation. Thompson's comments exemplify the power and hegemony of usable rebellion in rock and in this case within the context of free jazz. The rebellion and subversive behaviors that Thompson describes, although seemingly countering the status quo, find substantiation in the capitalist order where sex, escape and style are all things to be bought. Music fulfills both ends of the bargain in packaging this subversion into usable forms for audiences who seek escape and social location in the subversion and criticism of dominant forces, while the music successfully uses these very same systems to spread its message and sound.

The modern music industry, despite its capability to reincorporate and sell the language of rebellion, still offered the best path to express dissent for band members like Kramer and Rob Tyner. The need to justify their notion of High-Energy music came through continued interactions with authorities and the increasing polarization of political life around them. As Kramer explains, "After a while you want to back up your argument." To accomplish this, he says, "we found a language and a vocabulary in the language of revolution, in the images of Che and fighting the oppressors and certainly the Black Panther Party. We saw in them people who took this revolutionary language and, at least what we knew then, were applying it and had the balls to carry guns and law books to confront the police of Oakland." He adds, "We found it inspiring, and we also found it patriotic that democracy required you, if you thought your country was going in the wrong direction, to do something about it" (Kramer 2006).

Interviews with Davis and Thompson especially highlighted a disconnect in this thinking. For them there was a complete rejection of political models accepted by the New Left. Dennis Thompson for example, in our discussion of the ideological construction of the MC5 and WPP, hoped to set the record straight on the MC5's political legacy. "I didn't read the *Red Book* ...Sorry people, I did not read the *Red Book*" (Thompson 2006).

Bassist Michael Davis echoes that their actual revolutionary dedication was paltry at best when compared to the perception of them by the authorities, including the federal government. All those directly involved freely admit that the WPP was only a small group of people frustrated with the system. But Davis says that the group got beyond its founders' initially playful intent at a very early stage.

> To me as one of the founders of the WPP, one of the people who were sitting around the table when the joints were going down and the WPP was founded, it was just a joke! It was one of our like let's goof on the audience things! This is just a cartoon! I didn't realize we were trying to be like the Black Panthers. But then I kept sensing ... like they would show film of Black Panthers in berets and Wayne was like yeah, yeah! [Davis 2005].

Davis felt more along the lines of, "What, what? Okay, it looks cool ... but you mean we have to do that? I don't think so. It kept getting more crystallized into being something ... something. I never thought it was anything more than tongue and cheek, absolutely" (Davis 2005). Davis continues this theme in some of his writings:

> As I recall, Rob and Sinclair were churning up a lot of propaganda, and Rob was taking on the spokesperson mission seriously. Between him and Wayne there was little air space left for words from anyone else about the intentions of the "revolution." Things were reaching rhetorical levels and it was starting to be embarrassing for those who weren't quite sure where this was headed. What had started as a satire was beginning to turn obnoxious [Davis "Diary"].

Davis continues that he saw this process affecting their performances. Looking back, he sees Tyner, as the group's literal voice, as being compromised by this process.

But the pressure to stay the course was in yer face all the time, and if you didn't stand up, you might be a counter-revolutionary. I think Rob became a victim of this stance. I hear these tapes, and I remember the awkward, uncomfortable silences at our shows, where Rob says something supposed to be inspiring, and after it's said, he shrinks back away from the microphone with no other words in his arsenal. You can hear mumbling in the background, noisy guitar switches being clicked, footsteps, shuffling, but nothing from a very large paralyzed crowd. You can tell Rob is demoralized and not in the moment by his self-conscious comments. Then Wayne attempts to fill the void, with equally irrelevant single-line banter [Davis "Diary"].

Wondering why "people didn't throw rotten vegetables at us," Davis clearly felt a great deal of distance from the frame created through their own propaganda and their reception in the media.

An affiliation with more formal revolutionary models left Kramer with a sense of ambivalence. He insists, "I don't regret anything and I don't close the door on it either. I know we made mistakes." Part of the WPP's reaction to continued harassment by the police and FBI was a series of promotional shots showing the members of the MC5 brandishing weapons. Kramer sees this as problematic: "The image of the gun was a mistake. The idea that we would use armed resistance was archaic" (Kramer 2006). Those archaic sentiments were ones that the government found of special interest.

These photographs reflected an increasing disconnect among the band members about the band's meaning and their role in "the revolution." John and Leni Sinclair have said self-defense was encouraged in a very Black Panther–esque sense through amassing some weapons in the group (John Sinclair, Leni Sinclair 2005). Davis, who testifies to having a disconnect with the focus of the Panthers, found the process a befuddling one, contributing to his distance from Panther rhetoric. "You're not going to have an armed conflict unless you have an army. And you see that's what they tried to make us do. All of the sudden there was thirty-odd-six and some M1-carbines around the house ... what's that shit do? We would go out and target practice [laughs] ... practice? I play guitar, when did I start playing a thirty-ought-six? [Davis 2005]

Thompson saw the armament of the WPP, in retrospect, as an instance of confusion. "There was a point where we started brandishing guns ... that was one of our tactical errors. We really didn't want everyone to pick up a gun and shoot the police ... that was never the intention" (2005). Kramer, who was elevating his awareness and political radicalism, points out that "we were young, we were crazy. We went too far with some things, but they went too far first!" He adds that there was a lack of communication among some members at the time, which may have exacerbated any confusion of direction for the band, especially regarding its role in the White Panther Party. "I know a lot more about how my colleagues feel today that they didn't talk about back then" (Kramer 2005).

The brandishing of weapons in these promotional shots demonstrates a discrepancy in individual ideals and goals for the band. The White Panther Party, while potentially expressing a foundation for revolutionary thought and dissent, was not the entity that critics have perhaps wanted to believe in. For example, *Bang Magazine* claimed that the MC5 were "the one and only in-your-face, capital P political band" (*Bang* 2). Instead, the members of the band, whose political thought varied from passionately invested to intentionally distant, could perhaps, find some middle ground in thinking that they would not have to partake in an armed struggle. Though the rhetoric did increase as the band and the WPP faced an increasingly hostile police force both in their homes and at their performances (Loren 20), direct, violent action was not something any member was willing to partake in.

Somewhere Between Chords and Discord: Ideologies as Separating Factors

Neither the MC5 nor the WPP had a pure ideological voice. Contemporary forces like the Black Power movement and the Vietnam War did actually affect all members of the organizations in some way. The realities of Detroit and the nation were continuously shaping perspectives among the party and the band. Detroit's increased oppression of the band forced the collective to move to Ann Arbor to avoid future violence. The collective had been the target of arson, and became a target for police harassment (Sinclair 1972, 44). The MC5 and the WPP's call to revolution in reacting to these numerous pressures appears to be where the opinions of those involved disagree. Other factors added to the confusion, including the incarceration of Sinclair on a drug charge, the increasingly radical political awareness of individuals like Kramer and Rob Tyner, and the stepping up of authoritarian controls, both by the Department of Defense and the local authorities. As the band became more popular, the authorities became more concerned with its rhetoric and actions.

John Sinclair, the band's manager and key player in the White Panther Party's development, was incarcerated "on a 9–10 year sentence for possession of two marijuana cigarettes and held without appeal bond for 29 months" (Loren 21). The harsh imprisonment added to Sinclair's extensive record of marijuana use. The band that had ultimately found success through Sinclair's promotion had for some time leading up to the incarceration felt itself drifting from Sinclair and the community.

Davis comments that Sinclair had "neglected to keep his eye on the business end of the 'revolution.'" He thought that the band was quickly thrown into a compromising position when the crackdown on the WPP and Sinclair occurred. "When the shit hit the fan, Sinclair was on his way to prison, and the MC5 were the sheep in the wolf den when it came to wheeling and dealing" (Davis "Diary").

Thompson believes that the initial success of the band, signed to Elektra Records in May 1969, was indeed an extension of the experience in Sinclair's Detroit based communes. "The message was inside the music. We were nurtured and nourished by Trans-Love Energies and John's people— their thought, intelligence and freethinking. That was the beneficial information we received from being with them. There was so much more than "we must destroy what exists with a Godzilla-like mentality, we must smash it down and build it all over again." But it was the idea of alternative thinking" (Thompson 2005). But Thompson continues that as Sinclair faced jail time, a gap began to widen between the band and community members more focused on political upheaval.

> When John went to jail ... it was like well, this man had gotten us this far. His politics became more aggressive, and combative and he was going to jail, and we were not going to profess the politics ... we're not going to jail. If it was our asses up against the wall and we were on the stand I think we might have escalated our politics even more so ... but we didn't want to go to jail. We wanted to be free to make the music, make records, to tour and to be a rock and roll band. Ultimately the real design of the MC5 in the beginning was to be one of the best rock and roll bands in the world [Thompson 2005].

Four. Sonic Anarchy: The Making of the MC5

Kramer agrees that escalating tensions were occurring within the band due to factors like increased commercial success and repression from authorities at national and local levels. These were heightened when combined with the harsh realities of Sinclair's impending sentence.

> John really believes in the power of art to change people, to enrich our lives ... that is the basis for the things that John does and for the things he does with the MC5. When it became clear that the MC5 was an ongoing business concern and John's legal difficulties started to conflict, it reverberated in personal problems. It took form in resentment. I don't know if you know many people who have done time ... but most people freak out before they get locked up. It is such a traumatic thing to face and you want to blame somebody. And John blamed me, the MC5 ... but mostly me because he was really close to me and that's what we do, we lash out at the people closest to us [Kramer 2005].

The band and Sinclair, by the time they were signed to Elektra Records in 1969, had suffered a long history of frustrations and torment at the hands of local and national authorities. The most intriguing evidence of this is in the footage of the band taken by the Department of Defense during the 1968 Democratic National Convention. The Yippie festival was supposed to be held in Chicago's Lincoln Park while the convention was meeting. The MC5 was the only band to show up, as tensions in Chicago had been nationally broadcast, dissuading others. Says Tyner of the performance, "There were helicopters flying low over me and people who looked like Lee Harvey Oswald walking around with funny-looking packages and it was scary, man. There were guys in suits with blue sunglasses walking around, talking in walkie talkies. People were milling around something terrible. Plus on top of that, everywhere they were giving out these brownies that were full of psychedelics and hashish. These babies were hitting people like a ton of bricks and ... people were getting very, very high and real, real nuts" (Sheppard 25). As chaotic as it sounds, the presence of the MC5 at the event caused a great deal of further interest in the band from listeners as well as the government. The performance and the band's national contract with Elektra Records pushed Sinclair into the limelight as a countercultural guru. Tyner admits that the band embraced its new-found fame, "and I think we started getting cocky once we were signed to the record company" (Sheppard 13).

Thompson thinks that the government had taken notice of the band as a catalyst of anti-authoritarian rhetoric and singled out Sinclair as its main target. "The idea was if we take this manager out of the equation, maybe this MC5 thing will go away. There was probably someone who said that sitting around at some backroom table" (Thompson 2005). One could certainly see this potentiality in the 9½ to 10-year sentence leveled against Sinclair for possession, an affirmation of Thompson's fears. Along with this targeting of Sinclair, the indictment of Pun Plamondon for his supposed role in a September 1968 bombing of the Ann Arbor CIA office reflects an established interest in the WPP by state and federal intelligence communities. This increasing interest in the New Left and groups associated with it, targeted key individuals within these organizations that were seen as domestic threats to national security.[1]

The crisis of thought in regards to Sinclair and other party members that Kramer discusses above can be witnessed in the increasingly militant rhetoric utilized by Sinclair in party press releases. A May 1969 release states:

> We will not allow these creeps to stomp us out, and we will defend ourselves by any means necessary against the fascist terror. This means using every possible weapon at our command, including the pig's own technology. We will rob that motherraper blind, we will steal his machinery, his media, his money, anything he lets us get our collective hands on we will snatch up and take back to our communities where it will be put to use for the people by the people with the people. All Power to the People! The spirit of the people coupled with the strength of the pig's technology in the hands of the people will enable us to turn the pig out of pasture for good! [Sinclair 1972, 153]

One can see a marked contrast to the program of "rock and roll, dope and fucking in the streets" advocated at the inception of the party. Sinclair, in his book, *Guitar Army*, sees the WPP as a reactionary force which was "struggling for survival." The rhetoric was "getting so extreme that it began to turn them [the MC5] off too, along with the people we addressed ourselves to"(Sinclair 1972, 50). The group became reactionary, according to Sinclair, because instead of providing a clear alternative to the "death culture," the MC5 was reduced to keeping its head above water defensively in the face of increasing authoritarian pressure. As Sinclair struggled for his freedom, the MC5 struggled for its. Feeling isolated and repressed by local and national powers and fearing that it would become a target caused the band to split from Sinclair. Kramer reflects,

> We were struggling to find our way. John was really our mentor ... he was the snowplow that cleared the way for us to be the MC5 and once he was out of the picture, we were in trouble. The more his legal problems increased the less

he was available to us and we were really struggling and trying to find our own voice. What John was able to do was articulate things that we felt at a gut level. John was older than us; John was better educated than us. John had a clearer worldview than we did [Kramer 2005].

After the separation the band would make two more albums. The path was not easy. Davis states, "We dumped the commune and then officially now we were going to just be a rock and roll band. Then there was real hell to pay ... because you jumped horses in midstream. The press, the fan base is saying hey, hey that's not cool! People are very eager to point out when you step over the line ... and that was stepping over the line" (2005). But according to the interviews, dropping the White Panther affiliation seems to have been a means for the band's survival, and it still wanted to be a musical force. Thompson explains that the pressures were numerous, and including the continued wrath of a government that, as Attorney General John Mitchell stated, "was looking to gather intelligence information deemed necessary to protect the nation from attempts of domestic organizations to attack and subvert the existing structure of the Government" (quoted in Wilson). This pushed the band into a state of doubt and confusion.

Thompson continues: "The band was finding itself, who we were. Don't forget all the things that were happening to us at the same time. Losing John Sinclair, confusing our fan base a bit ... from the first album to the second album ... two different schools of music entirely.... We were losing ourselves ... we were beat up. We were taking some pretty nasty drugs, and that is another large part of the reason that the band separated, because the drugs the band were taking were these death drugs" (Thompson 2005). The band had moved on from drugs like LSD and marijuana to heroin, a reflection of larger trends of the time, especially in urban centers like Detroit. Two albums after its debut with Elektra, drugs would become one of the most prominent causes of the band's demise.[2]

Reducing the Rocket: Making Sense of the MC5 and the White Panther Party

The MC5/WPP relationship allowed a plethora of uses, of meaning, and of significance for those involved. Did the relationship between the MC5 and the White Panther Party truly reflect a revolutionary move in the annals of American history? The answer varies, based upon members' perspectives. Time has taken away the voices of Rob Tyner and Fred "Sonic" Smith. This further complicates the spectrum. What can be discerned from the three remaining members is that the MC5 and the White Panthers were an organization built upon an array of perspectives, some seeing radicalism as tongue-in-cheek and some declaring its authenticity. These perspectives were complicated when the group amassed national media attention. This media attention provided the five young men a massive audience through a national recording contract. Members, whether believing in the possibilities of change through cultural revolution or whether basking in the limelight the band had collectively sought, saw the MC5 and White Panther Party become an amorphous organization that could fulfill numerous potentialities. But the coalition also alienated the less politically motivated members of the band, an increasingly apprehensive Thompson and Davis. The MC5 quickly devolved into numerous interpretations by the band members themselves. Far from a cohesive unit, the group was an often-conflicted collection of views and intentions about what the MC5 was supposed to represent in popular culture and the political world.

Different levels of communication and of loyalty to rock and/or to social upheaval allowed for this multiplicity of perspectives among band members, among party members, and between the two entities. The interviews reveal a band divided. Rob Tyner and Wayne Kramer are commonly seen as the most connected to Sinclair and the social, cultural and political visions of the White Panthers as expressed in the party's rhetoric. Davis points out that decisions about the WPP's marketing and its adoption of increasingly formal political and revolutionary rhetoric were made through a filtering process that began progressively to involve more of those excited by the political and cultural debate the band was inspiring. "So our information kind of got filtered down through innuendos and jokes," he said (2005). It appears that an ineffective and incomplete form of communication occurred as the band stepped up its rhetoric and ran into greater repression from authorities. My interviews with band members and WPP leaders reveals a rough chain of rhetorical flow. The determination of revolutionary rhetorics and image mostly centered around Sinclair, Plamondon and Kramer; secondary to these initial discussions were Rob Tyner, and other WPP members like Leni Sinclair, Gary Grimshaw and Dave Sinclair; and finally, at the bottom of the rhetorical divide, were those mostly concerned with the band's career, with little concern (or at least, comparatively less) about its political role, including Thompson, Davis, and Fred Smith.

The party was meant to create a sense of community for those persons that felt frustration in their daily lives. It was not an army, and the MC5 never intended to wage a physical attack on the power structure, but instead looked to culture as a tool of change. As Thompson notes, the revolution was not at the end of a gun barrel. "The basic revolution that was taking place to me was one of consciousness, one of thinking. I think the revolution that was going on was in people's personal lives and the way that they looked at the world. I think the effect that the MC5 may have had on people over time was that yes you could kick out the jams in your own life, yes, you could do something different ... you could be unique" (Thompson 2005). Kramer, who is still active in political and socially focused causes, retrospectively interprets the band's place in the counterculture and its sometimes de facto association with the New Left in a similar fashion.

> We were sincere about what we did and it was expressed in the work we did. There is something keeping this whole thing alive. Why has the work of the MC5 been recognized by a generation today when we weren't even recognized in our own day? I think the message holds up pretty well. The fundamental message was that you could make a difference but you had to do it wholeheartedly. You have to make a commitment. You have to kick out the jams; it doesn't mean you have to nudge out the jams.... Will the MC5 be looked on as a cheap revolutionary hype rock band that a bunch of people were naive enough to swallow ... I don't think so ... I think the sincerity comes through. Given all that remember what we said in the beginning that the idea of a rock band being political is an illusion. It was in fact a marketed sense of revolution. We knew that then ... this isn't a new revelation to me [Kramer 2005].

Kramer states that the band intended to use Elektra Records and mass media. They allowed the band to reach and influence a mass audience, carrying, according to Thompson, a basic message: "We're carrying a message a positive message a powerful message a message of self-efficacy that I think is a useful message" (Thompson 2005).

These perspectives have been developed and refined by the individuals chronicled here for nearly four decades now. The MC5 lives above and beyond any single member's wishes or intents. Intent can only mean so much to a group that has carved out its own spot in popular music and the social and cultural history of this country. Davis comments, "The legacy is cool,

I'm grateful for it, I'm grateful for the fans and the people who have come out and like the stuff we did. So much of that is in spite of everything, in spite of yourself, in spite of all the mistakes, in spite of whatever you thought about it ... that's what you meant. I have no control over the legacy, and I'm fine with that" (Davis 2005). Dennis Thompson acknowledges that authenticity remains an issue in regard to the MC5's political/cultural legacy. This nostalgic view of the band as an uncorrupted foot soldier in the countercultural revolution is just as constraining, musically and generally, today as it was for the band at the time, he says. "It's an illusion ... there is a lot of MC5 fanatics that would like us to remain pure, in other words they would want to let the sleeping dog lie. That we were this entity at a certain point and time and they want to preserve it. They want to dip us in plasticine and say geez ... you're not allowed to evolve" (Thompson 2005). He adds that those that have invested a sense of authenticity in the band remain adamant even today as the band confronts ongoing debates on genuineness and intent. "People who are the fanatics ... it's like whoa.... You're stepping on their holy grail. This is the way I perceive it ... you can't change my perceptions of it!" (Thompson 2005).

At the time, this sense of authenticity was heavily invested in by some, and written off by others. The debate has yet to subside, as demonstrated in press and popular reaction to the band's *Sonic Revolution* project in 2002–2003. A posting by "Bob D" on a Wayne Kramer message board on i94bar (an online rock zine from Australia) showcases the continuous battle over meaning in the MC5 narrative:

> These guys have had tough lives and who could begrudge them making a living from the past? On the other hand, putting yourself out there as a public figures and espousing a certain morality opens you up to this type of criticism when you turn 180 degrees and bend over for the MAN. ...Brother Wayne, brother Michael, brother Dennis ... I'm ashamed of you and for you. Fuck Levi's! You guys should know better ["Kick Out the Jeans"].

The search for a pure means of rebellion that would allow fans and critics to take part seems intrinsically tied to these perspectives. This usability of rebellion is sacred to some. Perhaps some of this dedication can be attributed to the fact that the MC5 and the White Panther Party really did, despite themselves, provide a usable text through which audiences could rebel and voice their dissent. Significant investment has come from audiences in the music of the MC5 and the work of the White Panther Party. They allow an energetic and autonomous space for questioning society that can be obtained merely through going to a show, wearing a t-shirt or putting on headphones. Kramer explains this momentous power to offer a space of dissent. "[For] each generation throughout history ... one part of that youth is that desperate desire to figure out who I am ... who the hell am I in the world. And one way I find it is in my music and when I find my music, that is my fucking music and you can't take it from me and that's part of who I am" (Kramer 2005). In effect a kind of authenticity is created for the listener. The power of the music is an outlet that feeds on this energy of change and challenge, wherever the boundaries may be. Indeed, it can be shaped by the bands and those controlling their images, but it can also be a deeply personal experience where one can use or not use or buy into or discard the messages of rebellion and angst. Somewhere between intended frames and successful poaching of musical products, the life of the music hybridizes and changes to fit numerous contexts. This question of authenticity in the music and life of the MC5 and the White Panther Party was not relegated just to their audience. The local and national authorities also questioned what exactly the White Panthers could mean to national security.

Messing with "The American Ruse"

In retrospect, the MC5 and the White Panther Party were not capable of creating a complete social revolution, nor did it seem that they ever intended a physical revolution. Yet the intensity of police and government attention was overwhelming to the group and to Sinclair. The creation of the party had fueled much more than the success of a band, and become much more than an outlet of creative expression about social ills. Davis comments,

> We frightened the shit out of them. They didn't know how to deal with it. We recognized that we were cool, we know we're cool, let's leave it at that. That's powerful shit. Because when you reach 10-year-old or 12-year-old kids and they just think you're the coolest and they want to be just like you ... you don't think that scares the government? That scared 'em ... big. There weren't too many ROTC recruits coming out of that group! [Davis 2005]

FBI files of the time reveal that this possibility of recruitment was especially frightening to the establishment powers, who at the time were actively investigating links between the group and a growing number of activist organizations. These groups employed violence and terror tactics, and included the Weather Underground and the WPP's own Pun Plamondon and John Sinclair, according to some allegations.

Davis points to perhaps the most powerful effect of revolution through cultural standards — being merchants of cool. The power of media and their effect on culture afforded the MC5 a significant voice whose energy equaled political clout to many a teenager. For Dave Marsh, the MC5 experience was total. "So, the MC5 remain the rock concert experience against which I measure all others, because getting lost in that music, as you were meant to, became a vehicle for finding yourself. It was as scary, as exhilarating and as worthwhile as it sounds. No wonder the men who made it happen were so depleted" (Marsh 90).

The media did not control interpretation of the message or whether it reflected the individuals in the group. Here again, comparisons to the Yippie movement can easily be drawn. Fiends of media manipulation, the WPP and Yippies put power behind image and sound, blurring the line between Aronowitz's notions of a divided counterculture of the political and the cultural. Media did not allow for a clear dividing line, and the WPP and the Yippies acted as sonic and semiotic tricksters, with the WPP merging the mischievousness of the Yippies' street theater intimately with their musical output.[3]

John Sinclair and Rob Tyner describe a unified vision in the power of media in *The Sun*. Sinclair postulates, "And now we're talking about a return to an oral culture, less and less people read, and people are getting what they know off the radio, off the records ... you can hear it, and that makes it more immediately REAL." Tyner follows up, "So we have to start taking over the mass media, because that's where it's at — that's where the consensus of the people's thinking comes from. It's part of their lives. We just have to show them that there's more than what they already know. What you can understand is limitless." Sinclair reflects the frustration with media frames that Gitlin would talk about several decades later in *The Whole World Is Watching*. "And that's the trouble. They want somebody to tell them everything, without going through it themselves." This prompt by Sinclair pushes Tyner to express a foundational hope for the use and exploitation of mass media:

Four. Sonic Anarchy: The Making of the MC5

What we need is a sort of well-rounded home, man. Because like, calling ourselves a community, that sort of thing, we need the mass media. Because like you've mentioned to me in the past, man, we've just handed out too many handbills. It's definitely not easy. But if we had some people who were together enough to put together some radio shows, some hip TV shows, I'm sure that since we've already taken over the newspapers, we might as well hit them with all the barrels [Sinclair "Rob Tyner Interview"].

The possibilities of the media screamed to a generation dependent on them. With TVs flashing and transistor radios spewing out culture and ideology en masse, baby boomers naturally looked to media for a voice in a world seen as having the old and outdated at the controls. The frustration of media frames pigeonholing the generation into sound bites caused like-minded individuals like Tyner, Sinclair and Hoffman to want to be able to create and maintain their own media images. They had little idea how difficult these images from the established media and their own media would be to harness and control.

Although it participated in the Festival of Life and shared a common view of media power, the band did not have the formal ties to Yippie leaders like Hoffman and Rubin that Sinclair did. However, through Sinclair, the band felt their influence. Says Kramer, "We all learned from each other. I thought that they were brilliant agit-prop political theatre artists. Wearing that American flag shirt ... that's why my guitars are painted in the American flag motif. We wanted to say we're super-patriots. You're the one following the fascists. We're for good old American justice" (2006). This sense of learning and camaraderie did not mean a formal relationship or formal methodology for change among the WPP and the Yippies. Neither the WPP nor the Yippies had any real organization as a "party" (Miller 285). Says Davis, "We understood what Abbie Hoffman and Jerry Rubin were up against. What they were dealing with was the repression of the political society that we rejected. That's what they had to deal with within the boundaries because that was what the law was." He continues, "I respected those guys, I related to them, I knew what they were going through. I knew it was tough, I knew they would have to stand up in court and people would laugh at them. They would have to do radical absurd things, make public statements that were going to fry them" (2006). The cultural and the political delineations of Aronowitz's notion of the counterculture were blurred by the Yippie and the MC5 approach, mixing the political and the cultural.

As the establishment increasingly targeted Hoffman and Rubin as subversive forces, some band members, including Thompson, felt no need to align themselves with the targeted individuals.

> What we had in common was the idea that change needed to take place. It was natural youthful rebellion. We wanted to end the war, legalize pot and have some sort of effect on bigotry and racism. Those themes we shared. But as far as sitting down and having pow-wows with them ... planning strategies.... Na, I wasn't ever involved with that. Didn't care to be. Whenever the call came [from the Yippies] for us to show up somewhere ... we went [2006].

All the members of the band did not necessarily buy into the supposed ideological underpinnings. Davis confirms,

> We knew what they were talking about, but did I want to be part of their court case? No. As far as going to Chicago, I don't remember ever having a relationship with those guys. I might have met them ... we might have said hi, we might have passed a joint back and forth. But I didn't sit down and have a talk with them about what the new world would be like. Sinclair may have. He was really our connection with all of that. He kind of passed down his edicts to whoever was going to be the next link in the chain of puppetry [laughs] [2006].

Even though the MC5 did not formally align themselves with Hoffman, the two groups tested the power of media in creating real or perceived threats to the establishment. Its opposed to the romantic vision of the master media manipulator portrayed in the Abbie Hoffman biopic film, *Steal This Movie!* (2000), the Yippies and the WPP often fumbled their on-the-spot experiments in media exploitation. Kramer explains, "In a sense we were all babes in media manipulation. We were figuring it out as we went. It's not like today where Karl Rove and the White House are geniuses at media manipulation. We were just making our bones" (2006). These rudimentary approaches to using the media as a stage for political theater and personal expression soon made these now-celebrated figureheads targets of national security interest.

As was the case with the Yippies, Kramer and Thompson see the establishment as linking the White Panther Party with violent dissent and rebellion, no matter how ignorant they were of their own power in the realm of popular culture. Claims that the band might now make delineating between culture and politics were not nuances the government sought to understand.

Four. Sonic Anarchy: The Making of the MC5

The threat was that their hypocrisies and inconsistencies were obvious. The MC5 was one small part of a generation that disagreed with the direction the country was going in that was directly affected by decisions that were made in Washington. He [Nixon] viewed the White Panthers and the MC5 along with the Yippies, and Black Panthers, and the Students for a Democratic Society and any one who stood up and said we don't want this war; we don't want what's happening in this country. You expand that out to the connection between the anti-war movement and the civil rights movement ... these were very powerful social movements [Kramer 2005].

Thompson explains that the very alignment of the White Panthers with these other groups created a reactionary response, which in turn propelled the band to higher levels of fame and myth. The band wanted to give up the hyped and unfamiliar path, jumping between the popular and the political. "Because they wanted to stop this ... this is where the purists might have a point, because of the way the establishment reacted to us. All of it was running counter-posed to their ethic, a fundamentalist Christian ethic" (2005). The anti-communist paranoia of the time was probably more to blame than Christian fundamentalism for the fear of upsetting the status quo. "Fundamentalism," which became a movement later, was in this context a kind of Protestant ethos guiding the American mindset. Nonetheless this is an important reminder that legacies are often read in contemporary terms. Overall, though, it is evident that the establishment's reactions to the band only added to its popularity and to the myth Thompson speaks of.

Perhaps this is why the debate continues. The terms of the debate over the band's legacy are framed in part by the media, and by participants' decision whether to buy into the historically entrenched and institutionalized youthful rebellion in rock. The reputation of the MC5 has come to strike a balance of sorts. As stated on the back of their recent *Sonic Revolution* DVD, "The politics and drama that surround the group's legacy may have enhanced their legend, but what really counts is the music they made" (Day/Kramer/ Samways). In the end it is the music that does the talking, but what "really counts" is that the musical voice is combined with the sometimes harmonious and sometimes dissonant aura that follows the music as it reaches new generations. The music and the myth combine to create something unpiloted and uncontrolled by its authors.

Rather than a mass-media product that imposes a dominant frame, popular culture icons like the MC5 prove that audiences of all varieties (individuals, fans, critics, governments, etc.) should be looked upon as active agents, like those described by Kramer, who make the music and the potential sense of rebellion their own. Simon Frith says that music "has been an important way in which we have learned to understand ourselves as historical, ethnic, classbound, gendered subjects" (149). A significant practice that proves this logic is in audience investment and use of the MC5 and the White Panther Party. Investments are drawn from audiences through numerous facets of the band's performance, including lyrics, stage presence, musicality, self-generated propaganda, and the media's presentation of the group. "How far would they go" in a revolution inspired by class, race and war is a question that is not likely to find any coherent answer soon among audiences and fans. This past is too usable for definite answers.

The ability of audiences to invest in these areas of performance by the band allows for a multiplicity of uses for a wide array of stakeholders. Frith argues that in essence we come to find identity through music by possessing it. "In 'possessing' music, we make it part of our own identity and build it into our sense of ourselves" (143). This creates questions about intent and authenticity. Authenticity is, of course, problematic to gauge, as music is rooted in "the person, the auteur, the community or subculture that lies behind it" as well as in listener communities. Despite the fact that music in the twentieth century and today is "a commercial form, music produced as a commodity, for a profit, distributed through mass media and culture" (Frith 136, 137), this is still the case. An interplay of commercial, revolutionary and individual thought and culture coalesce in the MC5, conflating absolutes in terms of these questions of political and musical intent.

The final product — beyond politics, beyond music, beyond the band's "high energy" approach — is ubiquitous, and seems to have etched a place in sonic, visual and written culture. The MC5 still effortlessly fits itself into the formidable ethos of rebellion in rock through continued touring, DVD releases, album releases and in the press in such periodicals as *Mojo* and *Uncut*. Simply put, the band is successful because of its ability to demand fevered investment, disdain and debate regarding its validity in the political and social world as a musical act. Detroit/Ann Arbor–scene contemporary Iggy Pop of Iggy and the Stooges eloquently describes this fluidity, observing,

> The MC5 went beyond having a sense of humor about themselves; they were a parody. They acted like black thugs with guitars. In Detroit, if you were a

Four. Sonic Anarchy: The Making of the MC5

white kid, your dream was to be a black thug with a guitar and play like one ... I can't say how political the MC5 are, but I certainly didn't feel it. But on a basic level, would they share their peanut butter with me? Yeah. So they were a decent bunch of guys — a nice bunch of guys to have around to blow up your local CIA recruiting office [Hasted 82].

CHAPTER FIVE

Guns and Guitars: Revolutionary Style and Substance?

The MC5's image was the product of an aggressive synergistic marketing campaign by the WPP community that linked the group to the radical, musical, and political landscapes of the late 1960s and early '70s in both local and national contexts. This campaign, whether the group liked it or not, has successfully framed the band for several decades, demonstrating the possibilities of performance and the place of usable rebellion in rock. Questions such as "Is it possible to thrive or merely get by in the music industry and to still have a voice capable of dissent?" and "How authentic were its aims?" followed the group. Throughout the band's career and association with "the revolution," the audiences asking these questions have had various investments in creating meaning through the band's performances. The programs of performance that made up this synergistic campaign propelled debate about music's role in social change.

The MC5 represented, depending on one's view, an all too real threat to national security and "American values," or an elaborate charade, showing how divisive popular culture could become in the modern political and cultural world. Regardless of the intentions of the MC5 or those involved in the WPP community, the authors soon lost control of their intended frames, as the image morphed beyond a single, comprehensible whole.

Supporting a Baudrillardian perspective, preceding chapters have shown how critics, and even some group members like Dennis Thompson, saw the political realities of the WPP as a "paper tiger;" as a non-functioning model. Yet several hundred pages of a documents from the FBI, CIA and other organizations including the Michigan State Police are now available through the Freedom of Information Act,[1] showing that the MC5 and its association

Five. Guns and Guitars: Revolutionary Style and Substance?

with the WPP was taken quite seriously as a threat to national security and concerned people such as Richard Nixon, Gerald Ford and J. Edgar Hoover. Beyond governmental interest, numerous music journalists, musicians and others took an interest in the program of performance the band put together. From this came a discussion of authenticity in regards to the group and its political associations, centering on the question of how far its members were intending to go. Critics, the FBI and those involved in the group make for strange bedfellows in the following pages, but the views of all will be used as gauges to measure notions of dissent and rebellion.

Various parts of the synergized campaign of performance that elicited responses from Lester Bangs to Richard Nixon will be broken down in order to understand the role of these parts in the larger operation The first aspect dissected will be the lyrics. The band's three albums will be examined with a particular concentration on the first album, *Kick Out the Jams*. This focus is warranted, as the album is the only one actually representative of the band's association with the WPP. The following two albums mark a deliberate attempt by the band to distance itself from the political and cultural rhetoric of the WPP. The group's output over the three albums demonstrates a wide range of lyrical themes from sex to drugs, with a surprisingly small amount of political content. Primarily the focus is on the pursuit of hedonistic desires. These focuses actually reflect the hedonistic mantras of the WPP such "as rock and roll, dope and fucking in the streets." Yet politically aware and challenging lyrical themes do occur in such compositions as "The Human Being Lawnmower" and a cover of "Motor City Burning." These messages, do not, however, constitute an overtly politically message or rhetoric.

The second area examined will be live performance, both the sonic makeup of the group and its stage presence. Live performance consists of a combination of music, dance, and onstage antics. Musically, the band fluctuated heavily in its sound. A live, raw and loose aesthetic dominated the first album, *Kick Out the Jams*. The second album, *Back in the U.S.A.*, which was released after the break with the WPP, showcased a much more precise and meticulous band, with most tracks barely reaching three minutes, reflecting much more traditional rock arrangements. The third album, *High Time*, finds a meeting of the first two albums, reclaiming a certain rawness in the compositions that is balanced by the musical discipline of the second album.

Rather than in album sales, the band found its real success and fan base in live venues, especially in the greater Detroit and Ann Arbor scenes. The MC5's stage show was a spectacle not only of music, but also of choreographed dance, with costumes and numerous onstage antics. The power of these live performances led Jac Holzman and Elektra Records to issue the band's first album as a live album. This was a risky and bold move in the record industry at the time. Negative run-ins with the law and promoters like Bill Graham also furthered the band's mythic existence as a live force to be reckoned with and sometimes feared.

The last and broadest area concerns the propaganda and press associated with the band and its association with the WPP. The WPP and Sinclair were behind an intricate network of live performances, photography, newspapers, flyers, art exhibits, poetry publications and readings, buttons, bumper stickers and numerous other means of creating and distributing the image and sound of the MC5 and White Panther initiatives. Here the home-cooked synergy orchestrated by Sinclair helped the MC5 create successful local and regional markets, with marginal commercial success to follow nationally and internationally. Hence, these sources are considered an important part of the larger program of performance. Here, just as within their lyrical content and live shows, specific roles were being played and presented by the band to audiences trying to make sense of what this was all supposed to mean. The propaganda and use of the MC5 as the financial core of raising funds for the WPP greatly aided in the aura of usable rebellion that the band commanded from fans and critics, as well as increasingly drawing attention from the authorities.

The life of the MC5 exists both inside the music as well as in ideological spaces outside of the music itself. This space between is demonstrative of the power and potential of popular culture as a means of expression and dissent. The program of performance that was amalgamated through lyrics, music, live performance, and propaganda contributed in creating a group that was loved, feared, and ridiculed for its experimentation with the usable space of rock in creating, or at least creating the image of, sonically incarnated rebellion and revolution. Live performance, lyrics, and propaganda all are responsible for this mythos. The MC5 myth has been dependent on these areas functioning together and through each other. All the while, the audience's reactions to the band have provoked considerations of authenticity and intent.

Moon, Spoon, and Revolution? An Examination of Lyrical Themes

Lyrical themes should be of direct benefit to audiences in figuring out intent. For a group whose legacy often centers around questions of authenticity in regards to political subversion and rebellion, the lyrical content, the most immediate and obvious tool for a musician to communicate a specific ideological message, is primarily focused on the traditional conceptions of rebellion in rock. As Ochs notes, this is a concentration on "teen topics of interest — automobiles, assorted fads, sexuality, rebellion, escape, energy, life, death, loneliness, dancing and dating" (Ochs, 10) and not on politically revolutionary thought or rhetoric. Lyrically, the MC5 explored notions of rebellion in much the same way as numerous predecessors in the rock canon. Isolated, the lyrical content of the songs of the MC5 could easily be overlooked in regard to revolutionary themes when considering other musical fare of the time such as "Street Fighting Man" or "Volunteers." The content at most offers a push to hedonistic pleasures found in dating, sex and drug use. In other words, nothing revolutionary for the time. These messages speak to a level of usable rebellion, yet not one that directly threatened the security of the nation or advocated for socialist or communist revolution.

Valuable in this regard is a perspective from Rob Tyner, in Sheppard's 1988 interview for *Ugly Things Magazine*. As Tyner was the primary vehicle delivering lyrical content and themes, Sheppard's interview captures a voice now lost, discussing the meaning and possibility of the words that he delivered.

Generally, the band's first album, *Kick Out the Jams*, is filled with brooding and unapologetic sexuality. Vocalist Rob Tyner actively mimics an orgasmic climax indicative of this theme in "Come Together," a song steeped in double entendre and machismo. The song ends with Tyner imitating the path to orgasm, pulling the audience unashamedly along for the ride. If we had not been given a clear enough indication of intent, the band, when thanking the applauding audience as the song ends, beseeches, "We hope you all did ... come together." Although potentially a message of brotherhood and community, the band unapologetically points us to a voice of sexual desire through lyrical forms.

Throbbing machismo abounds as well in such tracks as "Rocket Reducer No. 62," where Tyner proudly gloats about being an "ass pincher" and not caring about the repercussions. Numerous other tracks on the rest of the album and on the other two LPs echo these sentiments. A cover of "Tutti Frutti" opens *Back in the U.S.A.* and shares a teenage vision of sexuality that by the time of the release of the album seemed very unthreatening when compared to other lyrics in the music industry at the time, when best-selling groups like the Beatles were asking "Why Don't We Do It in the Road?" But the band quickly re-establishes its swaggering tone on the track "Teenage Lust," where Tyner unweaves a tale of unbridled sexual angst and want that boils over in an admission that if this energy isn't directed soon, he may explode.

The lyrical content bends between the extreme and the flaccid throughout and into the next album, *High Time*. Songs from the MC5's last two albums demonstrate unashamed sexuality in tracks like "Call Me Animal" on *Back* or "Miss X" on *High Time*. The latter work describes in great detail bodies undulating and dripping in sweat. But other tracks such as "Let Me Try" on *Back in the U.S.A.* present a fairly commercially digestible and traditional notion of sexuality in lyrical content inspired by the blues tradition. Tyner delivers an intimate, pleading message that promises satisfaction as well as tenderness. This sentiment does not much more challenge the sexual mindset of the American public than individuals ranging from Muddy Waters or Mick Jagger had done by the late 1960s.

The work of the MC5 carried a very real tradition of sexuality in lyrical form, both obvious and as metaphor. One could easily make the case that sex thematically dominated the MC5's lyrics. Politically, the sexual theme was not a real threat to the nation or to notions of dominant American values. When held up to other musical examples of the time, the subject matter of sexuality was old news. The second dominating theme of the lyrics — drug use — might be considered somewhat more of a threat. The topic of drug use, far from a rarity, was commonly found in music of the time.

The celebration and encouragement of drug use among Trans-Love Energies and the White Panther Party was far from a tightly guarded secret. Drug use was advocated within the basic platform of the WPP and was a focus of police interest directed at John Sinclair and his marijuana advocacy. The band cites drugs as an integral influence on performance in "Kick Out the Jams," which describes a pot haze encompassing their dressing room before a show. The theme continues in "Rocket Reducer No. 62," declaring

Five. Guns and Guitars: Revolutionary Style and Substance?

a dependency on chemical inspiration in the form of marijuana and beer. Michael Davis says that "Rocket Reducer No. 62" is actually the name of a chemical solvent used to strip paint off engine blocks. Several of the individuals involved in the group and the WPP community would soak rags in the solvent to get high (Davis 2005). Such overt references are less prominent in the latter two albums, as general themes of youthful rebellion and sexuality became the focus.

A general sense of youthful rebellion, the usable theme so present in the rise of rock, is honored and heralded concretely throughout all three albums and through a teenage perspective. Embracing this youthful play, the band members decree themselves hell-raisers on the first album. The cornerstone piece on the first album, the title track "Kick Out Jams (Motherfuckers)," possessed a demand for energy and a usable challenge to any power structure the listener wanted to insert in the blank. Says Tyner,

> I think "Kick Out the Jams" was kind of like the battle cry of the White Panther Party. Nobody understood exactly what it meant then; it was sort of like whatever you wanted it to mean. The beauty of rock 'n' roll on a lot of levels is that people can hear the sound that you make and they interpret it however they want, because it's kind of open-ended. You try to keep the songs with enough room so that people could put their dreams on it [Sheppard 13].

Such sentiment fits in succinctly with the notion of usable rebellion. Fans, critics, the government, and, perplexingly enough, the band took this musical raw material and used it to create their own meanings.

The next album (which marked the separation from the WPP), *Back in the U.S.A.*, overtly pulls in a '50s teenage rock aesthetic meant to be more succinct. "Tonight" and "High School," for instance, describe familiar narratives of teenage angst. "Tonight" posits the MC5 as the voice of youth, yearning to escape the dullness of the classroom to get to a local rock show. Tyner feverishly describes the urge to see a band play that night and to dance uninhibitedly to the music. Significantly mirroring this theme, "High School" claims that the concern of the "kids" is, in the end, to escape the drudgery of the institution and to get a little crazy and dance to the music. In the end a warning is issued that these wild *Blackboard Jungle*–esque youth will eventually take over. Implied here is the idea that adults should heed the song as a warning. Again, the themes dominating the group's work thus far, although sometimes crass, still follow Ochs's notions of teenage rebellion in music.

Political themes did indeed make an appearance in the lyrics of the group, but in terms of considering direct political challenges, a general sense of youthful insurgency was much more present than any formal plan for revolution. Vietnam is predominately the focus over the three albums of politically overt messages in the lyrics. These messages are less pleas for direct action and more part of the general commentary in popular music of the time. Such messages could be found in the lyrics of numerous other groups such as Country Joe and the Fish, Credence Clearwater Revival, Jimi Hendrix, and even the Lovin' Spoonful.[2]

The anti-war theme is explored on the band's second album, where Rob Tyner sings about receiving a letter from the Army. He decides that he does not want to take part, not due to laziness, but due to an overwhelming case of sanity. One of the most overt commentaries on the Vietnam War and the state of American society on the same album comes in "The American Ruse." Society in 1969 is cited as being in "terminal stasis." The band rejects the America of its youth where freedom was taught, but now feels more like repression. Now facing the Army beckoning them to Vietnam, they become fully aware of the "American Ruse." As Tyner told Doug Sheppard in 1988, "That was about the unrest in the country." He continues that in addition to wanting to communicate the importance of knowing your rights,

> another thing that I'm glad about that tune is I got a chance to say "take a look around" to people. I kept repeating that over and over and again, because I think that is real important. At that time, what people needed to hear from me was that the price of freedom is vigilance; you gotta really watch and make sure that your rights are not slowly eroding away. That's what the "American Ruse" is [15].

Similar in sentiment is the song "The Human Being Lawnmower," where the Vietnam War is equated to a mindless death machine to which youth blindly submit themselves. Says Tyner, "'The Human Being Lawnmower' was kind of like a poetic way of describing what was going on in Vietnam. It's like this huge meat-grinder that's happening. I can't put it any other way. There was all these people with this huge lawnmower running through ... it was like a metaphor for all the horror that was going on" (Sheppard 15).

Such perspectives are continued on *High Time*, with numerous songs questioning the war and its contextual relationship to modern American life. "Gotta Keep Movin,'" "Poison," and "Over and Over" discuss frustrations with Vietnam and American life. Here the band is taking part in the

Five. Guns and Guitars: Revolutionary Style and Substance?

usable rebellion in rock that had evolved as social upheavals played themselves out on the battlefields of Vietnam, on the streets of cities and on campuses across the nation. Music offered commentary and a place for audiences and consumers to vicariously or directly challenge social and political concerns of the time. Some of these messages offered a sense of empowerment without a clear path to tearing down the status quo. *High Time's* most direct comment on social change and rebellion came in "Future/Now," where a plea for autonomy says that those in power are only looking out for themselves.

Yet such pleas advocating rebellion to a new and usable level were not a central focus of concern for the governmental agencies that considered the band, the party, and individuals like Sinclair and Plamondon possible extremist factions in the New Left. In terms of *Back in the U.S.A.* and *High Time*, this was probably because the band already had publicly split with Sinclair and the WPP. However, when formally associated with the WPP during the recording of *Kick Out the Jams*, the band's lyrical content was the focus of some concern for those governmental agencies trying to understand the WPP and the musical organizing force that propelled it financially, the MC5.

The government largely ignored lyrical themes while focusing on other aspects of the band. Most of the interest in the MC5 as a tool of extremism was generated by its propaganda, with very little interest paid to lyrical content outside the band's use of profanity. For example, a letter dated March 20, 1969, addressed to the president of the University of Michigan, the Justice Department, the FBI, and the Michigan District Attorney from a concerned "parent and taxpayer" was placed into the band's FBI file, a file that was opened as early as 1967.[3] The writer, collecting quotations from WPP propaganda, hoped to provide some local insight to what he or she saw as a moral threat to the immediate community. The writer wants to "enforce the sedition laws against the White Panther Party." The writer says that the "moral tone of this trash" is not protected by the First Amendment. The writer of the letter, whose name is classified, then goes on to cite numerous pamphlets and rhetoric associated with the group. Such examples are the standard among the intelligence gathered on the band and the WPP. Lyrical content receives little attention in the face of Sinclair's fiery rhetoric.

Lyrically, the band did draw some attention for its performance of "Motor City Is Burning," a song popularized by John Lee Hooker.[4] An FBI memo dated February 25, 1969, describes a *Time Magazine* feature published on January 3 that year. The article says, "The group also performed Al White's "Motor City Is Burning," and there was no mistaking the message: 'All the cities will burn.... You are the people who will build up the ashes.'" Concern about the article in the memo seems to center around the contention that "the MC5 are taking protest one step further to get attention by practicing what they preach, as is shown by their string of arrests on charges of noisemaking, obscenity, and possession of marijuana" (Special Agent-in-Charge 25 February 1969). The article is used as an initial frame, from which the memo's author is attempting to make general sense of the band.

For Tyner, the lyrics were a commentary on the 1967 riot—a song that was sung "because we lived through it." Although having left the city himself, he sees the song as a reflection of the madness that surrounded the band, along with what he witnessed personally on his way out. "The other people in the band didn't get out of the city. A bunch of 'em wound [sic] going to jail. The cops just came and picked 'em up and threw their ass in jail" (Sheppard 12). The song, although an expression of rage, according to Tyner was also an expression of confusion and even fear for the future of their city.

The same article that contained the information harvested by the FBI said, "Just as clearly, even their most aggressive songs are only that—songs, not bricks or guns. It may be that the first victim of their metaphorical revolution will be the overused word revolution itself" ("The Revolutionary Hype"). Even with such condescending tones concerning the role of music in social change, state and national authorities would not take any chances. Interest in the band and the WPP grew until the authorities believed they were dangerous extremists.

The effective synergy that helped to garner audience investments did not come from lyrical themes. Along with lyrical content, performance would greatly add to the band's reputation among fans, critics, and governmental authorities. Musical performance both in a sonic and theatrical sense also contributed heavily to the MC5's image—either a face of the revolution, or the face of an unashamed marketing campaign drawing on the social and political upheaval of the world at the time.

Five. Guns and Guitars: Revolutionary Style and Substance?

Marshall Stacks and Norman Mailer: Musicality, Performance and the MC5

Sonic structure and live performance were key to the reactions the MC5 garnered from its fan base, from critics, and from authorities. This was especially the case during their affiliation with John Sinclair and the WPP, when a close eye was kept on the band's performances by fans and federal authorities. Elektra Records' risky decision to record the band live for its first album is indicative of this connection between music and live performance. The musicality and stage performance of the group was the most immediate and lucrative means of creating a link, or the fallacy of a link, between music and social change. As Baudrillard says, "A myth of power — and a myth of origins: whatever it is that man lacks is invested in the object." Essentially, he contends, "it has become a sign" (82). As Thompson saw a "paper tiger," critics like Lester Bangs see an empty signifier in the guise of a "revolutionary rock band." Or, as in Norman Mailer's view, the music could be a revelatory experience that could speak volumes about social change and development. The band's sonic construction and its dramatic live shows were the most immediate form of performance that allowed audiences to gauge the validity of the band in relation to its supposed revolutionary objectives.

In 1968, while chronicling the Democratic National Convention in Chicago, Norman Mailer came across the MC5 performing in Lincoln Park. The performance was one that Mailer spoke of as a revelatory sonic pronunciation of the counterculture and the potential energies contained within, an experience that shook the foundations of an elder generation whose ears had been raised on "Star Dust."

> He knew they were a generation which lived in the sound of destruction of all order as he had known it, and the worlds of other decomposition as well; there was the sound of mountains crashing in this holocaust of the decibels, ears bursting, literally bursting, as if this was the sound of death by explosion within, the drums of physiological climax when the mind was blown, and forces of the future, powerful, characterless, as insane and scalding as waves of lava [Mailer 142].

The author claims that he was "as affected by the sound (as affected by the recognition of what nihilisms were calmly encountered in such a musical storm) as if he had heard it in a room at midnight with painted bodies and kaleidoscopic sights" (143). This same performance was filmed by the Depart-

The MC5 in performance, Mt. Clemens, Michigan. Front (L to R): Wayne Kramer, Rob Tyner, Fred "Sonic" Smith. Back: Dennis "Machine Gun" Thompson. Michael Davis is just outside the frame (courtesy Leni Sinclair).

ment of Defense with perhaps a differing revelatory intent (Day, Kramer and Samways). Others such as Bill Graham and various promoters and venue owners could have cared less about ideological implications of the band's performances, good or bad, and were much more concerned with the band's reputation and penchant to involve local authorities. Manager John Sinclair, writing in his book *Guitar Army*, describes the band's numerous run-ins with the law over noise, drug and obscenity violations. Perhaps the most notorious of these run-ins occurred at Graham's Fillmore East, where an anarchic group called "The Motherfuckers" demanded free entry. A brawl ensued and Graham's nose was broken with a chain.[5]

How, then, is it possible that the MC5's live shows could contain both the spirit of Woodstock and the dystopia of Altamont in one space? A great carnivalesque atmosphere a la Bakhtin was created in the MC5's live environment that was hard to predict. What the band did, the music it played, and what the band represented to groups like the Motherfuckers who ini-

Five. Guns and Guitars: Revolutionary Style and Substance?

tially saw the band as the sonic vanguard of the revolution all drew investment from the audience. A symbiotic relationship grew among all of those involved. As Davis says,

> To me, our performances were about spectacle ... multimedia presentations that went into infinite possibility where anything could happen. In the back of my stoned consciousness there was some nirvana ... that we would all just wind up somewhere and that everybody would be cool. It was a fantasy, but back then fantasy was a big part of my deal. We were stoned on weed and hash all of the time and taking this and that ... anything we could get our hands on to expand our consciousness [2006].

This attempt to reach nirvana within concert venues and stages around the nation, and the immediacy of exposure to the band and the WPP in these venues were a concern for authorities, who kept as up to date on the band's live schedule as the fans. Whether the revolutionary rhetoric was authentic seems moot as so many actively negotiated meanings were constructed within this space of identity and community.

Davis's nirvana spoken was not loosely amalgamated but was focused on creating this carnivalesque environment where both the group and the audience were the intended targets. The concert space offered a usable and sometimes highly dramatized environment from which to escape everyday life, focused through the band's concept of "high energy" performance. This meant complete immersion in the music for the band and its audience. Kramer recalls:

> The performance and the spectacle ... we called it high energy. We had a high-energy lifestyle, we had high-energy music, and we had high-energy performance. That peak energy ... we were drawn to it and fed by it. When I would go to see another band and maybe one or two guys in the band were really deeply intensely doing what they were doing, I would connect with them more than the guy just going through the motions. It was a matter of passion and commitment. When we talked about that and incorporated that consciously into our performances and our music, we got that reaction back from our audience. We would win people over, we would convert them. We would make believers out of them! [2006]

Research on the MC5 revealed that this notion of "high-energy" music and performance was the only concept the remaining band members agreed upon. "High-energy" music and performance is arguably *the* ideological connection that links all three remaining members across politics, the music business, and the band's career path. Michael Davis asserts that this ingredient in creating the band's live sound and presence was intrinsic to the band's limited success nationally and internationally:

> It's an attitude ... it's a hard thing to define, to describe in words. It's almost as if you tap into a beam where everything you do is just focused. It doesn't mean you focus on anything; it's just focused period. When you play, the way that I interact with your drum part or guitar part ... the way that my instrument sounds, the band as a unified sound is intense ... it's an intensity. You just can't kick back. It's condensed into the smallest, strongest beam possible; it's all about strength. It's not about speed, fast or slow it's something you feel. It's kind of like losing consciousness. I've heard it said that in the sex act the moment of orgasm is almost a loss of consciousness. It's almost a dream state. High energy ... that is the closest thing that I can bring it to ... it is that intense. It's sort of like living on the edge ... going around that corner and not knowing if the tires are going to hold or not. It's like taking it to the edge of sanity [2006].

Davis continues, "We were in our early 20s at that point and we thought we could do damn near anything. Our point was to shock people ... coming out of their suburban coma" (2006). Dennis Thompson agrees with Davis's assessment, adding, "We were brutally assaulting their senses. We did it with the sound, with the music" (2006).

Davis says that in the end, the energy was what propelled the band. Even in the face of supposed weaknesses, the notion of energy overcame members' faults. Davis remembers in his "Diary of a Mad Dog" that "in the beginning, Mick Jagger was pulling them in by sheer sexuality. This is what Tyner had to compete with on the stage. Skinny legs, paunchy middle, a gap in his teeth, and the kinkiest hair ever for a white boy—not an easy prescription for a singer in a world full of pretty boy guitar bands. But his gut was charged with rock and roll fever and whatever he had to do, he was determined to get there" (Davis "Diary"). Such sentiment, even between two individuals in the band that had a sometimes contentious relationship, showcases the focus of the band on intensity and energy in performance. Such drive was considered a mark of investment in the project at hand. But different members of the band and WPP had different ideas about what that project was, exactly.

In an interview done in 1969, Fred "Sonic" Smith, Wayne Kramer and Rob Tyner discussed how this notion of "high-energy" performance fit into the larger interest in social change and development.

Five. Guns and Guitars: Revolutionary Style and Substance?

The MC5 with Rob Tyner at the vocal helm. West Park, Ann Arbor, Michigan, 1968. (L to R): Wayne Kramer, Michael Davis, Rob Tyner, Dennis "Machine Gun" Thompson, Fred "Sonic" Smith (courtesy Leni Sinclair).

> FRED: There's a parallel there then to the whole Movement too.
> WAYNE: Right, that each person who involves himself has received another person's energy, and it is only a matter of time until there's enough energy to....
> ROB: To cover all levels. That's the basic principle involved here, all these different people, all these different groups, and different organizations, are each covering a level; the Black Panthers cover a level, and the Motherfuckers cover a level, and the SDS cover a level. Fusing all those energies together, it's going to spread. That's because everybody is jostling for position on these levels, you know, who's going to cover what level [Walley "Interview"].

The band's musicality and its arena of performance are seen here by these three band members as inherently connected to the larger structure of the New Left movement.

The MC5 and Social Change

Here, Van Gosse's idea of a "movement of movements" is shown in practical application. Notions of cultural, political, and social separation were quite blurred for many involved. Music, to the three above, played a part in a larger structure of social change and development. Granted, all members did not agree on this role within an increasingly contentious climate. Still, just as those who invested in the MC5 as fans did, the members saw a possible means for expression of dissident, rebellious thought and emotion. The expression of this musical voice was powerful and meaningful for some.

Such investment in meaning and musicality was far from universal. The band's musical legacy is still debated among critics and fans. Lester Bang's review of the MC5's first album in a 1969 issue of *Rolling Stone* that lambasted the group's revolutionary tactics as a ruse exploiting the politically charged times (Bangs 34) mirrors similar discussions three decades later. A 2003 issue of *Bang Magazine* describes the group's first album with the following mischievous words: "Politically correct it ain't; slick it is not. It couldn't be dumber or less grown-up. It's a rushed, garbled, rambling, patchy snapshot of an overhyped and under-rehearsed band who were totally off their ugly, white-afroed heads on tons of stupid drugs and the sheer power of their own ridiculous self-mythologising. And it was wonderful" (*Bang*). The release of the MC5's boxed set, *Purity Accuracy*, in 2005 elicited similar musical comment. Nick Hasted in *Uncut Magazine* claimed that the live CDs were "more grueling, as the band bravely attempt free jazz freak-outs with inadequate musical ammo" (123).

In terms of authorities who were collecting intelligence on the band and the WPP, the sonic qualities of the group were not of interest, beyond the labeling of the group as a "'hard' or 'acid' rock group," as identified in a 1969 Secret Service report on John Sinclair. It cited "individuals involved in illegal bombing or illegal bomb-making," and "identified as member or participant in communist movement" as the cause for the intelligence gathering (Secret Service Report 19 September 1969). Local and federal authorities were much more concerned with the band's onstage antics and the crowds that the band was capable of drawing.

Part of what sold the band to the public, the media, and the authorities who would label the group as an extremist threat was the elaborate stage show. The show incorporated music, dance, display, and White Panther rhetoric. (Concerts were a favorite spot to pass out literature and items embla-

Five. Guns and Guitars: Revolutionary Style and Substance?

zoned with the WPP logo.) John Sinclair wrote to *Creem Magazine* in 1970: "The stage show grew directly out of the music, all the dope we were smoking, and out of our culture and our collective history. As the music got more frantic the stage show got farther out, and the people responded wildly and it got more and more wild. It was a beautiful demonstration of the principles of high-energy performance: as the performer puts out more, the energy level of the audience is raised and they give back more energy to the performers" (Sinclair 11, "A Letter").

The presentation, according to Kramer, was based on several ingredients that included choreography, agit-prop theatre including, once, a faked assassination of Rob Tyner, hype-men, a fake religion, and costumes that went along with the musical presentation.

> There is physicality to it ... the performance the dance. I always admired performers that danced ... interpreting what's happening with the music with your body. My idols of course are James Brown and Jackie Wilson and Tina Turner ... people who really knew how to move on stage. Even ballet dancers, modern dancers, jazz dancers ... you're trying to carry a message, you're trying to tell a story. So what is your media? Do you have paints, music, dance, theater? We were trying to incorporate as much of that into as we could. We used to talk about it in terms of "meat energy," put the meat energy into it! There would be that, the performance, the art, the science of the performance [2006].

Kramer asserts that the full intent of the shows was lost in favor of a reductive label of "revolutionary rock."

> It's almost as if what ended up being transmitted about the MC5 was not really was what the MC5 was. We really did have a much broader artistic agenda. By the time it filtered down into "revolutionary rock" it got reduced down into the simplest sound bite. We were trying to really open doors to all new stuff. The stuff Dennis told you about [a faked assassination of Rob Tyner while on stage] ... bands didn't do this kind of thing.... incorporating agit-prop street theater into the performance. I mean this predates Alice Cooper or any of the stage theatrics of today. We learned from the living theater ... Julian Beck and their production of *Paradise Now* where the actors came out and said, "I'm not allowed to take my clothes off" and then they took their clothes off. "I'm not allowed to smoke marijuana" and then they smoked marijuana. To me this was real, this was intense! So we would actually sit in a room and brainstorm theatrical productions that would make some kind of social comment or statement ... or just good entertainment value! But we would try to keep it to something that would have a larger meaning to it. Of course these

stories are lost in the vapors, they were never documented, they were never filmed [2006].

Mirroring boundary-pushing performances of other such controversial bands like the Doors, the band's performances became a target of concern for authorities. Sgt. Clifford A. Murray represents what seems to be a general feel of moral panic when discussing the band's ability to draw audiences at live events, and to turn performances into flashpoints of debauchery and rebellion. He testified before a U.S. Senate Internal Securities Subcommittee in 1970. "I would like to say at this time that it is the opinion of myself and that of my department that the White Panther Party is working toward obtaining control of large masses of young people for the primary purpose of causing revolution in this country." He continues, "The methods used to recruit these people is based upon a complete dropout of our society and the adoption of a system involving 'rock music' and the free use of drugs and sex" (Sinclair 1972, 31). The most immediate exposure to this feared communal environment was in the concert setting. Recruitment could be done there.

One of the first recorded instances of intelligence-gathering was when the FBI listed TLE as hosting the 1967 Detroit Belle Isle Love-In, "which ended up in a 'rock-heaving' and 'bottle-tossing' riot." This information was included in a report on the activities of John Sinclair up to that time (Hoover "Re: John Alexander Sinclair"). Whether the subject is really the band or the crowd and its behaviors is given further consideration in numerous documents. An FBI memorandum dated February 25, 1969, used the band's feature in *Time Magazine* to gather general information. "The article states that the MC5 now favor outrageous on stage stunts [such] as removing their clothes and burning the United States flag" (Special Agent-in-Charge 25 February 1969). By the time of this memorandum, the band had already been filmed by the Department of Defense during the Lincoln Park concert in Chicago. Indeed, the band had a lengthy relationship with authorities, resulting from marijuana violations and arrests, the use of profanity, and nakedness on stage and the desecration of the American flag during live performance. Sinclair proudly advertised these run-ins in periodicals including the *Fifth Estate* and the *Ann Arbor Sun*.[6] Fred Goodman in *The Mansion on a Hill* describes an evening's occurrences when the MC5 burned an American flag onstage, as an opening act for Cream. "The show climaxed with

Five. Guns and Guitars: Revolutionary Style and Substance?

Tyner ripping a plastic flag to shreds and then hoisting a 4 × 5-foot banner inscribed with a marijuana leaf and the word FREEK. To put just the right finish on the spectacle, a member of the lighting crew walked onstage naked and settled cross-legged at the lip of the stage, where he chanted "Om" as the final chord of the band's ear shattering performance faded into an electric hum" (163). Focusing on the band's drawing power among the countercultural community is a Michigan State Police inter-office correspondence memo. In one of the more entertaining bits of intelligence, the memo says that the MC5 are set "to play the Student Union at MSU [Michigan State University] on Saturday, November 2, 1968. This should draw all the hippies from all the counties around the Lansing area" (Schave). What this meant, beyond a generic threat, was not explored in the brief memo. It seems as if the warning of hippies gathering was enough to merit concern from the police.

The ability of the MC5 to draw concertgoers to their various shows above all was seen as a cash cow for the activities of John Sinclair, Pun Plamondon and the WPP. Confidential Michigan State Police reports through 1970 said the "great bulk of the financial support for the Y.I.P. [Youth International Party]–W.P.P. originally came from John Sinclair's percentage of the MC-5 earned in his capacity as manager" (Murray). In actuality, more than Sinclair's percentage was used to fund the WPP, which did not, according to interviews, maintain a formal relationship with the Yippies. The band functioned as the primary source of capital for the WPP. Another Michigan State Police memo looked positively on the incident with Bill Graham and the Motherfuckers that resulted in many concert venues blacklisting the band. "As of recent weeks, the MC-5 has run into problems because of the adverse effect of the White Panther activities and the publicity and because of this numerous appearances have been cancelled which results in a financial problem" ("Memo to Captain Walter Hawkins"). Both of these reports tried to gather a wide array of information about the WPP and the MC5's role in the group, focusing on finance, membership, location, and associated publications.

The reputation of the band through its lyrical, musical and performance contexts would have had little significance without the fevered use of media by Sinclair and the WPP. Instead, the band was surrounded by masterful town criers, which can be heard on *Kick Out the Jams*. Brother JC Crawford's (the band's hype man and the WPP's "Minister of Religion") pleading to "see some revolution" and asking the crowd whether it is part of the problem or part of the solution provides some of the most memorable propaganda associated with the band.[7] Although not all members of the group agreed on political content, they all believed an individual like Crawford was a valuable addition to the group, acting as an effective hype-man for the band's shows. This was not true for all of the propaganda and rhetoric put out by the WPP. Photos, underground press and other media became an additional focus of surveillance and concern for those who believed the band was fomenting rebellion through music to a much too usable level. Group members saw this as both adding to the success of the group and eventually leading to its downfall. Reactions from the national press made the band feel claustrophobic, and lent a general sense of greater authoritarian oppression by the industry and the government.

Watching Us, Watching You: The Press and the Framing of the MC5

The importance of the press and its framing of the MC5, taken together with the WPP's own propaganda, reflect a central framing process to create the MC5's mythos. Press pieces would play an intricate part in creating the notion and implications of "revolutionary rock" and the band's aura of usable rebellion. This usability entails not only fan and critical response and usage, but also includes the reaction of the government and the surveillance that resulted. Print media proved especially useful to the group and the White Panthers in trying to define and spread their message, and also allowed convenient frames for authorities and the public to understand the lyrical messages and performances of the band and their supposed intent. Conveniently, press sources that promoted interest in the band and its myth became a tool of performance that the band depended on, as well as a tool used by audiences to help determine meaning and intent.

As Todd Gitlin discusses in *The Whole World Is Watching*, the mass media seek to "*process* social opposition, to control its image and to diffuse it at the same time, to absorb what can be absorbed into the dominant structure of definitions and images and to push the rest to the margins of social life" (5). This absorption and disposition of information into usable forms also seems to apply to federal surveillance methods, which utilized media frames to establish basic perspectives about the MC5 and White Panther Party. The use of the *Time* article "The Revolutionary Hype" by the FBI to frame its investigations points to accessibility of media framing, which describes the makeup of the group for an interested party, in this case the FBI. This media frame also details the extent of increasing attention for the group in national media outlets. The report references the band being featured in a "well-known widely circulated weekly'" (Special Agent-in-Charge 25 February 1969). FBI files about John Sinclair and the actions of the band and the WPP also cite news sources such as the *Detroit News* as sources for their information ("Secret Service Report"). FBI files reference other media sources that featured information on the MC5 including Barry Kramer, editor of *Creem Magazine*, who was investigated as a possible accessory to the actions of the WPP and MC5 ("Memorandum to Director"). Other publications like *Rolling Stone* and the *Village Voice* featuring the group could have been used for similar purposes, but that's hard to determine because of redactions and the destruction of some documents. Using media outlets set a precedent in intelligence gathering, for example the Michigan State Police's use of *Detroit Free Press* sources in its investigation of the MC5's role in the Belle Isle Love-In in 1967, or, as the report referred to, an "Assembly of Hippies" ("Detroit Police"). Much like the public at large, it seems that the United States intelligence community depended on press reports and frames to establish an understanding of the MC5 and its association with the White Panther Party.

The use of press sources is part of intelligence gathering and the use of these sources in reference to the MC5 and the WPP should not be considered exceptional. What should be considered exceptional, especially in regard to the New Left and associated groups, is that the media played an increasingly central role in determining meaning, even to potentially repressive state apparatuses such as the military. This created, as Gitlin calls it, an active "notion of hegemony," where the press naturalizes complex entities into usable frames for the public, the authorities and even perhaps members of the group themselves (10). Major media outlets were trying actively to either dismiss or embrace the themes of rebellion put forth by groups like the White Panthers, SDS, the Weather Underground, and the Black Panthers. These frames can actively shape the political and social world and the ways these groups are received. Dennis "Machine Gun" Thompson sees these media frames as intrinsically shaping the reception of the band by the public at large. "The

MC5 got tagged by the media as the vanguard of the revolution. Speaking for myself that is not what I wanted to do. Once they gave us this political tag, it made it tough for us. We were a threat. We were more of a perceived threat. Like someone can get tried for murder in the media. It's how fast things are compressed in this modern day world. The MC5 was guilty" (2006).

Yet isolating one entity like major press as *the* reason for the MC5's lasting relationship to audience discussions of rebellion, authenticity and music and social change would be ignoring a major and conflating perspective on media at which the White Panthers excelled, the creation of their own press and propaganda. This contributed to creating a level of usable rebellion in audiences, including to the governmental interest that considered the band a legitimate threat. Thompson and other group members testify to the importance of this media onslaught and its creation of a revolutionary rock mythos.

Thompson explains, "The perception of what we were was manufactured by ourselves to a slight degree. For a while we had swollen heads ... we thought we were going to change the world. That was youthful naivety" (2006). What Thompson is describing was the flyers, newspapers, photographs and other propaganda used to obtain funds for the band and the White Panther Party. These materials often were intended to exacerbate and highlight tensions between the groups and the authorities. Run-ins with the law and other "heroic" feats were chronicled by manager John Sinclair in periodicals including *Guerrilla, Hard Times, The Fifth Estate,* and *The Ann Arbor Argus* as well as newspapers created by the WPP, including *Sun/Dance,* the "national organ of the White Panther Party" (Sinclair 1972; 60). Michael Davis places a central importance on frames such as Sinclair's "Rock and Roll Dope" series in *The Fifth Estate* in creating further media attention. "First, any kind of government intervention into what we were doing or our performances was always viewed as positive! It was just like that famous picture of the girl [sic] sticking the daisy in the National Guard guy's rifle barrel. How do you fight that? It's an insurmountable argument ... checkmate!" He continues, "I always thought anything the government did to repress us was good publicity for us and not just for us but for what we were wanted to do" (2006). Guitarist Wayne Kramer sees this independent and sometimes self-generated media as responsible for later, mass-generated frames.

Five. Guns and Guitars: Revolutionary Style and Substance?

> I don't have the sense that we got a lot of play out of mainstream media. Most of the work we accomplished was in the underground press, through our own media. The underground press was an entire syndicate of newspapers in every city in America and around the world, and it was called UPS, the Underground Press Syndicate. It was pretty well organized. These were young entrepreneurs who saw that there was a need for a cultural voice as an alternative to Walter Cronkite and *The New York Times*. That's where we found our exposure [2006].

Much like the debate over authenticity and intent that continues today across audience lines, Kramer says the band's aims were even then sharply debated outside its own self-generated press. "We would get hammered pretty hard from the Left, because they would question how we could be revolutionaries and charge money for gigs. These were kind of tough questions for us in those days. I wasn't that well-versed to articulate our position. John was better suited" (2006). The writings of Sinclair in these publications and in WPP literature, as opposed to lyrical content or performance, are some of the most direct and outspoken ideological pieces of the MC5 puzzle. Some of those involved, such as Kramer and Rob Tyner, felt invested in and helped shape these ideologies.

Pun Plamondon admits that, like the band, he felt he was performing a role as minister of defense. "It was very much me performing. Like I say, I had always been the roughneck, the violence-prone individual, and now I started wearing a black beret." He copied behaviors from a smattering of revolutionary figures. "I can remember having to go to places to speak, and I always wanted to speak like Fidel, 'cause Fidel was known for his extemporaneous, off-the-cuff speeches. Fidel's dead-straight-away speaking at the United Nations after the Cuban Revolution lasted eight hours. I always wanted to be able to do that." But he was never completely pleased with his "performance." "It always comes down to: 'If they don't listen to us, we're gonna kick their ass.' That gets pretty stale, and it's very shallow" (Larabee 116). Such messages, no matter how Plamondon viewed his "performance," contributed to the serious reception of the groups.

Some, like Michael Davis, felt increasing pressure from the propaganda.

> It started getting away from my ideal of being a rock and roll band. The images I thought were more important at the time were being the tough guy, the Rolling Stones, or performance artists like The Who ... things that I thought were more critical for us. They were more important to me than

standing on stage and saying, "these guys are no good and these guys are no good." I got really tongue-tied. Am I saying the right thing here? Maybe this is counter-revolutionary? Maybe I'm offending somebody ... maybe offending these guys? Listen ... I'll just keep my mouth shut.... I know that I would like to see society agree on what a real life is ... I felt like that we were heading in that direction and then all of a sudden I felt compression ... then I felt ... better watch your step now ... it wasn't freedom anymore. It was from within ... it was with us really! [2006].

The writings produced by Sinclair and other WPP officials such as the following example from "Rock & Roll Dope #5" highlighted altercations, which defiantly challenged the police and government, in this case a dispute over pay and obscenities in the band's performance.

Fred leaped into the pile of pigs who were beating on me, but two of them pulled him off and beat his ass with clubs. They subdued both of us, got us handcuffed and dragged us over into the corner before they started clearing the room. A bunch of sisters, righteous MC5 addicts who came to all our gigs, came over and started wiping the blood off of us, but the pigs grabbed them and pushed them down the stairs [Sinclair, 1972 92].

Such self-generated press, along with more prevalent works like Sinclair's liner notes, which reached an international audience on the band's first album, stated that the band was a "free high energy source that will drive us wild into the streets of America yelling and screaming and tearing down everything that would keep people slaves."[8] Such sentiments, apart from framing the group to numerous audiences including the media, underground press, fans, and critics, were also of central concern for the FBI and Michigan State Police. This certainly could have contributed to the heightened interest in the band and the WPP which created the "compression" Davis complained about.

FBI and Michigan State Police records obtained through the Freedom of Information Act indicate a concerned focus on group propaganda. FBI reports as late as 1975 focus on media outlets created by Sinclair and affiliated parties including the WPP, using themes of drug use, dependency on rock to spread ideological messages, and personal defense ("FBI Correlation"). An FBI memorandum to the agency's director dated April 24, 1969, examines the *Sun* in detail and its potential readership, especially in the Ann Arbor/Detroit area. The *Sun* was *the* central publication of the White Panther Party, and the publisher of the "White Panther Statement." The paper is tracked

Five. Guns and Guitars: Revolutionary Style and Substance?

down in the file to an Ann Arbor residential address. The report states, "The paper is cut on a stencil and is being run off on a duplicator owned by the MC 5, a rock band headquartered at 1510 Hill, and managed by Sinclair. Sources further advised that the paper is made available to high school students from the Detroit Metropolitan area at 1510 Hill, Ann Arbor and they are encouraged to take the paper to their respective high schools for distribution to their friends" [Special Agent-in-Charge Detroit April 1969]. The report also links the paper's funding to the MC5's earnings, with more investigations promised to determine "further information regarding the financial, editorial, and extent of domestic or foreign influence regarding the captioned paper" (Special Agent-in-Charge Detroit April 1969).

The following month a "security investigation" was launched in response to the above memorandum stating that Sinclair, as the founder of the WPP, and his "professed anarchist beliefs" demanded additional investigation. Further investigation would include government surveillance such as wiretaps on individuals like Sinclair and Plamondon, even after the MC5's departure from the WPP (Memorandum to J.B. Adams). Further references to WPP–produced literature appear in numerous other FBI documents, including a letter from September 25, 1970, addressed to then–Minority Leader Gerald R. Ford Jr. from J. Edgar Hoover that discusses the WPP and pamphlets produced by the group. The letter was produced as a follow-up to Ford's "inquiry concerning the White Panther Party which you raised during our conference with the President on September 22, 1970" (Hoover). Even though the band had disassociated itself from the WPP that same summer, Hoover still discusses rock as a spearhead of the WPP attack. The letter from Hoover focuses on Sinclair and Plamondon as the main targets of investigation, but it still depends on earlier information involving the band and Sinclair. It draws Ford a biographical sketch and promises continued active investigation.[9]

Thompson says that as the rhetoric became more heated, certain messages heightened the sense of threat felt by local and federal authorities, especially the publication of a series of photos taken by photographer Leni Sinclair in which the group was brandishing both musical instruments and guns. "There was a point where we started to do PR pictures with us holding guns. That's when I think they started really taking us seriously" (2006). At the same time, Sinclair and Plamondon would also become suspects in the bombing of an Ann Arbor CIA office.

As Gitlin points out in *The Whole World is Watching*, the MC5 and its relationship to the White Panther Party was a complex and multi-layered process of making news events, as well as larger media frames that packaged them. It is a fight over hegemony when an entity like the WPP tries to construct itself but is also held to dominant interpretation by media frames. Along the way, the WPP and the MC5 discovered the difficulty of managing the media frames they constructed themselves and how they were interpreted through the national press and by the government. The members of the MC5 did not want to be a formal political entity and a political movement. They did not want to pick up guns for aggressive actions. But because of their own publications and their reception in the mass media, the message became beyond the control of any one individual, especially since the band and WPP were by no means unified in their vision. Says Davis,

> The people were looking to us for answers and we were just one part of it ... the performance part. There were other people like political prisoners and political activists of the day who were in the spotlight. Then there were those who were the invisible guys ... the terrorists really. The underground people that were setting up booby traps and who would actually go out and do something about it.... The population at large was receiving many messages and not really knowing what the big blob was going to do. That's the thing with a mass of people. Nobody really wants to stand out and be apart ... there are some that like the attention. But the majority of people are looking at each other before they do anything. It turns into those kinds of forces. Well our side was kind of fragmented. You had the MC5, which wasn't just five people but all these people in the MC5 organization who were pushing for what they think is right. You've got John Sinclair, Pun Plamondon, the women, the political guys, guys setting off homemade bombs. What does the blob think? You don't know, they don't know. They're looking to you for door number 1, 2 or 3. We had a problem finding the door!... It grew and grew until it didn't have any more room to grow. And the things that were growing next to it ... everything got squeezed. The message got, I think, got corrupted, polluted. We had too many inputs ... we didn't function as a unit of five anymore, we were a unit of who knows how many [2006]?

The media, performance and lyrical content created a larger picture from which the MC5 revolutionary mythos was created and received by numerous audiences. An active synergy was created across these areas that led to the continued debate over intent and the role of music in political and social change. As Baudrillard contends, an object dependent upon popular culture to create and maintain meaning can easily become an empty

Five. Guns and Guitars: Revolutionary Style and Substance?

shell, invested in by those desperate for some kind of frame. Style over substance.

Articles written as late as 2003 like "Have the MC5 Sold Out?" or "Fever to Sell" desperately seek authenticity and intent. The band's 100 Club reunion show and the debate over Levis' role are more examples of the continuing fight for meaning in the MC5. Articles like "Kick Out the Jeans, Motherfu-Sorry, Brothers and Sisters ... or Does It Suck To Make A Buck," or fan postings like "Let's hope there are NO more MC5 gigs and people can cherish their very real memories, forged from truly experiencing the fierce intensity of one of the world's greatest bands" show the deep level of investment and meaning among fans who see the band in the mythologized light of revolutionary musical anarchists. The post continues, "Let them cash their checks and be done with this fiasco" ("Kick Out the Jeans"). Something almost sacred, according to this individual, was marred by the realities of capitalism.

The lyrics, music and propaganda left by the MC5 are still actively deconstructed and debated to determine if the band was a hollow shell selling records under the guise of social revolution. These are the very same questions asked at the advent of their career.[10] Audiences continue to perceive the relatively small amount of texts left behind by the band in disparate and contradictory ways. Now with members making their way into a whole new kind of 60s, and two members deceased, the MC5 and its life with the White Panther Party continue to challenge new generations of listeners. Whether dismissive or embracing, listeners hear different things. And as Tyner explained, the band seems to have left enough of a space so that "people can hear the sound that you make and they interpret it however they want" (Sheppard 13).

However, one needs to balance perspectives of revolutionary facades with the very real uses of the band by fans, critics, individuals involved in the WPP and the government itself. This popular culture product was applied to notions of revolution and social change. A fake facade would not make sense to those who made very real investments into the career and life of the MC5 and the White Panther Party, but it should be included in the discussion as much as the MC5's potential exploitation and use of revolutionary models. Here J. Edgar Hoover and Lester Bangs meet from beyond to discuss the power and possibility of popular music and popular culture to affect the political and social world. The band's ability to mix lyrical content, performance and media usage created an entity that lives and breathes on its own as the years have progressed. Somewhere between a farce and a usable tool from which individuals could create rhetoric and a path to rebellion, the band continues to be a focus of discussion over how popular culture can, or has, contributed to social change and development.

CHAPTER SIX

Managing the Legacy of the Sound and the Fervor

As the previous chapters have shown, the MC5/White Panther Party relationship was a complex concoction of participants, state interests, and audiences that looked to a cultural text in a way that was and continues to be disputed. From vanguard of the revolution to "revolutionary hype," the uses were varied and the investments in authenticity or lack thereof continue to follow the MC5 into the new millennium. The investment from those in and around the group and from the authorities, who made it their job to quell the band's actions, would follow participants long after the band folded in the early '70s. This chapter will explore the period following the MC5's break with the White Panther Party and the subsequent downfall of the party and the band. The aftermath deserves some consideration.

Band members, WPP leaders, and fans continue to be affected and shaped by this brief experiment. Several levels of study show this, including a micro-level investigation of the personal effects on band and WPP members, an examination of the band's musical legacy as contrasted to its political and social legacy, a look at the group's downfall and its disputed place within the New Left and that movement's disintegration. A look at the effects of governmental interest in the group will show how these remain part of the story of the MC5 in the four decades following the band's short career.

The people involved were re-consulted in the spring of 2008 regarding the fragmentation of the band and the White Panther Party. John Sinclair, Leni Sinclair, Pun Plamondon, Michael Davis, Wayne Kramer, and Dennis Thompson, as veterans of the association between the MC5 and the WPP present a spectrum of interpretations and narratives about legacy of the time, the experience of the groups, and the continuing story.

For many, the narrative doesn't get any easier. Their actions in the band or the WPP shaped many of their years to come, and some would say still very much do. A band trying to maintain a presence. Individuals struggling with drugs, prison, and continued litigation. People still besieged with a drive to change the world around them. The years following the demise of the band and its relationship to the WPP community presented a whole new host of challenges to people who already felt they had run the gauntlet.

The band's musical legacy as a usable product of rebellion will be closely examined. The MC5 has been a favorite of musicians and fans, who believe it was a cornerstone for the rise of punk and heavy metal, and propagated rock's subversive possibilities to new generations of fans. The band's sonic assault was both heralded and damned, all because of doubt over members' commitment to politics and social change. Audiences had a wide array of reactions. Echoing Norman Mailer's appreciation of the band in *Miami and the Siege of Chicago*, musicians such as Lemmy Kilmister from the group Motorhead and Jack White of the White Stripes and The Raconteurs openly cite the influence of the MC5 as central in their musical development (Jonze and Day).

Never the commercial success members had hoped for, the group still manages to have a mythical status in the history of rock. The myth ranges from importance as the godfathers of punk, or condemnation as poseurs. The MC5's inability to garner a spot in the Rock and Roll Hall of Fame, unlike peers like Iggy and the Stooges, shows that its legacy is far from universal among fans and critics. A lot of this has to do with the lingering question of their political posturing.

The pressure of government investigation of the MC5/WPP aligns with the larger disintegration and repression of the New Left. This disintegration of the MC5 and WPP will be measured specifically against the downfall of the larger New Left. Again, despite criticism, the MC5 and WPP faced many of the same pressures as the New Left, and similar government repression. The division between the serious political and the hippy-dippy rest of the countercultural movement is obscured by how these groups were viewed from the top, and by the similarities in how these groups all fell in the 1970s.

The legacy of the MC5 and the White Panther Party continues. The split between the WPP and the band as a creative unit continues to follow those involved, and pulls in successive listeners and audiences. Rather than a story about individuals, this is the story of a whole that exists beyond any of its parts—the band, the WPP community, the fans, or the critics. This story speaks of the promise and the difficulty in figuring out music's role in dissent, rebellion, and social change.

The Roses Are Ramblin' On: Personal Perspectives on Disintegration

According to this most recent set of interviews, confusion about the meaning of the whole experience and over how to manage its legacy only seemed to worsen as the band dealt with firing Sinclair and the aftermath. The idealism and swagger of the band that filled the *Kick Out the Jams* album and Panther propaganda was fleeting. The brotherhood, in effect would be quickly diluted as members faced increasing pressure from the government and the music industry. People inside and outside the band had differing views as to what the WPP association meant. The firing of John Sinclair further pushed these differences to the forefront among fans, the government, the WPP, and the band.

This separation deserves some more attention, as it has, for some time, been a mark for critics proving that Sinclair was the singular, ideological dominating force. Trans-Love Energies and the White Panther Party were organic creations among some of the band and the WPP community. Like its formation, the separation of the band from the WPP moniker involves a multiplicity of perspectives and use values. This would be the same whether you want to damn or verify the band's "revolutionary" potential. This round of interviews presents a clearer picture of the separation and its meaning for all involved.

The interviews support the earlier findings that the split was far from easy. Wayne Kramer saw that Sinclair was engulfed in the fallout from the MC5/WPP rhetoric and action. "John is not a drug dealer ... he never was! John is a poet, a beatnik, an artisan, and an artist ... so he wasn't prepared to resist this kind of pressure. So, ultimately John had been taking on these cases for years." Kramer spoke of an immense pressure that he describes as pushing Sinclair up against a wall.

The MC5 and Social Change

So it comes to the point where it looks like he might get this sentence, they might actually go through with this because we knew they were not joking. They're trying to send a message and they're serious. And we're hearing the message, and the message is "you fucked with us so badly, that we gotta do something to you." The attitude had been for years when is someone going to do something about the MC5 and John Sinclair? So John became the scapegoat for the MC5. He became the martyr. They're going to hammer him and hopefully that will send a message to the rest of these crazed youth to straighten up and fly right. Which of course was never going to happen! [Kramer 2008].

Much like Kramer, Dennis "Machine Gun" Thompson felt the pressure of Sinclair forthcoming sentence for giving two joints to an undercover police officer, but he saw the disintegration as less abrupt: "That whole thing was disintegrating around the trial, but you might say it was disintegrating slowly before that." He continues, "There was a dissipation of focus, a dissipation of intensity, a dissipation of commitment. This is real, this is very real. When you are in the middle of it all, riots and things ... people polarize ... they get polarized. A contingent were willing to be White Panthers, a very small fraction were willing to go the distance." Thompson, as one of the members in the band who was less invested politically, saw a line being crossed that he couldn't support. "When it comes down to just wagging your finger at someone and threatening to fight, versus a knock-down drag out fistfight ... you might lose some teeth, you might get hurt, cut, shot ... I think a lot people will walk away. And personally I think that is what happened" (2008).

The finger wagging he speaks of was taken to a new level, more intense, and more threatening toward the success of the band. "It got more real and wet, blood wet ... and I started backing off. You had to make a personal decision in your own lives ... am I willing to get shot and killed or do I know what I am fighting for? You had to make a personal evaluation of what you felt about politics, about the war, about your lifestyle" (2008). Thompson wasn't prepared to increase his investment in revolutionary ideology. He thought the experiment had gone far enough. "We played it and shit hit the fan like it was supposed to and that's all we could do. It wasn't our job to shoot people, or to shoot the cops. Our job was to inform the people that the war could be ended, that there were alternative possibilities in your life" (Thompson 2008).

Much the same could be said for Michael Davis, who likewise expressed the necessity, in his eyes, of splitting with the WPP and especially those in the WPP family who were becoming more invested in revolutionary ideology and rhetoric, including Pun Plamondon.

> I really kind of didn't have a connection with Pun. I didn't realize Pun was such an integral part of the situation. I was so overwhelmed and involved with the music, the show, and my fellow band-mates. I didn't pay much to attention to what they said. The things that I did learn about, I didn't like. Like, so and so are on the FBI's list and they are running from the police, they bombed such things, they did this ... it was all sort of like wait a minute, what does this have to do with being successful? I think that is where the band started to detach itself. Because these people are going around doing covert things and that had nothing to do with playing guitars and having a good time at the rock and roll show. We started to break away from that kind of stuff. It's not going to take the band long to fall into the same ... we're going to be the fugitives, you know? [2008]

Davis describes a sense of loss and pragmatic concern for the continuation of the band that echoes Thompson's views on a line being drawn.

> Things really started getting weird. Sinclair is getting more and more militant and rhetorical and the band is getting more rhetorical, and then some guys go out and do something ... and it's like what are we really all about?... Though everybody likes the idea of reforming society or whatever, when it comes down to if you are going to get your ass thrown in jail and you won't be able to do what you want to do ... it kind of creates a line in the sand. Really what is happening is our confidence is eroding; the idealism that we started out with was crumbling. We were losing spirit [2008].

As earlier interviews have shown, the responsibility did not lie only with Sinclair and Plamondon. Instead, the responsibility for the pressure was widely distributed, including, for individuals like Davis and Thompson, an increasing discomfort with some of the other members of the band. In essence, the fracture existed far beyond a band/community level. It existed among each person. Disagreement over the direction of the band in this pressure cooker of government repression and criticism from the Left and the music industry over the WPP was magnified. Davis began to feel that a line had been crossed. "If we could have held the line, without going overboard ... when we started to disagree on how to get there, it created resentment" (Davis 2008). The differences among band members at this stage would seed later incidents of anger and disconnectedness that even their split from the WPP wouldn't heal.

Kramer sees the disintegration of the band as a brotherhood as being a natural by-product of the increasing political pressure. This pressure hurt the band's ability to function.

> You got that pressure on the MC5 and then you have the political pressure. That industry and economic and career pressure takes the form of the gigs aren't coming the way like they used to come. There's new bands ... it's a very competitive world. And the political pressure on the band; they don't like the things we sing about, they don't like what we represent ... this also takes a toll on the band. Then, the personal dynamics inside the band start to deteriorate. That one for all, all for one kind of gang, family, tribe mentality starts to break down when you're not working and there is no money [Kramer 2008].

Kramer, one of the most ideological voices in the band concerning the WPP, expressed a sense of fight or flight with the "fight" side looking pretty murky. "I was ... we were in a position where I was like, John, if you go to prison what am I going to do? I've got a band to run." In Kramer's opinion, the survival of the band was the decisive reason for the split. It was not looked upon kindly by Sinclair or other WPP members.

> I didn't fuck anybody over and this idea that the MC5 sold John out is wrong. So that in itself creates some distance between us and the White Panthers. Then there were ideological differences. We had been touring the world now, and we had to go out and confront radical political students and leaders and now we had to defend our positions; we had to argue our points. And we quickly came to see that the idea of armed love, or violence, or rebellion ... was not what we wanted to talk about. It really wasn't going to work. That in fact that was part of the problem ... that guns were the problem, that war is the problem, that violence is the problem. We had a disagreement with our brothers in the left on that subject. I started to develop my own ideas on how politics could enter the picture and what the role of a band is [Kramer 2008].

Members of the WPP indeed saw the split in a much different light. John and Leni Sinclair and Plamondon all expressed a sense of desertion, seeing the music industry, not political oppression, as the powerful force separating the band from the WPP community. Says Leni Sinclair, "With the 9–10 years in jail, the band didn't have much hope to have a manager any time soon." The earliest indication of troubles at hand came to her shortly before the band fired John. "I think the first thing that happened that we didn't like that they did was after they got their own house outside of Detroit in Hamburg, Michigan, they fired J.C. Crawford. Now J.C. Crawford was not a member of the MC5, he was the announcer." She believes the music industry pushed the guys into the move. "The whole machine took over, the music business machine, telling them this revolutionary stuff has to go" (Leni Sinclair 2008).

Plamondon echoed this thought. "Of course some elements in the band were more revolutionary than others. With Sinclair in prison, the influence of music business types [capitalists] had undue influence on the band with no counterbalance from the righteous" (Plamondon 2008). Unlike the band, these two represent the other side of the art versus commerce debate concerning the band and its attachment to the WPP. Not surprisingly, John Sinclair himself, at the time, echoed these sentiments, but had a less extreme view.

A level of hurt still popped up in the interview. Sinclair says, "It was a month before I went to prison, at least, that they fired me.... They fired me, J.C. Crawford and Bob Rudnick in one fell swoop and they said they were through with the White Panther Party." Not mincing words, Sinclair says, "At the time I was enraged that they were traitors." Time, however, has given him some perspective on the split. He sensed a feeling of frustration coming from the band rather than a practical concern for its manager going to jail. "Nobody, starting with me or my lawyers, ever contemplated that they would send me to prison. So they say they knew I was going to prison; no one knew I was going to prison. They did it because they had dedicated themselves 100 percent to the idea of being this revolutionary band and a revolutionary party and it didn't work for them. It took me about 40 years to understand this" (2008). He notes, after years of retrospect, "I realized that they sincerely tried everything they could and it didn't work and that they were being attacked not only by the establishment but also by the lefties. They couldn't do anything right according to anybody" (Sinclair 2008). The difficulty of fitting into the New Left was a lasting theme for the band and the WPP.

The increased repression of the group by local authorities and the threat of jail was one of the most important points of contention among the band and the WPP community. For Sinclair, the band was the means to take on issues.

Of course, I never would have mounted my energetic campaign against the marijuana laws and the police like that if I hadn't thought that they wouldn't be behind me. That was my big strength, that I had a rock and roll band behind me and alongside me as well. So that really gave me the courage to do what I did, and then of course I wound up doing 2 years in prison as a result. But I dealt the hand ... so I had to play it [Sinclair 2008].

The WPP's use values for the band, and the band's use values for itself created a point of divide that caused a fracturing from numerous angles, not one clean break. Different factions lost a sense of investment and possibility as the band began the second phase of its short career, after the split. This was important to critics and fans at the time who argued over intent and authenticity just as they do today.

As the invested parties went down their separate paths, their time with the MC5/WPP would continue to follow them through the coming decades. As the myth grew, the fracture ran deeper. In fact, many of those involved would have a hard time making sense of the interest that the MC5/WPP relationship brought to the band and those in the WPP community.

A dominant theme in many of the band interviews was that drugs became a key element in how the band functioned after its break with the WPP. Kramer claims that the ramifications of the White Panther relationship continued, both from the music industry and political pressures. "Of course this opens the door for the pain-killing properties of Jack Daniels, Budweiser, and heroin. They bring with them a whole new host of negative power" (Kramer 2008). Thompson echoes the sentiment. He says downers plagued the MC5's career as a rock band. "The drugs of choice were changing ... people were doing less psychedelics, and they were doing more downers" (Thompson 2008). The "death drugs," as the individuals interviewed were prone to call them, drained the idealism and search for success, and tore apart the brotherhood so apparent in the band's early career. Davis comments, "If you are doing drugs, and you are fucked up all of the time, you just can't think, write. You are not rational." The pain-killing effects of these drugs tore through any notion of community within the group. "You're really losing touch ... even if though think you are doing what you want to do; you are actually creating a stasis in-between the people you are with." He emphasizes, in regard to the effects of the drugs on him personally, "The more I got into my high or whatever it was, I was creating more distance between myself and the band ... you're in your own little world" (Davis 2008).

Kramer sees drugs as the natural by-product of the pressures they were feeling from the industry and the political environment of the time. Kramer asserts that their marketability as "revolutionary rock" was short-lived in the music industry. "The forces of the nature of the music industry work against it [maintaining a career in music]. They are always keyed to the new, because the corporate structures make most of their money on new artists. So they only like you while you are new and dumb, and they get the biggest piece of the pie" (Kramer 2008). The continued effects of the band's extended liminal status after parting ways with the WPP continued to plague members through their next two albums. With an industry casting them to the side, their marketability up in the air, and the increasing use of drugs in the group, it would only take a short time for the band to completely fracture under the weight of poor album sales and difficulties finding venues. Rob Tyner in a 1988 interview discussed this myriad of concerns. "There were money problems and personnel problems and chemical problems and all kinds of different symptoms, but the one underlying cause was probably the frustration." He says the pressure cooker wore band members down. "We had been blasting away at this for so long that even us guys with our unshakable meanness, you know — you just run out of time for it. Maybe that's the clock again, you know?" (Sheppard 17).

Thompson asserts that there was still some sense of hope in the languishing days of the band to keep it all together and rise from the ashes. But before that could happen, members would have to address the drug use. "When I quit the band, I quit it to go to a rehab clinic ... I said at that point that we don't have to end all of this, but I need to get off of heroin" (Thompson 2008).

This was not to be, as other members struggled with drug use and the pressures placed upon the band as they tried to salvage their careers. Davis ultimately places the blame on band members. "We made our decisions ... this is how we are going to react to it." The decision to self-medicate was complemented by personal issues within the band, with many feelings still lingering about control, as was the cast during the WPP days. "I think the whole break-up of the band was from within. We stopped communicating. When we first started up as a band there was fair amount of equality, at least in the broad sense, that we all respected each other on an equal basis. After a few years, we got tired. We started to be unequal. Some of us started taking on more a decision capacity while others started walking away from decision capacity" (2008). Davis continues, "Then your group really isn't a group anymore." Finding a successful direction for the group after the WPP split was a difficult hurdle to commercial success. They could not overcome it.

Following the demise of the group in early 1972 (after numerous personnel additions, subtractions, and re-additions) the sense of liminality continued mostly due to the continued influence of drugs, as the band tried to find outlets for musical expression. I asked Kramer, one of the most ideologically focused members of the band during and after the WPP, if he still felt a sense of political connection and purpose.

> Because in my personal life the band was gone ... I only know this now looking back on it, but I suffered a loss. I had my entire identity invested in who I was: Wayne Kramer from the MC5 and now I wasn't Wayne Kramer from the MC5 anymore because there wasn't any MC5 anymore. My four best friends were the guys in the band and they weren't my best friends anymore. I denied it. That denial is very powerful and creates a lot of problems. It was incredibly painful, but I denied the pain with drugs and alcohol. And they worked pretty good for awhile. Unfortunately, they bring their own additional difficulties with them [2008].

Kramer's increasing dependence on drugs and alcohol culminated in prison time. "That Nietschean idea of that which doesn't destroy me, makes me stronger ... that wasn't my experience. What didn't destroy me, continued to diminish me. I drifted into lower and lower circles." Kramer was unsure of himself and how he fit into the real world after the group's demise. His habits overtook him, causing him to take part in criminal activity to feed his habit. "I was an active alcoholic and a drug addict, and these things cost a lot of money." Kramer asserts that in the absence of an identity as a rock star, he wasn't quite sure how he was supposed to fit in. "I would try to find esteem in doing wrong." This would lead to his eventual imprisonment.

Even after serving two-plus years in prison for selling cocaine, Kramer still struggled with dependency issues. "My time in prison didn't actually help me. I came out more cynical and more embittered. Outside of the fact that it gave my body a couple of years' break from the degree of drugging and drinking that I was doing." He adds, "I came out determined to do better and had nothing but willpower to go on. Of course that won't get you very far. By example, join a band with Johnny Thunders, the most notorious heroin addict in music of that time period.... He was the new Charlie

Six. Managing the Legacy of the Sound and the Fervor

Parker at least in terms of his drug usage...." Kramer joined the band Gang War. He would continue to wrestle with drugs for years to come, as many band members did. Kramer admits, "I still had a long way to go" (Kramer 2008).

Thompson also wrestled with drug habits formed during his time in the band, and found himself working, while continuing to play in various groups. His hope was to sometime again make a living in music, "I started playing music with my brother in bars around Detroit. I did that for a while for a living. Then dad got me a job where he worked as a tool maker. I was a tool maker for about twenty-three years. But I didn't give up on music." Thompson says many others in the Detroit scene of the late 1960s and early 1970s were running in similar circles.

> I think most everybody was doing that. The Stooges had broken up.... They were doing it. The other guys in other bands in Detroit ... everybody was doing the same thing. Original bands that may have broken up, but they were still trying to make a living with music. But it was impossible. After the "scene" in Detroit ... it fizzled around here. It pretty much died in the '70s. The '70s were a dead decade. Nothing much was happening, so you had to get out of Detroit [2008].

Davis, who had been dealing/using drugs when the band ended and into his post-band life, would work with Fred "Sonic" Smith and Thompson in the short-lived group Ascension (Callwood 144–145). Davis would go on to work with Destroy All Monsters with Ron Asheton, a former member of the Stooges. As with Kramer, alcohol and drugs continued to be a problem.

Rob Tyner continued his pursuit of music as well, producing as well as playing in numerous groups. One of these groups was a reconstituted New MC5 not involving any of the other members. Kramer had briefly experimented with a similar idea. Both eventually stopped using the MC5 moniker. The issue was contentious, irritating the frayed relationships from the former brotherhood of the MC5.

A 1977 issue of *Bomp! Magazine* highlighted this frustration among various ex-members when Fred "Sonic" Smith, then performing with his group Sonic's Rendezvous Band, criticized Tyner for using the MC5 name. "They're imposters," comments Sonic. 'It's as if they're each taking turns being the MC5. I was as much the MC5 as they were and I'm much more concerned now with moving Detroit rock into its next phase. I saw Tyner recently—

he's putting on weight and has a wife and kid. It's just a cheap shot'" (Baker 30). Smith comments later in the article that he still feels an investment in music as well as in the Detroit scene. "'I don't know if it's quite my style to be out tooting the horn for the scene as a whole,' he says. 'But I'll be around to help Detroit rock move into its next place'" (Baker 31). Even as the years progressed, disagreement over the meaning, legacy, and usability of the band by its members differed significantly.

At least to Davis, Smith represented a positive assertion of what post–MC5 life could be like.

> I saw Sonic's Rendezvous Band for the first time at the Hilltop Inn off of Interstate 75 on the way to Brighton. I had just come out of seclusion and was slightly bewildered by the atmosphere of rock and roll. They were pretty solid. This was in early '77. A few months later I caught them at Second Chance in Ann Arbor. By this time they were starting to get a reputation as the formidable band on the set. They began their show with what can only be called a wake up to the "sonic sound." It was an ascending tempo intro to a song that bore the intensity that was nature to Fred Smith — a very Chuck Berry riffed rocker that just chugged into your brain. Each song in the set was unique in its own way, without giving any sense of repetition. They were in control and Fred handled the crowd with the same off handed charm that I had watched him perfect in the MC5. A very cool customer was he, with that little secret you were anxiously waiting to hear. And he delivered without actually telling anything — it was just his way [Davis "Diary"].

Davis gives insight into the ghost that the MC5 had become to its members. The pressure cooker of the music industry, drugs, politics, and each other created something which ex-members, years afterwards, did not know what to think about. In his writings Davis describes a reunion of sorts with Rob Tyner.

> After I was released from custody of the bureau of prisons, I went over to Tyner's house one night. It was an unannounced visit and I was with someone who was a friend of Rob's wife's. I went into the kitchen where Rob had stationed himself, apparently to avoid talking to me. He seemed unusually agitated. I thought he was going to panic. I asked him what the problem was. He said that it was just kind of weird. I asked him why. He said it just was. I suppose that he was right. Why should I expect to be warmly welcomed? I should have called, but that would have been even weirder. I left and never saw him again [Davis "Diary"].

Six. Managing the Legacy of the Sound and the Fervor

With the death of Fred "Sonic" Smith in 1994, any hope for a storybook ending failed. The pressures and difficulties that the band faced during its tumultuous time in the spotlight, including the weight of its association with the White Panther Party, caused a break that could not be mended. As Kramer says, the fallout from a small group dynamic can be significant because of the intensity of the relationships formed in a common pursuit. "The MC5, like any group of artists that band together for a common purpose, if they're focused and have definable goals, they can generally achieve those goals." He adds, "You get five or six people pulling together ... you can make something happen. I mean look at the neo-cons ... how many are there of them? A dozen, maybe ten? Look what they did. They destroyed America and killed millions of people. Hitler had maybe a dozen people and almost destroyed the world." In the case of the MC5 and WPP, a small group of people created an entity that is deeply rooted in the history of popular music and society. Notions of what music can or cannot accomplish have met over their unstable legacy.

Effects of the MC5/WPP relationship continued to be felt by the Sinclairs and Plamondon. Their lives as well would be marked for decades to come by the MC5/WPP experiment. Sinclair's lengthy jail sentence for two joints was seen as a direct result of his status as the manager of the band. As his then-wife Leni says, the imprisonment made many community members want to maintain their investment in WPP ideologies, but leave behind thoughts of "armed love."

The attention paid to John during his legal struggles and his imprisonment actually helped the group get further exposure and interest around the world. "While John was incarcerated he became kind of a poster child for all political prisoners and we had a lot of friends around the country and we had a lot of chapters around the world. We had chapters in London and as far away as Australia. We said anybody wanting to start a White Panther Party chapter can do so and call themselves White Panthers" (2008). Such free use of the WPP name created difficulty for the party, as it had no control over any chapter's actions. The degeneration of control was one of the factors that caused the group to change its name to the Rainbow People's Party.

Despite the confusion and the fact that the leaders of the group were behind bars, "that's when we had to spring into action, otherwise he [John] would stay in there for ten years," Leni Sinclair says. "I was busy with the

Free John Now campaign, two small children, and a houseful of teenagers who barely knew how to make their own beds! There were about twenty-seven of them. I became kind of a house mother for a lot of things, plus I was still doing my photography. Also, all the things we did that were political: legal, demonstrations, and all of that stuff I was involved in organizing" (Leni Sinclair 2008).

Plamondon and Sinclair re-examined their notions of change, thanks to generous time for reading in prison. Plamondon was awaiting trial for his role in the Ann Arbor CIA bombing. Says John Sinclair, "The prison experience had a big effect on me and Pun Plamondon.... The positive effect was that we did a lot of studying of revolutionary history. We didn't know anything; we were just ruled by emotion when we started out." The two read works by Ho Chi Minh, Kwame Nkrumah and others. The experience, according to Sinclair, helped changed their reactionary perspectives. "It added intelligence and history to our emotional commitment. The first thing we realized was that being the White Panther Party and threatening the police and all of this was contraindicated in terms of organizing people.... It just frightened them. It just got us into a lot of trouble and we were never going to win anything that way" (John Sinclair 2008). Sinclair saw this approach as not appealing to their target audience, hippies. He explains that the band decided to tone down its verbal aggression: "One thing the hippies hate was violence ... nothing a hippie hates worse than violence! So we thought the first thing we have to get rid of is this violence thing. All that it is doing is putting us in prison. We had never done anything to anybody. But we hollered and we screamed ... we sold a lot of wolf tickets" (John Sinclair 2008).

Leni Sinclair says that even with the elevated levels of persecution, and the WPP effectively folding when the band left, some were still willing to continue the program, and in her eyes had to continue the program. "We had to keep the party up in order to keep up the struggle to get John out more than ever.... After John went to jail and started studying a lot of books, he came to the conclusion that we needed to change the image from what it was" (2008).

The Sinclairs and Plamondon as key WPP community members insist that the ethos of change was very much alive and demanded some recontextualization. John Sinclair describes the change taking place in the group. "It became, in the middle of 1971, the Rainbow's People Party. It was the same people, in the same place, doing the same kind of things. It lasted longer than the MC5, I'll say that much." Though Sinclair says things were done in a similar fashion, ideology was changing in the group, especially with the leaders who had felt the sting of government in the WPP experiment. Sinclair separates this new vision from other radical groups proposing an increase in violence.

> The bombings and that whole Weather Underground thing it just drove the so called vanguard of the revolutionary movement farther and farther away from the "broad masses" of the people who were hippies! They were against the war; they didn't want anyone bombing anybody. We wanted to disassociate ourselves from that. When we won our case it was like being liberated finally from that whole period of trying to be bad-assess you know? No one is as bad-ass as the United States government! Hahahaha. You can never beat them! They're the baddest assess in all of human history! They're the only ones who dropped the weapon of mass destruction on some other people and they don't even care!... We had this vision of a rainbow culture and society where everyone got along and it was very positive. We thought we would be a lot better off projecting this than some kind of mutant animal that is out there blowing people up and shooting them [John Sinclair 2008].

Leni sees the time after Sinclair's release as positive, full of possibility.

> After John got out, let's start again where we left off before all of this happened. Let's build a community, let's have a free daycare, free food, free medicine, let's have a free ballroom, let's dance and have fun and do the things we were put on earth to do. We were real energetic after John got out. He went back into managing bands, and putting on concerts and organizing the world famous blues and jazz festival [2008].

Leni would continue to be politically active as well pursuing photography further. Plamondon wrestled with drug and alcohol abuse, and eventually became an author/activist. Much of his work, as is the case for the Sinclairs, comes back to experiences with social change and development in the '60s and '70s, namely their roles in the White Panther Party. Like the band members, they are forever linked to the events chronicled in this book. Although it only lasted a short time, the association of the MC5 and WPP affected their members for the rest of their lifetimes and beyond.

"The Legend Business Doesn't Pay"

The legacy that began to develop around the band, in part, concerned its musical place in popular history, and its social place as a text of rebellion. It is impossible to discount the association with the WPP in examining the MC5's musical legacy. The association with the WPP gave the band greater credence in expressing the fundamental ethos of rebellion in rock — or lesser credence in the minds of those who saw this association as a marketing gimmick. The "revolution" was sacred to those who participated, and levels of authenticity and commitment were constantly tested and debated among those claiming to take part.

The main focus in this section is on the musical lineage of the band, especially in relation to the rise of punk and heavy metal, two musical genres dependent on an ethos of rebellion. The interviews revealed that this legacy is qualified by members of the MC5. Just as they were surprised by the amount of political pressure put on the band, its members are also surprised that they are seen as musically influential figures.

To measure the influence of the band on musical circles and with fans, one does not have to look far. There is a great deal written on the band and its connection to the developing genres of punk rock and metal in the 1970s. For instance *Rolling Stone* offers, "The group's loud, hard, fast sound and violently antiestablishment ideology almost precisely prefigured much of punk rock. There was, however, one crucial difference: The MC5 truly believed in the power of rock and roll to change the world" (George-Warren and Romanowski 630). The musical heirs were left trying to figure out how this energy could be put to use.

Punk is a cornerstone of popular music in the twentieth century, and the most referenced form of music in terms of the MC5's musical legacy. *Maximum RocknRoll*, a now 20-plus-year-old independent zine, regarded as one of punk rock's most revered periodicals, writes of the band as a genesis of the music. Chris Davidson penned "The MC5: Pioneers of Punk" in a 1995 issue of the magazine. The article on the band was part of a series "examining killer bands of the 1960s and '70s that directly influenced the 1976 punk revolution and, consequently, planted the seeds of contemporary punk." Interestingly, the author is quite absolute in looking at the band's musical influence, and in distancing himself from the political overtones. "Let's isolate the MC5's energetic power chording, their excellent second album, and the fact that they purposefully broke away from the fruity politics to get back to basics. And let's shy away from the hippie-noodlings. Believe me; you'll like 'em more this way" (Davidson). He continues:

Six. Managing the Legacy of the Sound and the Fervor

A second 45, "Borderline"/"Looking at You" was recorded on January, 1968, under the supervision of Sinclair and released on the Ann Arbor–based label, A-Square. Another heavy duty coupling, this single shows the band steering towards the distortion and endless jamming of free-form jazz. The 5's punk instincts are certainly intact, but it's clear to these ears that things were going wrong [Davidson *MaximumRockNRoll*, 1995].

The author then goes on to admit the importance of *Kick out the Jams*, "as an historical precursor to metal and other undesirable sounds. Its heavy power-riffing, frantic drumming and half-shouted atonal singing is evidence of this. But that's not enough in my opinion, to launch the LP into legendary status" (Davidson). For Davidson, the band's tenure with the WPP seems to be suspect and demonstrates musical excessiveness. Such sentiments don't match the perspectives of those like Paul Friedlander, who surmises, "Detroit-based MC5 exhibited a combative, cultural-activist stance and monotonous driving lead vocals by Rob Tyner that were also reflected in punk" (249). For Friedlander, the connection of the band to rebellion and the WPP "activist" stance was an essential part of developing the punk rock genre. Much can be said of the album's inclusion in *MOJO Magazine's* "Big Bangs: 100 Records That Changed the World" list in its June 2007 issue. However disputed, the theme of rebellion and challenge to convention was as significant as the musical production of the band. Together they created an aura that was taken into the fledgling musical form of punk.

The MC5's role in punk had as much to do with the band's attitude as it did with any musical concerns. Dave Marsh, in a piece on the group in *Musician Magazine*, says, "What survived was the band's guitar sound, expropriated by the Doll's Johnny Thunders and handed down to Glen Matlock and Steve Jones of the Sex Pistols. And, among musicians, a vestigial wariness of revolutionary politics as profound and well-embedded as the fear of snakes among ordinary mortals" (88). One would be hard pressed to isolate the "combative" stance of the band from the aura of rebellion created by the group's "hippie-noodlings."

He continues that the MC5's legacy is very much intertwined with the volatile times in which the group was flourishing. It was a music of aggression and challenge. "The frenzied frustrations of Motor City R&B's spiritual energy clashed with the intellectual anger of Midwestern bohemian dreams crashing to earth amidst the multiple disasters of racial backlash, psychedelic crapout and Vietnam psychosis." The environment that spawned the band, the WPP, and their relationship affixed itself to the music that the band produced and the aura of rebellion that surrounded the band throughout its career. Marsh laments, "Today's misunderstanding of high-energy Michigan rock is exemplified by the fact that most historians credit the Stooges, the Five's exquisitely comic doppelganger, as one of the era's and the area's pre-punk prime movers" (86).

The marketability of the band depends on this sense of rebellion that was created in its early career. Formalized notions of politics are obviously seen as problematic by some of these authors, but such activity is part of the foundation of the "punk instincts" that are credited to the MC5. The aura of rebellion is of the utmost importance here. As Kramer said, "Punk is really talking about the age old defiance of youth against the generation before them. Every generation has to claim its own identity and its own sound and its own art ... this is what we're about" (Kramer 2008). The "punk" aesthetic renews itself generation after generation, through themes of youth and rebellion.

Kramer asserts that this "aura" is what is most commonly absorbed by audiences. "The influence of the sound of the MC5 really is just outside of the message of the MC5, that yeah, everyone picks up on that the MC5 rocked like fuck, that they were political, that they were hard-core, but they never go below the surface, or rarely." Kramer sees the MC5's links to punk as somewhat problematic. "I noticed these bands that claimed to be influenced by the MC5 had not moved the sound forward at all. They were taking kind of the surface of it: they were taking the aggressive guitar tone, the up tempos of the lyrics, the up tempo of the arrangement but they weren't advancing it technically. To tell you the truth it kind of started to lose me" (2008).

Davis concurred. But for Davis, the true influence of the band on punk rock came in the first album. "The whole *Kick Out the Jams* thing is what puts us on the map ... the energy and the live show. The connection with the audience; it was the live album."

Davis, who of the group was furthest from any specific political ideology or cause, believes that the association with the WPP produced a significant energetic moment. Any certain ideology beyond that was to be taken or left behind. "The energy between the band and the crowd is undeniable; it was something that was never done before. There were live albums, but you couldn't hear the audience's connection to the band" (Davis 2008).

Six. Managing the Legacy of the Sound and the Fervor

The notion of audience connection to artist as well as a notion of energy and commitment became important factors in the rise of punk rock. As "hippie" as it might seem, an ethos was established in this work. Davis understands the generation gap that was created, leading to his inability to see the direct connection of the band to punk rock. "After the '60s there was such a backlash against the whole hippie movement/peace-love generation and then it took a while before people thought of it as anything worthwhile.... The punk rockers thought the hippies were just like the most fucked-up people who ever lived!" (2008). Musically, the debate rages.

A similar debate occurs when looking at the MC5's possible influence on heavy metal. In his *Running with the Devil*, Robert Walser says,

> These groups of the late 1960s, now identified as early heavy metal bands, favored lyrics that evoked excess and transgression. Some, such as MC5 and Steppenwolf, linked their noises to explicit political critique in their lyrics; others, like Blue Cheer, identified with the San Francisco–based psychedelic bands, for which volume and heaviness aided an often drug-assisted search for alternative formations of identity and community [9].

Walser sees a disconnect between the San Francisco–based scene, what could be considered the core of hippiedom, and the metal impulses of the MC5 as a "political" band. Kramer, like the others, expressed appreciation for those creating these links. "To know that the guys in all of these bands always gave the MC5 mad props was always encouraging to me and of some conciliation being that we never got paid!" In addition to highlighting that the legend business doesn't pay, he also expressed a sense of confusion:

> There was another branch that started off into heavy metal and these were the guys who could really play. They weren't doing what the MC5 was trying to do either! They had some technical ability but they missed the point as far as I was concerned, which had to do more with free music and going beyond the beat and the key. Going into a more pure sonic dimension, like my heroes were doing, like Sun Ra, John Coltrane, and Albert Ayler. I just didn't hear the metal guys going for that [Kramer 2008].

As with punk rock, measuring the influence of the band on heavy metal depends on a mixture of musical and social/political ascriptions. Values are connected to the music that help audiences accept or reject the band's place in the canon of musical creation. Perhaps this is why so much emotion is tied up with concerns of authenticity. How rebellious was it? Was it something to believe in or something merely exploiting the historical context? John Sinclair weighs in:

> They were charged with starting punk rock but that didn't really have anything to do with them ... that was just their attitude. The Stooges were the pioneers of punk rock. When they started they didn't know how to play and they didn't have any tunes, they just had a lot of attitude and a lot of nerves. That describes punk rock in a nutshell to me. I'd hate for the MC5 to be pinned with it because they were very skilled musicians who worked very hard at their music and their presentation. They didn't just get drunk, get up there and fall off the stage and curse on people and all that ... they worked very hard; they were artists. But the attitude seems to have influenced a whole generation of people [John Sinclair 2008].

The attitude, the posturing, the promise of rebellion, still clings to the band and discussions of their authenticity as a musical and social force. This gritty, in-your-face realism was showcased in the group's musical output. Tyner touches upon a notion of "rawness" in rock communicated through the group's attitude, as well as a sound that spoke of the same rebellious, gut-produced expression. "Well, we proved that you could play really raw and you could sing really raw, and get an audience going crazy" (Sheppard 9). Lester Bangs, whose initial impression of the MC5 was not favorable, expresses a fondness for that rawness in sound and attitude later in the decade. "As the Seventies drew to a close, it appeared that heavy metal had had it. Records by bands like Kiss, Aerosmith and Bad Company could still be found on the charts, but they didn't hit the nervous system with quite the same electrode barracuda bite that early Led Zeppelin, MC5 and even Grand Funk had" (Bangs "Heavy Metal" 462).

The discussion here has moved beyond whether the embracement is a pure or tainted musical influence, and points to the group's embracement of rebellion. Bangs showcases a need for a pure product from which to measure the process of musical degeneration discussed in Chapter One. Rock demands a pure product of rebellion. Audiences and critics, while attempting to create a definitive narrative of popular music, sometimes overlook the fact that this is sacred space, and that audiences, including the producers themselves, can assign and specify legacies for products of popular culture.

Like its relationship to the WPP and its authenticity and intent there, the band's musical legacy is one that is hotly debated. Tyner saw this as a theme that ran throughout the band's career, especially in the wake of its breakup with Sinclair and the WPP. "People were freaking out; they didn't know that that was possible for the MC5 — to go up on there without any pretensions and without any politics or none of that stuff and just have fun" (Sheppard 18). Even at that time audiences were not sure what to make of the band and in Tyner's view were surprised that the band could still function. Questions about and an identity attached to the possibilities of "revolutionary rock" continued to follow the MC5. The WPP will always be a part of the discussion, no matter who is debating the MC5's legacy and influence, as it is so closely tied to a search for usable rebellion within the genre and sub-genres.

Thompson sees that part of the problem of dealing with musical legacy and the MC5 stems from the wealth of influences on the band: they owed a great deal to other artists in terms of its sound.

> We would just stretch and play with the sound in any way that we want. A lot of people in the early days didn't like it. What we were doing to them was sometimes strange and scary. We took our influences from so many categories ... James Brown, Motown, Jimi Hendrix, the Who, the whole jazz library of John Sinclair, the Beach Boys ... you name it ... we took our influence from anything that rocked ... that moved [Thompson 2008].

In essence, the band was part of a regenerating pattern in music. Its members took what they wanted from popular culture and used it for their own means. They used these raw materials to create their own structures of meaning. The process continues and as the research has demonstrated, those who produced the music long ago lost the ability to control the band's destiny and its legacy.

As Leni Sinclair sees it, the band's legacy is fundamentally tied to its time with the WPP. "The main thing is that the MC5 and their involvement in the political process back then is what keeps them from dying out." She continues, "Two or three generations since then ... want to find out more about it." The link is so strong for Sinclair that she sees the band's time with the WPP as accomplishing something remarkably significant. "They already did enough, if they never did anything else after what they did ... they did enough to have an influence. The influence is what carries on..." (2008).

Either as villain or rock and roll savior, the MC5 continues to be tied to a legacy of rebellion. As Thompson sees it, "The more time that passes, the stronger the myth will become. When we die off it gets locked in stone.

There is nobody left to refute it or tell the truth about it. People don't want to hear the truth about their heroes: that they're just regular people" (Thompson 2008). To those finding either value or a charade in their work, they have become much more than a static musical product. This musical legacy, much like the band's political legacy, stretched beyond any member's realm of thought. As Davis says,

> I'm surprised that the MC5 is the iconic figure that it is. We just kind of crashed the car and walked away from the wreck. To have us be so documented is beyond my wildest imagination. I never figured ... I thought we were just a big issue in Detroit and we kind of just flashed on the world scene. Here today, gone tomorrow or here today, gone today [2008].

The flash in the pan that Davis sees as the MC5 continues to attract discussion of musical influence, and is a cornerstone in discussions concerning the place of music in social change and development.

Legacy and the Left: The MC5 and WPP's Parallel to the Disintegration of the "Political" Left

The last key to connecting the legacy and myth of the MC5 from its heyday to today comes in measuring its role or lack of role in the New Left as compared to other groups that are traditionally considered part of the New Left.

The MC5 and WPP as products of historical memory now represent a larger discussion about the legacy of the baby-boomer generation, a legacy that is of intense focus and scrutiny, as the baby-boomer generation attempts to try to shape it.

The pressures the MC5 and WPP felt from outside and from within mirrored the experiences of those considered to be within the "proper," "political" New Left. Todd Gitlin says movements like the New Left that function through a dependency on mass media can be made weaker several ways (285). This can include fundamental questions about leadership and direction. Many groups like SDS faced a difficult situation as their organizations grew. The split with Sinclair demonstrates a sense of ill-preparedness by those leading the media onslaught. Leaders like Sinclair, and the band as the organizing force, were not equipped to make sense of the feverish rise of the Left, nor the repression that resulted from it. Often cited as an intrinsic part of this difficulty was the youthful naivety that was such an implicit part of the movement. As John P. Diggins observes, "Participatory democracy was the naïve ideal of a generation that had been reared to believe that good will and 'togetherness' could bring instant change. Innocent of the realities of power and the slow pace of historical change, lacking personal experience with the psychology of poverty, young radicals were unable to cope with setbacks and defeats" (177). The MC5 and WPP saw music, along with drug and other lifestyle changes, as the vehicle which could ignite change. Davis saw this in his experience with the WPP. "The New Left as far as the ideas ... we all were under the cloud of the previous generation. The idealism of that time was one kind of movement towards breaking away. It's very storybook and more" (Davis 2008).

The "storybook" that Davis speaks of rests on the idealistic frame of opposition to the Vietnam War as the primary organizing force for the entire movement. Diggins claims that the New Left lost out in that it "could never successfully organize the disconnect that the war had spawned" (179). Instead, factionalism caused the movement to degenerate. As Doug Rossinow states, "The New Left was a messy agglomeration of national and local groups and initiatives" (241). Yet the Vietnam War was a common flashpoint from which various forms of dissent found a foundational wellspring. Identity politics, empowerment, sexuality, and drug use all seemed to depend on the climate of dissent that the Vietnam War presented. Numerous groups felt a disconnect from their government and were daunted by a climate of authoritarian control and power. Numerous voices of empowerment and challenge rose from the populace. "Inevitably the radical upsurge of 1968–1972 began to wane as the war ended and Nixon sank into the swamp of Watergate. Americans across the political spectrum felt a growing political exhaustion after years of division," says Van Gosse (188).

When asked about political involvement following their time with the WPP, the MC5 band members said they felt a sense of listlessness as they ended their careers as a band and moved on as individuals. Kramer says, "There was a sense that the war was in fact winding down" by 1972. "All of those things that we were fighting for were kind of fading from the screen. That great mobilization of youth, the civil rights movement, and the antiwar movement ... it wasn't on the front of my thoughts anymore." Increasing drug use and his frustration with the band caused Kramer, in part, to lose focus on the movement. "It was really tough because, to tell you truth ... I wasn't all that savvy with Fanon, Lenin, Marx, and revolutionary critical theory. I'm a guitar player; I'm trying to learn what the substitute chords for B-flat are! I was interested and committed, but I couldn't argue my case. I think maybe I could hold my own today but geez, it's forty years later!" (Kramer 2008). Thompson concurs that the movement was becoming stagnant." Yet Thompson sees the end of the Vietnam War as testifying to the power of the New Left. "It was a war that we were losing and it was finally ended, and I think that is because of the voice of the people got through to political leaders that it was not fashionable to be a proponent of the war any more" (Thompson 2008).

As he saw it, the movement, even though supposedly disintegrating, was still very alive in everyday life. Leni Sinclair expresses the same kind of sentiment, describing how she was encouraged by those who continued to maintain their ideals, even in changing and less "revolutionary times." "They stopped the war. That's more than you can say for anybody nowadays. It was a great movement and I admired people like Tom Hayden and other people in SDS who later on became university professors or sat in the state legislature. I admired people who transferred that idealism and activism into real political power" (Leni Sinclair 2008). In the eyes of such participants the environment of dissent that the Vietnam War had brought had been successfully harnessed in some sense. To many, though, the New Left simply was not enough to stop the war, but it did provide new modes of thought. As Gosse contends, "Although the New Left did not stop the war in Vietnam, it did much to foster sentiment against escalation and to publicize the complicity of industry and the academic community" (185). Fights over the legacy of the New Left point to the struggle to establish a dominant narrative of the New Left, an important part of a generation's legacy.

The New Left and the MC5/WPP experiment shared the atmosphere of repression that they encountered. This repression and interpersonal issues resulting from its fallout were incredibly successful in bringing down groups associated with the New Left. Diggins contends that a tide turned in the movement.

> Confrontation politics worked well on campus, where the New Left could force professors who identified with their antiwar goals to capitulate to ever-increasing demands and could effectively exploit the television medium to create the

impression that it spoke for the majority of students. Outside the sanctuary of the campus, however, confrontation brought a backlash of repression. The nasty awakening came during the Democratic Convention of June 1968 [180–181].

For some in the band this was a sobering awakening of how close it was to the front lines as a "revolutionary" rock band.

Plamondon says that any problematic relationships among WPP members was exacerbated by government harassment. This repression could be seen among the Black Panthers[1] and other groups who found themselves up against the wall. For some this would result in distancing themselves from the movement and the rhetoric. For others like the Weathermen, this pressure further pushed their sense of commitment and need to simply fight back.

> The government/Cointelpro had significant effect on WPP/RPP. This, coupled with several financial failures and the interpersonal contradictions that come with living for years and years under tremendous stress among our leadership ... ultimately we folded. This was similar to the stresses of the BPP and other New Left groups. I just moved on and didn't look back [Plamondon 2008].

Fortunately, compared to many other groups Sinclair says it was difficult to infiltrate their group for intelligence gathering.

> We were less susceptible to this than most, because first of all we were a commune. Our members lived together; it was a basic component of our concept. If you all lived together and someone wants to infiltrate your group they have to live there with you 24 hours a day, and fuck you, and cook for you, and answer your phone. We all did that for each other. We had an organized household in a sense [John Sinclair 2008].

In regards to the legacy of the New Left, the parameters become confounded due to the spectrum of identities in the "New Left." From Van Gosse's "movement of movements" (5), to Aronowitz's notion of two distinct countercultures: a political and social, the parameters of the "New Left" are far from absolute. This last series of interviews looked to measure just how much they saw themselves fitting in the New Left. As products of usable rebellion, could the possibility for social change exist among the texts of popular culture that are often thrown to the side as extraneous?

Echoing Aronowitz, John McMillian sets down a definitive boundary. "Briefly, the New Left can be defined as a loosely organized, mostly white student movement that promoted participatory democracy, crusaded for civil rights and various types of university reforms, and protested against the Vietnam War." He continues, "'The movement' on the other hand, was a much larger constellation of social protest activity that either grew out of the New Left (e.g., gay liberation, radical feminism, and the hippie counterculture), or influenced and inspired the New Left (e.g., the civil rights and black power movements.)" (6). Such definitions reflect a much more specific mindset than the "movement of movements" perspective. The MC5 for many, like the U.S. government, saw the same threat of change attached no matter where theoretical definitions lay. Says Sinclair,

> In retrospect we were all part of the same thing, there is no question about it. From the mildest protestors to the "Ban the Bombers" to the anti-nuclear campaign of the late 1950s, the Bertrand Russell campaign, and then the anti-war movement. This was all started by church people and liberal Catholics. They had the right orientation culturally and it spread all the way to the White Panther Party and the Black Panther Party [John Sinclair 2008].

Band members, regardless of their commitment to the WPP rhetoric, seem to agree with this unified vision of the time period. Thompson says,

> Our fame was small compared to the measure of our influence. If you wanted to use it as a parallel to the New Left ... I think the New Left changed the way that a lot of people look at things. In other words it freed up thinking in the country over a long time.... The hippie-ish way of thinking ... people had opened minds. That is the true legacy of the left, of the radical left or modern left, was that there are more roads to roam than one ... there are possibilities ... possibilities that are protected under the first amendment. You have a right to pursue your own happiness [2008].

Davis, who earlier said that "we all were under the cloud of the previous generation," says, "The MC5 part of that movement is just a small fraction of that." The two who were the least happy with the rhetoric and actions of the WPP, Davis and Thompson, maintain a positive vision of the possibilities for music in everyday life. Davis says,

> It's a great feeling to feel like you've contributed something to someone's life and you've never met them. That's a great feeling. Maybe that is where I get the inspiration for Music is Revolution [a non-profit Davis heads]. Through the MC5 ... and being in shock that what we did was valuable to so many people that we never met and cause them to find something they weren't aware of before that. That is where it all comes from, the ol' MC5 [Davis 2008].

Six. Managing the Legacy of the Sound and the Fervor

Kramer plainly states, "I'm not cynical about the things that the New Left accomplished in the '60s." He sees the MC5 as playing a part in that movement. Instead of being an aside to a movement of dissident, white college students, they played a role in the struggles at hand,

> I think we had a role to play in it as artists do. The role is not to have central committee meetings. The role is as messengers, as an underground news-service, and as a community meeting. If you hear a Bob Dylan song and you think the lyric speaks directly to your heart, and I know that song and I feel that song speaks directly to my heart, then we have met in that song, we have connected. The song can create a sense of community. This is what Woody Guthrie understood so well. "This land is your land, this land is my land." The songs themselves have the possibility of bringing unity, unity against the forces that separate people [Kramer 2008].

Kramer sees the totality of the New Left and claims that its effect can be witnessed in the protests against George W. Bush's war in Iraq. "There were millions of people in the streets of the world trying to stop this war before it started. It didn't stop them, but at least the people out there were trying. They were paying attention; they knew exactly what was going on. I think that is a direct result of the New Left of the '60s: that consciousness, that awareness of what governments are doing" (Kramer 2008).

John Sinclair expressed a sense of frustration with those who were drawing definitive lines of identity during the time. "We tried to be part of the New Left really hard." Being dismissed as products of popular culture with a political organization attached created a sense of resentment after some time to those involved, who saw the music as an intrinsic piece of the larger puzzle. Sinclair describes throwing up his hands.

> We just withdrew ... we just thought that the New Left was students. Basically it was a student movement. We didn't think students per se were a revolutionary force. We thought youth with their own culture was a revolutionary force. The students were likely being financed by their parents to take over their parents' positions in society. While they were at school they didn't have to struggle for everything and they had the time to agitate, but they lived in the dorms. Culturally, we just didn't think they were advanced enough [2008].

Kramer, as one of the most politically engaged members of the group, echoed this feeling:

> We were aware of it [a binary reaction of love or hate in terms of the band's role in the New Left] and we generally could make it work for us. Like when

we'd go to a new city and we'd play, generally we would win people over. We would always generate harsh criticism from a few ... journalists.... We really got hammered from the left, more than from the right! The right just thought, "Oh my God, this is terrible what these people are saying." But the left, they would tear into us with a vengeance because we weren't revolutionary enough for the revolution! I told this to Tom Morello[2] and it blew his mind! I said man, we used to get it, and he said, "I can understand that." And I said no, we would get it from the left! [2008]

Seemingly membership in the New Left was as contentious then as it is now as a product of political and cultural history. Questions about who was included in the New Left continue to be asked today. What are the enduring effects of the New Left and who has the right to take credit? Scholars have hailed the New Left as an extreme that eventually was quelled by reactionary means, as a success that brought marginalized voices to the stage, as a failure that fostered no lasting change in power and government, and as a success in normalizing the ability to question the government.

The MC5 and WPP actors share, like these scholars, a spectrum of ideas about the New Left. According to Plamondon, legacy issues are unresolved, but the New Left contains a basic universal across groups.

> It's too early to tell what legacies were left behind. I don't see that time and those organizations as failures. I have no political regrets. Personal regrets, yes. I see the MC5, WPP/RPP as part of a great historic struggle that includes Native American resistance to national government, slave revolts, the civil rights movement, labor movements and the struggle of people around the world to fight against oppression and exploitation. The fight goes on, the story is not finished [Plamondon 2008].

Davis warns that nostalgia can be an enemy of historical insight, and that the baby-boomers need to be careful in shaping their legacies. "The whole New Left thing and the period of time that you talk about is also romanticized and fantasized about. It has taken on a Disney-like character. The events and the people, the situation as I remember it from day to day was a lot more mundane than people make it out to be. There wasn't all this wonderful dancing around in the park" (2008).

Oddly enough, one of the lasting changes from the era indeed arises from the MC5/WPP experiment. The "Keith Case" was precedent-setting. As Damren reminds us, the "Keith Case," that involved illegal wiretappings used to charge John Sinclair and Pun Plamondon for the bombing of a CIA office in Ann Arbor in 1968, is a "beacon to the judiciary to vigilantly guard against attempts by the Executive Branch to secure an 'uninvited ear' to the private conversations of citizens" (6). "Warrantless wiretappings of Plamondon's telephone" were "found to be illegal and caused the government to finally drop the charges" (Christie 8). The case helped secure civil liberties even for dissident voices. It remains an important precedent in discussions about civil liberties today.

Wherever this question of legacy falls in the coming years, it is important to remember what culture and popular culture can provide a populace looking for a sense of social location and direction. The questions of legacy for the MC5 were shaped during its tenure with the WPP, as well as after. Still, the connection to the WPP for good or ill shaped the lives of band members irrevocably as participants in history, popular music, and popular culture. The fallout from their break with the WPP tells an important part of the story: the desire to manage legacy and meaning. Managing the legacy of the New Left is similar, and like the MC5/WPP, levels of identity and investment are richly interwoven into the discussion and debate.

CHAPTER SEVEN

Up Against the Wall: Music's Place in Revolution

The rise and fall of the MC5 falls into an intensely debatable realm, the interaction of rock and rebellion. The band offers a case study in music's role in social change and development. One can spend chapters and careers waxing nostalgic about artists, relating them to notions of generational and cultural change without specific correlation. The MC5 takes these real and impassioned notions of music's role in social change to task, investigating the realities and the shortcomings of culture's function in dissidence and rebellion. The MC5 acts as a gauge in the history of popular music and popular culture to help measure how well music is able to tear down walls of ideology and practice.

The MC5 was a band that pushed, through its association with the White Panther Party, the foundational ethos of usable rebellion in rock. Complexities and passionate feelings are engaged when a product of popular culture connects itself to political and ideological thought in everyday American life. Steve Waksman in *Instruments of Desire* sees the MC5 as in search of a "usable past, for a fusion of aesthetics and politics that seemed necessary" (Waksman 209). Usable rebellion builds upon this possibility of constructing the past, but looks to these moments as more active, distinct and necessary for the continuation of rock, as well as demonstrating the power of popular culture products and the sometimes intense and distinct lives they can live among audiences. The challenges or at least the appearance of challenges to these structures through musical forms actively prompts an ardent discussion about audience investment, intent and the realities of popular culture's role in determining the ways in which we interact with the world around us.

The career and life of the MC5 and its connection to the WPP showcases the interaction of media frames, audience, artist, management, politics, and critics' use of popular culture texts. Government agencies were engaged in the use or repression of these texts, taking an active interest in the MC5 as a possible tool creating countercultural ideology through the mass media. Numerous frames and perspectives on the band from outside and from within were actively used to make sense of a popular culture text that employed rock's tradition of youthful rebellion and actively connected it to a platform that challenged the realities of everyday life in the United States in the late 1960s.

The MC5 proved that culture could be the flashpoint, or at least a promissory note, for social change. But this doesn't guarantee specific actions or usages by individuals and groups. Like the government, the economy, the law, or moral codes, music is a way that we as individuals order and understand the world around us. It is a space for escape as well as for challenging our beliefs and practices. Christopher Small refers to the process as "musicking," a process of communication that is a basic function of our humanity. Hence, contentions that two countercultures existed, a political and a cultural, make too neat a division. The MC5's reception in the '60s demonstrates how these lines easily blur.

The following pages will examine music's role in social change and development and will utilize the MC5 as a specific and challenging example. No attempt will be made to create a unifying, holistic, theoretical perspective on the function of music in social change and in dissent. Individual intent, group intent, media frames, reception, and the role of technology are too interwoven. To promise an overarching theory would be overreaching. To universalize would be to miss the spectrum of uses and meanings that are consumed and utilized by audiences. The career of the MC5 allows for a concrete interpretation of how music can be connected to notions of dissent, rebellion, revolution and social change. The nature of its career tested these boundaries and helped showcase the challenges and triumphs of music as ideological tool.

Can You Dance to Ideology? Breaking Down the Boundaries Between Mind and Body

Aronowitz's contention that two countercultures existed — a political, concerned with institutional change and a cultural, "for whom the erotic revolution was a political movement" which "believed the struggle within the state and its institutions hopeless and beside the point" (36)—is a common separation. It occurs in numerous narratives seeking to understand historical movements like the counterculture, neatly placing logic to one side and emotion to another. Music has traditionally been seen in historical discourse as part of this cultural sphere and viewed at best as a rejection or escape from the realities of the political and social world. Adorno and his cohorts in the Frankfurt School famously labeled these notions of mass cultural expression as meaningless distraction.

This separation between culture and politics is not relegated only to the mass media. It actually extends to the foundational voices of Western thought. Carson Holloway in *All Shook Up: Music, Passion and Politics* extends this discussion beyond music in mass media to a rich history among heralded thinkers of Western civilization. He contends, "The debate over music is, in essence, a debate over the place of reason and passion in human nature, their proper relationship to each other in the soul, and the proper relationship of both to politics." Classical thinkers such as Plato and Aristotle, "asserting the primacy of reason, seek to use music to calm the passions with a view to the noble rule of reason in the soul and the city," whereas latter critics of modernity such as Rousseau and Nietzsche, "accepting the priority of passion but also seeing a need to reinvigorate it, resurrect the power of music, aiming to use it to inflame the passions and silence reason in the service of a new, more noble politics" (20). Musical practice in society seems to be consistently tied to humanity's carnal nature and is distinctly separated from cognitive processes.

If this historically heralded separation between mind and body exists, Elie Siegmeister coyly suggests, one must then logically accept that musicians exist within a vacuum in which they "will not question the social bases of the conditions under which they work, nor the social function of their work," and that audiences, without thought or question, must consume the musical products without hope of shaping the products themselves, as there is no real relation to the material world (12). In Aronowitz's view this is exemplified by the cultural contingent of the counterculture simply dropping out of the political world. Such clear delineations between cultural products and the political and material world become increasingly problematic when looking at the history and legacy of this contentious time. Instead, scholars should reflect the realities and uses of music in everyday life and

Seven. Up Against the Wall: Music's Place in Revolution

hence its effect on social and historical life. Although this perspective is convenient, the effects of music and cultural products are not isolated from the world and are deeply embedded in the forces of ideological creation and maintenance.

Not all scholars separate mind and body in regard to musical forms. Small sees music as an intricate facet of the human experience in *Musicking: The Meanings of Performance and Listening*. He annihilates the separation between musical practice and ideological life. "Music is not a thing at all but an activity, something that people do" (2). Instead of an autonomous entity, music, like speech or thought, is an intrinsic tool of human communication and meaning-making. Capitalism has further entrenched the boundaries around music in society. Small contends that the traditional partitioning of "operations of the mind" working "independently of the body, is all the more pervasive for being unrecognized for what it is: an assumption, by no means to be accepted without scrutiny" (52). Capitalism, then, has taken a false delineation and systemized it.

> Our present-day concert life, whether "classical" or "popular," in which the "talented" few are empowered to produce music for the "untalented" majority, is based on a falsehood. It means that our powers of making music for ourselves have been hijacked and the majority of people robbed of the musicality that is theirs by right of birth, while a few stars, and their handlers, grow rich and famous through selling us what we have been led to believe we lack [Small 8].

If one invests in the idea of a separation of music from meaningful, everyday cognitive practice, Aronowitz's notions of separate countercultures are extremely useful. However, if you believe with Small that this separation between mind/body and performer/audience is false, the MC5 becomes a much more usable tool of ideological creation and understanding. Critical analysis and interest in the group transcends body/mind borders. The band provides this intersection of debate because it prompted among some a desire for social change and development, including direct challenges to existing power structures and ideologies. Themes of youthful rebellion in rock's early life were an active agent in the creation of identity. According to Small, the process of "musicking" "is part of the survival equipment of every human being. To music is not a mere enhancement of spare-time enjoyment but is an activity by means of which we learn what are our ideal social relationships, and that is as important for the growth of an individual to full social maturity as is talking and understanding speech" (210).

The MC5's linking of this usable space of rebellion to revolutionary rhetoric and style, regardless of its members' individual levels of commitment, played a key role in testing the conceptualizations of music and media's roles in the creation of ideology. By blurring these lines, the band demonstrated the dangerous linkage that could occur when these two processes were combined and used as tools of social and ideological construction.

Gosse's concept of the New Left as a "movement of movements" is perhaps a more practical way to discuss the New Left. No matter how tempting the thought of a definitive dividing line between culture and politics, these threads were interwoven into people's experiences, and into the way that history has come to view the time. As Gosse states, the concept encompasses "all of the struggles for fundamental change from the early 1950s roughly to 1975." The broader definition allows for the inclusion of numerous movements that "overlapped, and each saw itself as part of a challenge to the established order. Therefore, it seems valid to assign them equal shares in what the New Left did and did not accomplish" (5). In the end, "it is hard to say where politics ends and culture begins" (7).

The interviews provided insight into the processes of musicking, and music as a potential agent of social change and development. Sinclair wrote in the liner notes to the MC5's first album that music should not be a sovereign entity. The theme of "separation is doom," as Sinclair described in the notes in regards to music, continues as an ideological center for the group. Michael Davis explains,

> We need to bring music to our children. We need to bring music to society as a more important facet of life. We need to not look at music as an extra, as a piece of candy on the side, as an appetizer to real life. We need to treat it just as if it is important as anything else ... as religion, as knowledge of the law, or of physics, or of anything. We need to bring it into focus, because music and art are really basic human tropes to represent a sense of what we see.... I think it makes [people] more human, it makes them more compassionate. It focuses on an experience within yourself that is beyond.... It is almost spiritual. It is religious. If you can share music with someone, it makes you worth something. It makes you worth something as a group. It takes away that sense of being abandoned, of being alone in a really cold universe.... We want every child, every person to understand the value of communicating with music.

Seven. Up Against the Wall: Music's Place in Revolution

This is my revelation, that music brings peace and a higher intellect, a higher understanding of who we are and where we want to go [2008].

When asked about music having a direct connection to the creation of ideology he said,

"Everything has a political connotation ... kind of sort of.... Sometimes it comes back to basic human needs of communicating honestly. I don't know how you could be dishonest and play music" [Davis 2006].

In 2006, Davis and his wife Angela aimed to put the above thoughts into action, founding "Music is Revolution," an organization that seeks to assist in the funding of school music programs, and to provide refurbished instruments to students. Davis hopes to put into action his ideas of music's centrality in education. According to the organization's manifesto, encouraging music education leads to "increasing the cultural and academic prosperity of this and future generations of public school children." Davis writes, "To play in an ensemble is an enriching process that teaches us the basis of community. When you consider the fact that all of us exist in concert as the human race, it becomes obvious that from this very parallel we can learn how to be better humans" (*www.musicisrevolution.org*). Instead of being a casual aside in educational paths, the organization focuses on music as a foundational absolute for development and growth.

Davis, like his cohort Dennis "Machine Gun" Thompson, would agree with Small's perspectives regarding the importance and everyday use of music to construct meaning. Hence, a possibility exists for its link to political and revolutionary thought. "Music is powerful stuff and it has an element of social change. It can change ... but I think it happens on the individual level ... that's the key here. It happens on a person to a person basis, not over movements" (Thompson 2006). Music, to these two individuals, is a practice within itself that does not lead and dictate the path of political and social change in isolation, but uses a larger network of political and cultural texts.

Wayne Kramer, who again, along with Rob Tyner, has been cited as the most politically impassioned in the band, mirrors his band-mates reflections with perhaps even more faith in music's role in social change movements. Yet he also does not believe music is strong enough in itself to create lasting change.

We try to infuse our hopes in there or our fears. When people come to the art, when they come to the message ... it's a meeting place. If you listen to "Masters of War" and say, "man, that's a great fucking song," and I listen to "Masters of War" and I say, "That is a great song," then we've just met, we've

Wayne Kramer (courtesy Leni Sinclair).

Seven. Up Against the Wall: Music's Place in Revolution

unified in a sense. It's eliminating the distance between us, which is the role of art ... to eliminate the gap between people. To show that we are way more alike than we are different.... It's not to man the barricades. Artists have a role in it all. Some people march in the street, some people write letters, some people go to law school, run for office and some people sing songs about it. Kramer agrees with the liner notes written by Sinclair in *Kick Out the Jams*.

Definitive separation of the cultural and political is false. It is instead a symbiotic relationship intrinsically shaping everyday life.

"The culture informs the politics, but the politics reinforces the culture. You can't separate them. Our political life is as real as our cultural life. I'm certainly on the cultural side, but I can't deny that the politics inform a lot of it. Trying to sing songs and tell stories and be honest about the human condition and the human condition is managed by our political systems" (Kramer 2006).

Kramer has continued to maintain a presence in this blurring of politics and culture. In 2005 he participated in the "Operation Ceasefire" concert in Washington, D.C., that "drew more than 100,000 people." Kramer states, "It shows you put a few people's energy together and you can make a statement" (Bowe 12). Kramer more recently has been a key player in the Axis of Justice tour. The organization and tour was created by Tom Morello (of Rage Against the Machine) and Serj Tankian (of System of a Down): "Its purpose is to bring together musicians, fans of music, and grassroots political organizations to fight for social justice. We aim to build a bridge between fans of music around the world and local political organizations to effectively organize around issues of peace, human rights, and economic justice" ("Our Mission," 2008).

Kramer felt strongly about the tour. "It was the coolest thing I ever did in music. It combined the two things that I most interested in ... rocking the fuck out and social justice ... about being of service to my fellows." Kramer was one of the featured performers on the tour. The tour went to various locales; part of the tour included projects in the cities they stopped in. "We fed the homeless in L.A., we cleaned up Katrina debris in New Orleans, we helped push forward a living wage movement in Asheville, we visited with kids who were blown to pieces in Iraq at Walter Reed and worked with Iraq Veterans Against the War, which was really illuminating."

Tour members focused as well on "health care in Boston, the Service Employees Union in Chicago. So every day we did a concert and we spent a day in service. I don't know if it helped anybody, but it helped me!" Kramer felt that the rubber finally hit the road. "The whole thing to me was kind of like all of the stuff we have been talking about for forty years put into action really on a grassroots level. On the level where you can do something" (Kramer 2008). Based upon the tour's immense success, Kramer hopes to see the project carried further.

Much like the MC5 experiment, the Axis of Justice tour looks to harness the power of usable rebellion, so tied into rock's ethos. Through a program of music, the tour hopes to solicit energy from its audience, and, perhaps in a way that the Panthers were not able to do, direct the energy into a pragmatic and immediate program of action. The tour's website (axisofjustice.org) lists activist groups centered around issues like independent media, peace, homelessness, sweatshops, and numerous other areas of concern. Tour goers can donate to the organization(s) or sign up for action with one of the many groups featured. Much like the MC5, this product of popular culture is experimenting with harnessing the energy and rebellious voice of rock to express discontent, and to provide a potential flashpoint for change.

The role of popular culture in this search for change is one that continues to be debated. How much can it really do? The MC5 can be a template for such discussions. The band helped shape the minds of Davis, Kramer and Thompson in regards to music's role in social change and revolutionary thought, and it provided an incredibly usable space to measure the function of music in these processes for audiences. Former White Panther Minister of Defense Pun Plamondon asserts,

> Popular capitalist culture is only interested in promoting capitalist economy and capitalist politics. Revolutionary culture, on the other hand, is involved in promoting revolutionary economics and politics. I always felt that we could develop and promote a revolutionary culture prior to a political and economic revolution. A revolutionary culture would make the political and economic revolution easier. If the revolutionary culture was successful it would minimize the violence of the political and ec5onomic revolution since a large mass of people would already be living in a revolutionary culture. Understand, economics is the very foundation of society. Politics reflects and supports the economic system. Culture reflects and supports both the economic system and political system [Plamondon 2006].

As minister of defense, Plamondon was too progressive in his political aims and revolutionary thought for the band. The relationship with Plamondon and his increasingly combative rhetoric would attract greater governmental interest and create difficulties for the band. The usable space became a polymorphic entity: a jumping off point for Plamondon's revolution, a perceived direct threat to national security by the FBI, a marketing ploy, and the "compression" that Davis had suggested.

Tear Down the Wall! Now, What? Determining If Music Can Equal a Movement

As a basic mode of constructing identity, according to Small, music can help to negotiate feelings of belonging, community, history, and memory. Music also further perpetuates ideology. The MC5's success and downfall as a "revolutionary rock" band points out the discrepancies in possibility and interpretation by parties that are invested in music and its perceived roles. Perhaps music's greatest drawback as an autonomous and unified tool of social change is that music is an interpretive process in which modes of communication are not transparent. Hence, a group like the MC5, with so many parties involved in its life and career including media eager to frame the group as either the vanguard of the revolution or as imposters, quickly became the possession of numerous users. Because of this, it slipped beyond any intended frames from the individual creators themselves. This multiplicity of viewpoints can allow a sense of community and communal dissent, as well as represent divergent and sometimes contestable uses of the same texts. Small says that people making music are

> looking for different kinds of relationships, and we should not project the ideals of one kind of performance onto another. Any performance, and that includes a symphony concert, should be judged finally on its success in bringing into existence for as long as it lasts a set of relationships that those taking part feel to be ideal in enabling those taking part to explore, affirm, and celebrate those relationships. Only those taking part will know for sure what is their nature [Small 49].

Searching out different relationships through musical texts is exemplified by the numerous perspectives on what the MC5 did and could mean in society, either as a live act or through the capital-dependent recording process. Small contends recording causes separation between performer and listener. However, recordings could and did create meaningful spaces for constructing social identity for listeners. Interviews with group members concerning their upbringings, experiences with the music industry, technology, their surroundings, racism, and politics all showcase contexts in which they used the band. Those who were involved in the band's career and the life of the WPP such as Sinclair and Plamondon had differing use values. The fan base, supportive and damning critics, and the government had still different use values. All of these looked to a product of popular music to negotiate their perspectives.

For those invested in the band and its revolutionary potential, performance and musical practice created intimate spaces where memory and consciousness were shaped through mass-media forms (Lipsitz viii), either albums or, more immediately, in live performance. Here, temporary communities, or to borrow a phrase from Hakim Bey, "temporary autonomous zones" (TAZ), were created; utopian spaces of escape or collectivism that were beyond the reach of anyone beyond the person immediately experiencing it (Bey x-xi).

Bey's vision of a poetic terrorism where "ART SABOTAGE STRIVES TO be perfectly exemplary but at the same time retain an element of opacity—not propaganda but aesthetic shock—appallingly direct yet also subtly angled—action as metaphor" (11), is, when compared to the MC5 and WPP, significantly less formalized and funded. Yet the idea of a spontaneous, affecting "energy" is shared between the two. Bey urges readers to "kidnap someone and make them happy" (5). In essence, this is what the MC5 could do to people for small sections of time and space. Norman Mailer's description of the band in Chicago in 1968, or Dave Marsh's ability to get lost in the band's performance (and to continue carrying that event with him) all speak of successful transportation and effect.

Bey qualifies the TAZ as being "like an uprising which does not engage directly with the State, a guerrilla operation which liberates an area (of land, of time, of imagination) and then dissolves itself to re-form elsewhere/elsewhen, *before* the State can crush it" (Bey 99). This is another area in which the path of the band differs, and perhaps can be a warning to potential TAZ creators out there. The band in many ways did actively confront the state. But the power of media and the response to the furious rhetoric of the group was a shock to many involved. None of them could foresee that the authorities would find them such a direct threat. Their inability to foresee the immense impact of their combining the political with the popular caused the retribution that took them out.

In the end though, interviews with those in the band and those connected through the White Panther community exemplify these spaces of interaction among audiences and the MC5 and the individual notions of community that came with their experiences. Davis's hope for a communal nirvana through a symbiotic relationship between performer and audience through the practice of "high energy" music showcases the utopian potentiality of audiences who are united, if only for a moment. Regardless of whether participation meant investment in music and performance or in the rhetoric of the White Panther Party, a community could be established. This all came under the guise of music and art as *the* organizing force. Bey expresses a similar romantic perspective: "Part of my self-induced stupidity, I confess, is to believe (and even feel) that art can change me, and change others. That's why I write pornography and propaganda — to cause *change*. Art can never mean as much as a love affair, perhaps, or an insurrection. But ... to a certain extent ... it works" (Bey 77).

The perspectives that audiences are prone to create reflect a spectrum of meaning and possibilities in such explosions of expression. Shelia Whitely in *The Space Between the Notes* says that while "it might be argued that on stage the groups' sexual aggression was little more than formalised and ritualised violence, the music nevertheless has a neurotic element which, in its more frenzied form, evokes a pseudo-tribal paranoia" (82). Whatever the band's reputation for anarchistic sound, this tribal cohesion was still a possible outcome for its audiences.

Sinclair discusses this important notion of community and autonomy in *Music and Politics* at a local level, saying local scenes "are reflective of the unique social conditions" (21) of the area. In the case of Detroit, the scene is characterized by a "rock- and urban-soul-based music, an intense energy feeling, and a close, tight involvement with *its* audience" (22). Nationally and internationally, Lipsitz's notion that memory and meaning are created through mass media communities was proven over and over again through the MC5. These were made possible through the sales of their LPs, radio and television exposure, and continued media attention in international magazines such as *Mojo* and *Uncut*.

The professionalism that Small says creates false stratifications of performer and audience are here, but communities large and small can actively center themselves around these products. Such varying levels of local and global can be negotiated by consumers of popular music in relation to a group like the MC5. They can accept all or part, or misinterpret the individual authors' intents. The negotiation can also result in complete disregard of the text. This active process of negotiation is one that De Certeau calls "dancing on a tightrope" (73). Here audiences are able to create levels of meaning and belonging by their ability to recreate an equilibrium through the use and non-use of popular culture materials, thus making meaning of their lives through an endless supply of materials and signs. This creates a "ceaseless creativity of a kind of taste in practical experience" (73), including the creation of temporary communities based upon shared knowledge and appreciation of popular culture icons like the MC5.

Usable rebellion is centered in this process, in that participants in popular culture can use these texts for their own purposes, including framing the political and social world around them. Differing levels of investment can even, as Tricia Rose discusses in *Black Noise*, "produce communal bases of knowledge about social conditions, communal interpretations of them and quite often serve as the cultural glue that fosters communal resistance" (99–100). This was the hope of some in the WPP, to produce a cultural base for their notions of revolution. This contingent was on one side of the spectrum while at the other end was the band, providing access to cash and sex. These extremes represent the fluctuation in usability of the band and its association with the White Panther Party, from audiences, critics, the authorities, and from the members themselves. Where you stood in the spectrum reflected investment, or lack thereof, in the increasingly overt political rhetoric and associations of the group and its propaganda.

It is these same notions of usability by audiences that also constrain products of popular culture in the creation of ideology in everyday life. De Certeau refers to popular culture as "a dark rock that resists all assimilation" (18) because texts like the MC5 cannot communicate or create an absolute voice. Users of popular culture are like "nomads poaching their way across fields they did not write, despoiling the wealth of Egypt to enjoy it themselves" (174). In the case of the MC5 and of rock in general, this usability was the case for those constructing the text themselves. The ability of media to frame these entities and the uses that audiences, critics and governmental interest had for the text reveal a vast contingent of poachers using a product that did not even have a complete understanding of itself *internally*.

For some like Davis and Thompson, directed youthful rebellion became problematic too quickly, whereas for others like Sinclair, Kramer. and Plamondon, experiences with the group and its political life gave glimmers of hope for music's power to change the course of the world around them.

Because of these multiple frames of reference from individuals associated with the group, varying levels of meaning creation were employed by media outlets seeking to frame the band and the WPP, and by audiences and the participants themselves. As Small argues, "In fact, in neither verbal nor gestural languages is there a complete one-to-one relationship between signifier and signified" (60). Here, the MC5 was used as a raw material in which identities were negotiated through the music itself as well as through the political associations of the group with the WPP.

Even with media frames seeking to create clear and concise interpretations of social and cultural forces like the MC5 and the WPP, the power and reach of popular cultural products in the creation of ideology and perhaps direct action is subject to these interpretive processes by those using the product for their own means. Siegmeister contends that the complexity of this meaning-making process of using and interpreting musical products is oblique and does not equal direct influence. "Social influences do not act in an immediate, direct, simple way. Often the effect is delayed, circuitous, oblique; in most cases a broad effect, felt over a long period of time, not perhaps discernable in one particular instance, but evident in a broad collection of instances" (20). The connection of the MC5 to revolutionary and dissident rhetoric and image tested this supposed delay by connecting the social and the musical in a product that for some could ignite direct action and tear down notions of displacement and tepidness.

The focus on the band by governmental authorities is a telling reaction that did not separate the cultural from the political. The authorities looked to a cultural product as possibly demanding action and continued surveillance. The wealth of documents collected on the MC5 and the White Panther Party show that the government was not so sure about the "obliqueness" of music's influence in creating dissent. Says Thompson, "Back in those days they had nothing to compare it to. The FBI was afraid of it ... it might go the other way. Kids might start burning shit down; they just might start picking up guns and assassinating rich people and people in power" (2006). The direct action that was feared, according to Thompson, did not provide the spark that ignited the tearing down of the status quo. Power and its connection to music had a long history before and after the MC5. Music has been a focus of governmental concern globally, such as in the intense scrutiny of content in Castro's Cuba, and in the efforts of the Parents' Music Resource Center (PMRC) in the U.S., a group that rose to fame targeting figures like

Frank Zappa in the 1980s, concerned that music would be a "prime cause of unwanted mass behavior" (Fischlin 30).

The main fear is that as a product of mass culture, music is omnipresent, difficult to control and can easily reach vast audiences with challenges to the established order. Author T.V. Reed questions this line between culture and politics, saying there is a failure to "distinguish degrees or levels of cultural politics, or to think carefully about the relative scale of impact of a given practice or discourse" (290). With the MC5, such discussions of scope can be problematized.

Music, with its ability to create effective autonomous zones for listeners who can invest in, disregard or misinterpret authors' frames, represents a difficult to isolate, but still very real, space of ideological construction and community creation. This creation can be empowered or dissipated through its dependence on the technology of mass communication. Small's notions of immediacy and foundational social location found in the daily practice of music, for better or worse, have met the realities of interpretation in the mass media head on. The MC5, regardless of the revolution's promises or fallacies and one's investment or lack thereof in the group, provided a text under which these vast and powerful topics could be examined concretely, both from emancipatory and repressive perspectives. Such a case study can also offer significant insight into the realities of usable rebellion through music, and its place in future social change and development.

Looking to the Future of Music: Music's Role in Future Revolutions

By taking on the rhetoric, image, and, arguably, sound of an idealized revolution, the MC5 at the least demonstrated how connections between culture and politics could be made through musical practice. Practice here refers not only to the creation and spread of musical texts, but also their reception and use. Future discussions of music's role in social change, as the MC5 case study demonstrates, should discard the false parameters separating the cultural and the political, the mind and body. Although they are convenient categories, the realities of musical practice even within the technological and financial constraints of the modern mass media show that they cannot be separated. As false or idealized sonic incarnations of the counterculture and the New Left, the MC5 was a very real, usable focal point from which individuals confronted and questioned the world around them. The band was also a showcase of the immense investment and concern when these commonly separated entities are brought together.

Keeping in mind the meeting of music and politics, we should discard notions of music as a singular entity that can independently perpetuate mass social change. When tearing down these boundaries between cultural and political, we see the limits of this practice of usable rebellion through rock. Music is dependent on an array of use values. From impassioned to superfluous, the right of these texts to speak does not guarantee the right to be consumed in idealized purity. Instead, music can be regarded as an intrinsic part to a whole. Culture and politics in the end cannot be separated clearly, if at all. The practice of music and the spaces of autonomy that it offers, like all human practices, are interdependent processes through which we find cohesion, community, investment, ideological construction and questioning.

The ideal notion of music working as a sovereign tool of dissent and social change within itself is a falsehood that the MC5 case study helps us understand. This is not because music is not a powerful or cohesive form, but because it depends on media, technology, and variance of audience use values, and, in the case of the MC5, is susceptible to government repression. Music can be considered powerful and prevalent, capable of creating autonomous spaces where people can openly and actively confront and question the world that surrounds them. In Small's "musicking" approach, music is part of a process of learning about and questioning the world. Like writing and speaking, music shapes our daily lives. It is also a deeply personal process in its role in constructing social location. But as Small complains, music has been "hijacked" by a small set of professionals selling us "what we have been led to believe we lack" (8).

Hence, a means by which we see the world has been relegated to a process dependent upon capital, industry and the technologies used to distribute it. The goal of establishing a cohesive community through music is still a very real possibility and perhaps best reflects why the government was so concerned with the band. If media forms are used to distribute an anti-authoritarian message, and groups like the MC5 and WPP actively communicate that message, what will the ramifications be? The answer, in terms of this case study, is that the band and its associations were used in a wide-ranging spectrum by listeners, critics and the authorities. It was a springboard for revolution, a means to access cash and sex, a demonstration of shameless marketing, and a threat to national security. In addition, the group provides a forum to consider musical inspiration and musical hype, and to measure political fearlessness or selling-out. Very real communities could be united and just as easily torn apart when looking at the life of the MC5 and its involvement with countercultural life in the late 1960s and early 1970s. These numerous frames point to a great difficulty for future musicians seeking to create autonomous programs for changing the world around them. If you say you want a revolution, as the Beatles sang in 1968, you had best be prepared to create countless highly individualized revolutions for those listening in.

To create a truly "rebellious" music in the hope of generating direct action and social change you must be able to shape media frames, manage governmental interest and potential repression, and manage the consumption and restrict the usability of individual texts to audiences seeking to, as De Certeau would say, "poach" the useful parts, and leave the others behind. Simply put, music by itself, like political leadership by itself or laws by themselves, cannot guarantee direct paths to mass social movements. Instead, groups like the MC5 are part of an intricate whole of intercontextuality where these parts all function together in adapting to and creating social change and development.

Music's great power comes from the acute and impassioned usability of its texts for audiences to create meaning and engage in active questioning of the world around them. Rock, like jazz, great symphonic works, opera or hip-hop, offers spaces in everyday life where ideologies are put to the test and are offered new challenges. Bands like the MC5 are such great threats to governments and to critics because there is a great fear that such supposedly wide-reaching and affective texts can mean so much to their audiences — audiences they may see as desperate, in search of leadership, or simply as ignorant. Regardless, these are audiences who can nonetheless find pathways to new ideologies regardless of the authenticity involved in their creation, or, in the case of the MC5, the idealism, anger, youthful naivety, and self-indulgence that was mixed into an already complicated text before it ever assaulted the ears of their listeners.

If the contention is still made that the "revolution will be televised," music will provide the soundtrack and will be put into the hard drives, iPods, car stereos, portable players and collective memories of the populaces seeking to create change and challenging the structures around them. In the process, music can provide momentary escape, or a momentary autonomous zone from which we can safely question everyday life. It can also simply be left at the door on the way home after the concert. The MC5 and the White Panther Party tested these relationships of power, pushing past the doors and into the streets. Once they got into those streets, the realities of the America they were commenting on hit back violently. But their push — and connection of a band and a political party, however tongue in cheek, provided a space from which future generations can determine if music, indeed, is revolution.

Chapter Notes

Chapter One

1. See Sinclair's Guitar Army for a cross-section of the WPP's self-generated press. Consult especially the "Rock and Roll Dope" series for examples of various framing methods.

Chapter Two

1. Studies of the band such as McNeil and McCain's *Please Kill Me* and Goodman's *The Mansion on a the Hill* do distribute the political responsibility to some extent. But John Sinclair is usually the focus of investigations into the White Panther Party, specifically in such studies as Hull's "The White Panthers 'Total Assault on Culture,'" and Strausbaugh's *Rock 'Til You Drop*.

2. This mirrors the contextual class realities that Bradley discussed in *Understanding Rock 'n' Roll*, in the rise of the UK rock scene that was discussed in the first chapter.

3. See a more detailed discussion of these affiliations in Chapter Three.

4. The MC5 was recently featured in *Mojo Magazine's The Roots of the Sex Pistols*. Rage Against the Machine covered the MC5's "Kick Out the Jams" on 2000's *Renegades*.

Chapter Three

1. The Rainbow People's Party will be discussed in Chapter Six. This was the group that eventually replaced the White Panthers, with John Sinclair at the reins.

2. The Black Panthers established numerous colonies across the nation, including in such cities as Detroit, Chicago, New York and San Francisco/Oakland. The reach of the WPP will be discussed in following chapters.

3. The Yippies, or the Youth International Party, was in reality several individuals, such as Abbie Hoffman, Jerry Rubin, Nancy Kurshan and Paul Krassner, who utilized media to spread countercultural values. The Yippies are most widely remembered for their organized spectacles and demonstrations such as the "Festival of Life," in which they acted as pied pipers for youth.

4. See Chapter Five for further discussion of this.

Chapter Four

1. Chapter Five deals specifically with state and federal authorities and their targeting of Sinclair and Plamondon.

2. For further discussion of drug use within the band see Chapter Six, as well as Carson's *Grit, Noise and Revolution* and Simmons and Nelson's *The Future is Now!*

3. Chapter Five describes both the musical and visual output of the group in detail.

Chapter Notes

Chapter Five

1. The MC5 has been featured on the FBI Website's "Reading Room."
2. For the last and perhaps most surprising of these examples, see *Revelation: Revolution '69*.
3. Sinclair, Plamondon, and the WPP were all the subjects of surveillance.
4. The song was written by his manager Al Smith.
5. For further information, see Goodman 1997 and Simmons and Nelson 2004.
6. See *Guitar Army* for these collected works.
7. Crawford also led the Church of Zenta, a fictitious church that, as Kramer states, "was a complete hustle to scam some money from people in the audience." The money went to buy the MC5 family marijuana and alcohol.
8. These liner notes were eventually pulled by Elektra.
9. Sinclair by the time of this letter was actually in federal prison.
10. See "SleazeNation" and Robinson.

Chapter Six

1. Some would argue against the Black Panther Party being considered part of the New Left. See Rossinow in *The New Left Revisited*.
2. Morello, former guitarist for Rage Against the Machine, has worked with Kramer in several instances, including on the Axis of Justice Tour.

Bibliography

Albrecht, Robert. *Mediating the Muse*. Cresskill, N.J.: Hampton Press, 2004.
Alterman, Loraine. "The MC5: More Like One Big Musician." *Detroit Free Press*, 17 February 1967, p. 3B.
Altschuler, Glenn C. *All Shook Up: How Rock 'n' Roll Changed America*. Oxford: Oxford University Press, 2003.
Aronowitz, Stanley. *The Death and Rebirth of American Radicalism*. New York: Routledge, 1996.
Attali, Jacques. *Noise: The Political Economy of Music*. Minneapolis: University of Minnesota Press, 1985.
Baker, Cary. "Detroit's Guitar Army Is on the March Again!" *Bomp!* November 1977, 30–31.
Bangs, Lester. "Heavy Metal." In *The Rolling Stone Illustrated History of Rock & Roll*, edited by Anthony Decurtis, James Henke and Holly George-Warren. New York: Random House, 1992.
———. *Mainlines, Blood Feasts, and Bad Taste*. New York: Anchor Books, 2003.
Barnett, LeRoy. *Makin' Music*. Lansing: Michigan Historical Center, 2002.
Baudrillard, Jean. *The System of Objects*. New York: Verso, 1996.
Benford, Robert D., and David A. Snow. "Framing Processes and Social Movements: An Overview and Assessment." *Annual Review of Sociology* 26 (2000): 611–39.
Bey, Hakim. *T.A.Z.: The Temporary Autonomous Zone, Ontological Anarchy, Poetic Terrorism*. Brooklyn, N.Y.: Autonomedia, 1991.
Bodroghkozy, Aniko. *Groove Tube: Sixties Television and the Youth Rebellion*. Durham: Duke University Press, 2001.
Boucher, Caroline. "MC5 Problem." *Disc & Music Echo*, 8 August 1970.
Bradley, Dick. *Understanding Rock 'n' Roll: Popular Music in Britain 1955–1964*. Philadelphia: Open University Press, 1992.
Callwood, Brett. *MC5: Sonically Speaking: A Tale of Revolution and Rock 'n' Roll*. Church Stretton: Independent Music Press, 2007.
Carson, David. *Grit, Noise and Revolution: The Birth of Detroit Rock 'n' Roll*. Ann Arbor: University of Michigan Press, 2005.
Chapple, Steve, and Reebee Garofalo. *Rock 'n' Roll is Here to Pay: The History of Politics of the Music Industry*. Chicago: Nelson Hall, 1977.
Christie, Judy. "Keith Case: The Participants." In *The Court Legacy: The Historical Society for the United States District Court for the Eastern District of Michigan*, vol. 11, no. 4 (November 2003).
"Classic Album? Kick Out the Jams." *Bang Magazine*, no. 2 (May 2003).

Bibliography

Cohen, Mitchell and Dennis Hale, eds. *The New Student Left: An Anthology*. Boston: Beacon Press, 1967.

Damren, Samuel C. "The Keith Case." *The Court Legacy: The Historical Society for the United States District Court for the Eastern District of Michigan*, vol. 11, no. 4 (November 2003).

Davidson, Chris. "The MC5: Pioneers of Punk." *MaximumRockNRoll*, no. 145 (June 1995).

Davis, Angela. E-mail to the author, 15 April 2008.

Davis, Michael. "Diary of a Mad Dog." Manuscript in the collection of Michael Davis.

———. Interviews by the author. Pasadena, Calif., 6 July 2005 and 3 October 2006.

———. Interview by the author. Via telephone, 16 April 2008.

Day/Kramer/Samways. *MC5: Sonic Revolution: A Celebration of the MC5*. Dir. Dom Phillips. Muscletone, Inc. DVD. 2005.

de Certeau, Michel. *The Practice of Everyday Life*. Translated by Steven Rendall. Berkeley: University of California Press, 1984.

Detroit Police Department Detective Division Special Investigation Bureau. "Proposed Assembly of Hippies." 18 April 1967, John and Leni Sinclair Papers, Box 46, Bentley Historical Library, University of Michigan.

Diggins, John P. *The American Left in the Twentieth Century*. Chicago: Harcourt Brace Jovanovich, 1973.

Downes, Robert. "The Last Outlaw: Pun Plamondon's Radical Odyssey." *Northern Express*. 15 April 2008. <http://www.northernexpress.com/editorial/features.asp?id=978>

English, Ron, and John Sinclair. "The Artists Worksheet #4 Manifesto." The Collected Artist Worksheets. Detroit: Detroit Artists' Workshop, 1965.

Farley, Reynolds, Sheldon Danziger and Harry J. Holzer. *Detroit Divided*. New York: Russell Sage Foundation, 2000.

FBI Correlation Summary. "John Alexander Sinclair" dated 8 May 1975. John and Leni Sinclair Papers, Box 46, Bentley Historical Library, University of Michigan.

Fischlin, Daniel, and Ajay Heble, eds. *Rebel Musics: Human Rights, Resistant Sounds, and the Politics of Music Making*. New York: Black Rose Books, 2003.

Frith, Simon. *Performing Rites: On the Value of Popular Music*. Cambridge, Mass.: Harvard University Press, 1998.

———. *Sound Effects: Youth, Leisure and the Politics of Rock 'n' Roll*. New York: Pantheon, 1981.

Garafalo, Reebee. "From Music Publishing to MP3: Music and Industry in the Twentieth Century." *American Music* 17, no. 3 (autumn 1999): 318–354.

George-Warren, Holly, and Patricia Romanowski. *The Rolling Stone Encyclopedia of Rock & Roll*. New York: Fireside, 2001.

Gitlin, Todd. *The Whole World Is Watching: Mass Media in the Making and Unmaking of the New Left*. Berkeley: University of California Press, 1980.

Goodman, Fred. *The Mansion on the Hill: Dylan, Young, Springsteen, and the Head-On Collision of Rock and Commerce*. New York: Times Books, 1997.

Gosse, Van. *Rethinking the New Left: An Interpretive History*. New York: Palgrave Macmillan, 2005.

Hale, Jeff. "The White Panthers' Total Assault on Culture." In *Imagine Nation: The American Counterculture of the 1960s and '70s*. Edited by Peter Braunstein and Michael William Doyle. New York: Routledge, 2002.

Hasted, Nick. "Search and Destroy." *Uncut*, May 2005, 80–90.

"Have the MC5 Sold Out?" *SleazeNation*. May 2003.

Hebdige, Dick. *Subculture: The Meaning of Style*. New York: Routledge, 1987.
Hoffman, Abbie. *Steal this Book*. New York: Four Walls Eight Windows, 1996.
Holloway, Carson. *All Shook Up: Music, Passion and Politics*. Dallas: Spence Publishing, 2001.
Holzman, Jac. Letter dated 16 April 1969. Collection of Michael Davis.
Hoover, John Edgar. Letter to Minority Leader Gerald R. Ford Jr. dated 25 September 1970. John and Leni Sinclair Papers, Box 46, Bentley Historical Library, University of Michigan.
_____. "Re: John Alexander Sinclair" dated 19 September 1969. John and Leni Sinclair Papers, Box 46, Bentley Historical Library, University of Michigan.
Hull, Geoffrey P. *The Recording Industry*. New York: Routledge, 2004.
Hunt, Andrew. "How New Was the New Left?" In *The New Left Revisited*. Edited by John McMillian and Paul Buhle. Philadelphia: Temple University Press, 2003. 139–155.
Hunt, Darnell M. *Screening the Los Angeles "Riots": Race, Seeing and Resistance*. Cambridge: Cambridge University Press, 1997.
Jarrett, Michael. "Concerning the Progress of Rock & Roll." *Present Tense: Rock & Roll and Culture*. Edited by Anthony Decurtis. Durham, N.C.: Duke University Press, 1992.
Jonze, Tim. "Infamous Five." *New Music Express*. 29 March 2003.
"Kick Out the Jeans, Motherfu — Sorry, Brothers and Sisters ... Or Does It Suck to Make a Buck?" (14 March 2003). <http://www.i94bar.com/rant/jeans.html>
Kramer, Wayne. Interviews by the author. Hollywood, Calif., 7 July 2005 and 2 October 2006.
_____. Interview by the author. Via telephone, 9 May 2008.
Lait, Jack, and Lee Mortimer. *U.S.A. Confidential*. New York: Crown, 1952.
Larabee, Ann. "Interview with Lawrence 'Pun' Plamondon." *Journal for the Study of Radicalism* 1, no. 1 (Spring 2007): 111–127.
_____, and Mathew Bartkowiak. "Interview with John Sinclair." *Journal for the Study of Radicalism* 1, no. 2 (Summer 2007): 129–140.
Lipsitz, George. *Time Passages: Collective Memory and American Popular Culture*. Minneapolis: University of Minnesota Press, 1990.
Loren, Cary. "Poetry Is Revolution." In *John Sinclair and the Culture of the Sixties*. Edited by Karen L. Jania. Ann Arbor, Mich.: Bentley Historical Library, University of Michigan, 2004.
Lowe, Marsha. "'60s Radical Takes Long Trip Back to His Roots." *Detroit Free Press*. 27 October 2004.
Mailer, Norman. *Miami and the Siege of Chicago: An Informed History of the Republican and Democratic Conventions of 1968*. New York: Signet, 1968.
Marsh, David. "After the Revolution: The Legacy of the MC5." *Musician*, November 1990.
MC5. *Back in the U.S.A.* Atlantic Records, 1970.
MC5. *High Time* (Reissue). Atlantic Records, 1971.
MC5. *Kick Out the Jams*. Elektra Records, 1969.
"MC5: Sonic Revolution: A Celebration of the MC5." *Uncut*, May 2005, 148.
McLeese, Don. *The MC5's Kick Out the Jams*. New York: Continuum, 2005.
McMillian, John. "'You Didn't Have to Be There': Revisiting the New Left Consensus." In *The New Left Revisited*. Edited by John McMillian and Paul Buhle. Philadelphia: Temple University Press, 2003.
McNeil, Legs, and Gillian McCain. *Please Kill Me: The Uncensored Oral History of Punk*. New York: Penguin Books, 1997.

Bibliography

Miller, James. *Democracy Is in the Streets: From Port Huron to the Siege of Chicago.* Cambridge: Harvard University Press, 1987.

Murray, Clifford. Confidential Report to the Michigan State Police dated 7 July 1970. John and Leni Sinclair Papers, Box 46, Bentley Historical Library, University of Michigan.

Negus, Keith. *Music Genres and Corporate Cultures.* London: Routledge, 1999.

———. *Popular Music in Theory: An Introduction.* Hanover, N.H.: University Press of New England, 1996.

Ochs, Michael. *1000 Record Covers.* New York: Taschen, 2001.

"Our Mission." *Axis of Justice.* 18 May 2008. http://www.axisofjustice.org/mission.htm.

Pardun, Robert. *Prairie Radical: A Journey through the Sixties.* Los Gatos, Calif.: Shire Press, 2001.

Plamondon, Pun. Interview by the author via telephone and e-mail, 11 December 2006.

———. *Lost from the Ottawa: The Story of the Journey Back "Bootleg Edition."* Cloverdale, Mich.: Plamondon, 2004.

Reed, T.V. *The Art of Protest: Culture and Activism from the Civil Rights Movement to the Streets of Seattle.* Minneapolis: University of Minnesota Press, 2005.

"The Revolutionary Hype." *Time.* 3 January 1969, 49–50.

Rhodes, Jane. "Fanning the Flames of Racial Discord: The National Press and the Black Panther Party." *The Harvard International Journal of Press Politics.* 4.4 (1999): 95–118.

Robinson, Peter. "Fever to Sell." *New Musical Express.* 17 May 2003, 30–31.

Rose, Tricia. *Black Noise: Rap Music and Black Culture in Contemporary America.* Hanover, N.H.: Wesleyan University Press, 1994.

Rossinow, Doug. "Letting Go: Revisiting the New Left's Demise." In *The New Left Revisited.* Edited by John McMillian and Paul Buhle. Philadelphia: Temple University Press, 2003.

Special Agent-in-Charge (SAC) Detroit. Communication to the director of the FBI dated 25 February 1969. John and Leni Sinclair Papers, Box 46, Bentley Historical Library, University of Michigan.

———. Communication to the director of the FBI dated 24 April 1969. John and Leni Sinclair Papers, Box 46, Bentley Historical Library, University of Michigan.

Sale, Kirkpatrick. *SDS.* New York: Random House, 1973.

Schave, R. Inter-office correspondence to Michigan State Police Detective Daniel Myre dated 18 October 1968. John and Leni Sinclair Papers, Box 46, Bentley Historical Library, University of Michigan.

Sheppard, Doug. "Put That Mike in His Hand: A Vintage Interview with Rob Tyner of the MC5." *Ugly Things Magazine,* Winter/Spring 2008, 7–19.

Siegmeister, Elie. *Music and Society.* New York: Haskell House, 1974.

Simmons, Michael and Cletus Nelson. *MC5: The Future is Now!* London: Creation Books, 2004.

Sinclair, John. *Guitar Army.* New York: Douglass, 1972.

———. Interviews by the author. Detroit, Mich., 12 May 2005 and 13 August 2006.

———. Interview by the author via telephone, 16 May 2008.

———. "John Sinclair: A Letter from Prison, Another Side of the MC5 Story and (Incidentally) the End of an Era." *Creem Magazine,* January 1970, 9–14, 27, 30.

———. Liner notes to *Kick Out the Jams.* Elektra Records, 1969.

———. "Rob Tyner Interview." *The Sun,* Spring 1967. <http://makemyday.free.fr/sunint.htm>

———. The White Panther Manifesto/WPP 10-Point Program. 1 Nov. 1968.

_____, and Robert Levin. *Music and Politics*. Cleveland: World Publishing, 1971.
Sinclair, John and Leni, Papers. Letter [name classified] to the president of University of Michigan dated 20 March 1969. John and Leni Sinclair Papers, Box 46, Bentley Historical Library, University of Michigan.
_____. Memo to Captain Walter Hawkins dated 29 August 1969. John and Leni Sinclair Papers, Box 46, Bentley Historical Library, University of Michigan.
_____. Memorandum to the director of the FBI from the Special Agent-in-Charge Detroit dated 13 December 1971. John and Leni Sinclair Papers. Bentley Historical Library, University of Michigan.
_____. Memorandum to J.B. Adams from the United States Government dated 11 July 1975. John and Leni Sinclair Papers, Box 46, Bentley Historical Library, University of Michigan.
Sinclair, Leni. Interviews by the author. Detroit, Mich., 24 March 2005 and 22 April 2008.
Small, Christopher. *Musiking: The Meanings of Performance and Listening*. Hanover, N.H.: University Press of New England, 1998.
Smith, Suzanne. *Dancing in the Street: Motown and the Cultural Politics of Detroit*. Cambridge: Harvard University Press, 1999.
The State of Michigan vs. John Sinclair. Ministry of Information of the Youth International Party/White Panthers, 1970. Collection of the Michigan Historical Center, Lansing, MI.
Steal This Movie! Directed by Robert Greenwald, 2002.
Strausbaugh, John. *Rock 'Til You Drop: The Decline from Rebellion to Nostalgia*. New York: Verso, 2001.
Sugrue, Thomas. *The Origins of the Urban Crisis: Race and Inequality in Postwar Detroit*. Princeton: Princeton University Press, 1996.
Szatmary, David P. *A Time to Rock: A Social History of Rock and Roll*. New York: Schirmer, 1996.
Thomas, Richard. *Life for Us Is What We Make of It: Building Black Community in Detroit, 1915–1945*. Bloomington: Indiana University Press, 1992.
Thompson, Dennis. Telephone interviews by the author, 19 October 2005, 17 September 2006, and 23 May 2008.
Torres, Ben-Fong. "Shattered Dreams." *Rolling Stone Magazine*. 8 June 1972, 30–32.
United States. Secret Service. Report on John Alexander Sinclair Jr. dated 19 September 1969. John and Leni Sinclair Papers, Box 46, Bentley Historical Library, University of Michigan.
Varon, Jeremy. *Bringing the War Home*. Berkeley: University of California Press, 2004.
Waksman, Steve. *Instruments of Desire: The Electric Guitar and the Shaping of Musical Experience*. Cambridge: Harvard University Press, 1999.
Walley, David G. "Interview with MC-5." *Jazz & Pop*, July 1969. <http://makemyday.free.fr/intw69.htm>
Walser, Robert. *Running with the Devil: Power, Gender, and Madness in Heavy Metal Music*. Middletown, Conn: Wesleyan University Press, 1993.
Whiteley, Sheila. *The Space between the Notes*. New York: Routledge, 1992.
Willis, John. "Variations in State Casualty Rates in World War II and the Vietnam War." *Social Problems* 22, no. 4 (April, 1975): 558–568.
Wilson, Samuel. "Criminal Power." In History of the Sixth Circuit Web page. <www.ca6.uscourts.gov/lib_hist/cases/criminal.html>.

Index

The Activist 56
Adorno, Theodore 37, 170
Albrecht, Robert 24
alcohol (use of) 80, 146, 149, 153
Altamont 121
American Idiot (Green Day) 20
American Indian Movement/"Red Power" 56
American Society of Composers, Authors and Publishers (ASCAP) 23
Ann Arbor 44, 47–48, 61, 65, 69, 93, 97, 110, 114, 134–135, 150; CIA office bombing 82, 83, 100, 135, 152, 166–167
Ann Arbor Argus 132
Ann Arbor Sun 33, 75, 106, 128, 134
Anti-nuclear campaign 164
anti-war movement/perspectives 34, 38, 62–63, 70, 74, 108–109, 118–119, 153, 161–162
Aronowitz, Stanley 19, 36, 106–107, 163, 169–171
Ascension 149
Asheton, Ron 149
Atlantic Records 23
atomic age (influence of) 52
Attali, Jacques 76–78
authenticity 22–23, 27–36, 90, 102–105, 109–111, 112–115, 132–133, 137, 139, 146, 154–158, 184
Axis of Justice Tour 175–176
Ayler, Albert 157

"baby boomers" 3, 24–25, 53, 107, 160, 162
Back in the U.S.A. 59, 113, 116–117, 119
Baker, Cary 150
Bakhtin, Mikhail 122
Ballard, Hank 41

Bang Magazine 97, 126
Bangs, Lester 35, 90, 121, 126, 137, 158
Bartkowiak, Mathew 43, 45, 70
Baudrillard, Jean 112, 121, 136
The Beach Boys 159
beat movement 4, 45, 61, 79, 93
Beatles 59–60, 92, 116
Beck, Julian 127
Belle Isle "Love-in" 46–47, 128, 131
Benford, Robert 13, 34–35
Berry, Chuck 42, 53, 59, 79, 150
Bey, Hakim 178–179
Big Brother and the Holding Company 61
Birmingham School 8
Black Panther Party/ Black Power Movement 8, 14, 16, 47–48, 50, 51, 56–57, 65, 67–68, 70–72, 75, 79, 84, 89, 94, 95–97, 109, 125, 131, 163–164
"Black to Comm" 94
Blackboard Jungle 25, 117
"Blowin' in the Wind" 12
Bodroghkozy, Aniko 68
Bomp! Magazine 149
Boone, Pat 12, 28
"Borderline"/"Looking at You" 45rpm 155
Boucher, Caroline (*Disc and Music Echo*) 35
Bradley, Dick 26, 28
Breakdown of race/class through rock 26, 72–78
Breakthrough 47
Bringing It All Back Home 12
British Invasion 37, 59, 60
Brown, James 127, 159
"Brown Power" Movement 56
Bush, George W. 165
The Byrds 62

Index

Callwood, Brent 4, 10
Carmichael, Stokely 68
Carson, David 4, 10, 40–41, 46
Castro, Fidel 79, 82, 93, 133, 181
Catholic activists 164
Central Intelligence Agency (CIA) 112
Chapple, Steve 30–32
Chicago 49, 80, 99
Chicago Festival of Life 49, 81, 128
Chicago Seven/Eight 83
civil rights (movement) 38, 46, 49–51, 57, 65, 74, 109, 163–164, 166
cocaine 148
Cohen, Mitchell 56
COINTELPRO 47, 163
Coltrane, John 61, 92, 157
Columbia University 63
"Come Together" 115
Communism 109, 115
Cooper, Alice 62, 127
counterculture 10, 12, 16, 19, 21, 34–35, 49, 68, 94, 103–104, 121, 182, 184
Country Joe and the Fish 12, 118
Crawford, J.C. 129–130, 145
Cream 128
Creedence Clearwater Revival 118
Creem Magazine 127, 131
Cronkite, Walter 81, 133
Cuban Missile Crisis 52

Damren, Samuel C. 83, 166
Davidson, Chris 154–155
Davis, Angela (activist) 68
Davis, Angela (MC5) 7–8, 173
Davis, Michael 1, 2, 3, 4, 7, 9, 40, 49, 51–54, 59–60, 63–64, 90, 92–93, 95–96, 98, 101–105, 117, 122–123, 125, 132–134, 136, 139, 143, 146–147, 149–150, 156, 160–161, 164, 172–173, 176–177, 179–180
De Certeau, Michel 37, 180
"degeneration" (musical) 28–30
democratic centralism 71
Department of Defense 98–99, 121–122, 128
Destroy All Monsters 149
Detroit: history of/class, race, economy, community 37–49, 65, 76, 93; music scene 11–12, 14, 15, 48, 50, 59, 61–62, 64, 69, 87, 97, 101, 110, 114, 134, 135, 149, 155–156, 160; police 47, 70
Detroit Artists Workshop (DAW) 16, 43, 45–46, 51, 72, 78

Detroit Free Press 60, 131
Detroit News 131
Diggins, John P. 55, 161–162
Dixie Chicks 20
"DKT-MC5" (Davis, Kramer, Thompson) 7
The Doors 128
Downbeat Magazine 61
Dragnet 68
drug use/drug culture 49, 51–52, 54, 62, 68, 73, 80, 94, 97–99, 101, 113, 115–117, 120, 127–128, 134, 140, 146–150, 153, 155, 157, 161
Dylan, Bob 12, 59, 165

Edmonds, Ben 7
Elektra Records 63, 73–74, 85, 98–99, 101, 103, 114, 121
English, Ron 43
Executive Branch (Federal) 84

Fanon, Frantz 82, 162
Fear (band) 84
Fear of a Black Planet (Public Enemy) 2
Federal Bureau of Investigation (FBI) 4, 15, 47, 96, 106, 112, 119–120, 128, 131, 134, 143, 177, 181
Ferlinghetti, Lawrence 79
"Festival of Life" 107
Fifth Estate 33, 46, 61, 82, 128, 132
Fillmore East 122
folk revival 58–59
Ford, Gerald 135
Ford Motor Company 40
Frankfurt School 8, 37, 170
"Free John Now" Concert/Movement 82, 152
Freedom of Information Act 4, 112, 134
Friedlander, Paul 155
Frith, Simon 1 2–13, 30–32, 35, 110
The Fugs 30
"Future/Now" 119

Gang War 149
Garafalo, Reebee 12–13, 30–32
gay liberation 57, 164
genre constructs 31–32
Gibb, Russ 61
Ginsberg, Allen 79, 82, 93
Gitlin, Todd 13, 17, 34, 53, 58, 67–69, 106, 130–131, 136, 160
Goodman, Fred 128

196

Gordy, Berry, Jr. 40–41, 61
Gosse, Van 55–56, 126, 161–163, 172
"Gotta Keep Movin'" 118
Graham, Bill 114, 122, 129
Graham, Billy 25, 35
Grande Ballroom 46, 49, 61–62
Grateful Dead 61–62
"Great Migration" 39
Grimshaw, Gary 7, 102
Guerrilla 132
Guevara, Che 79, 94, 151
guns (use of) 50, 84, 88, 96–97, 134–135, 144, 152
Guthrie, Woody 165

Hale, Dennis 56
Hale, Jeff 10, 47, 66
Haley, Bill (and His Comets) 12, 25, 40
Hard Times 132
Hasted, Nick 126
Hayden, Tom 68, 162
heavy metal 18, 19, 58, 88, 140, 154–155, 157–158
Hebdige, Dick 27, 35
hedonism (of the band/WPP) 50–51, 74–76, 78, 113, 115–117, 128, 184
Hendrix, Jimi 118, 159
heroin 52, 101, 146–148
"high energy music" 59, 61–62, 74–75, 90–92, 94, 123–125, 134, 157, 179
"High School" 117
High Time 59, 113, 116, 118–119
"hippie(s)" 57, 68, 129, 131, 152–155, 157, 164
Ho Chi Minh 74, 82, 93, 152
Hoffman, Abbie 68, 80–81, 107
Holloway, Carson 170
Holzman, Jac 63, 114
Hooker, John Lee 12, 40–41, 59, 119
Hoover, J. Edgar 113, 135, 137
Hudson's Department Store 63
Hull, Geoffrey 23–24
"Human Being Lawnmower" 113, 118
Hunt, Andrew 55

Iggy and the Stooges 61–62, 110–111, 140, 149, 156, 158
Iraq War 165

Jagger, Mick 29, 116, 124
Jarrett, Michael 28–30, 32
jazz 15, 25, 45–46, 58, 61, 92, 94, 155, 159

Jazz & Pop 60, 92
Jefferson Airplane 12, 30, 32, 62
John Birch Society 47
Jonze, Tim 140
Justice Department 119

"Keith Case" 15, 82–84, 166–167
Kerouac, Jack 93
Kick Out the Jams (album) 1, 8, 50, 52, 59, 61, 73, 113, 115, 129, 141, 155–156, 175
"Kick Out the Jams Motherfuckers" (song) 63, 73, 89, 116–117
Kilmister, Lemmy 140
The Kinks 60
Kramer, Barry 131
Kramer, Margaret Saadi 7
Kramer, Wayne 3, 7, 9, 35, 40–41, 46–47, 49–51, 58, 60, 88–105, 107–110, 122, 124–125, 127, 132–133, 139, 141–142, 144, 148–149, 151, 156–157, 161, 165, 173–176, 180

Lait, Jack 26–27
Larabee, Ann 43, 45, 70, 71, 79–80, 133
Leary, Timothy 62
"legacy of the 1960s" 3
Lenin, Vladimir 82, 162
Lennon, John 82
"Let Me Try" 116
Levi's (brand) 7–8, 104, 137
Lewis, Jerry Lee 25
Licensing issues 7
Life Magazine 42
Lincoln Park, MI 40
Lipsitz, George 178–179
Lomax, Alan 58
Loren, Cary 97
Los Angeles 62
Lovin' Spoonful 118
LSD/acid 15, 45, 51–52, 73, 75, 80, 99, 101, 146, 155
lyrical content 18, 58, 74–75, 113, 115–120, 136

Mailer, Norman 18, 121, 140, 178
marijuana 45, 51, 73–74, 80, 82, 94, 97–98, 101, 108, 116, 120, 127, 129, 146
Marsh, Dave 106, 155, 178
Marx, Karl 162
masculinity 115–117
mass media 9, 11, 13, 53, 67, 69, 80–82, 87, 89, 93, 102–103, 106, 108, 129–130,

Index

132, 136, 160, 163, 169, 172, 178, 180, 182–183; frames 13, 16–20, 33–36, 38, 53, 58, 64, 67–68, 81, 88, 95–96, 105, 109, 112, 130–131, 136, 169, 180–181, 184
"Masters of War" 173
MaximumRock&Roll Magazine 154
MC5 1–5, 9–19, 21, 22, 27–52, 54–56; disintegration of/split with WPP 139–153; ideological influences on the band 93–98; interaction of music and social change 66, 69, 71–82, 117–120, 168–185; legacy 103–104, 109–111, 140, 154–167; music industry pressure 141, 143–147, 150, 177; perceptions of authorities 93–101, 105–109, 119, 121, 126, 128–132, 135–138, 139–144, 147, 153, 178, 181, 183; perspectives on meaning from band members 87–111; popular culture influences (on the MC5/WPP) 15, 37, 40–65, 159; relationship to the New Left 78–84, 160–167; reunion 7–8; rise of 58–64, 65; technological innovations (influence on band) 38, 49, 52–54, 77, 107, 169, 177
McLeese, Don 10
McLuhan, Marshall 68
McMillian, John 57, 163
Michigan 11, 41, 48, 119; State Police 112, 129, 134
Michigan State University 129
Miller, Jim 67
mind/body separation 170–171, 182
"Miss X" 116
Mitchell, John 101
Mitchell Doctrine 83–84
Mojo Magazine 110, 155, 179
The Monkees 68
Moore, Charles 43–44
moral panic 23
Morello, Tom 166, 175
Mortimer, Lee 26–27
The Motherfuckers 122, 125, 129
"Motor City Is Burning" 50, 113, 119–120
Motorhead 140
Motown Records 40–41, 44, 58, 61, 64, 159
Murray, Sgt. Clifford A. 128
Music Is Revolution Foundation 164, 173
musical influences (on the band) 38, 58–63
Musician Magazine 155
"musicking" 169, 171–172, 183

NAACP 39
Negus, Keith 12–13, 31–33
Nelson, Cletus 10, 40, 43, 45
New Left 3, 10, 12–14, 15, 17, 19, 34, 36, 54–58, 63, 67–68, 78–84, 88, 95, 100, 103, 119, 125, 131, 133, 140, 143–145, 160–167, 182
The New York Times 63, 133
Newsweek 34
Newton, Huey 68, 70
1967 Detroit Riot/Rebellion 14, 42, 47, 88, 120, 155
1968 Democratic National Convention 49, 99, 121, 178
Nixon, Richard 83, 109, 113, 135, 161
Nkrumah, Kwame 82, 152
nostalgia 29
Nugent, Ted/Amboy Dukes 61–62

Ochs, Michael 26, 77, 115, 117
Old Left 55–57
100 Club (London) 7, 137
Ono, Yoko 82
"Operation Ceasefire" 175
"Over and Over" 118

Pardun, Robert 63
Parents' Music Resource Center (PMRC) 181
performance/spectacle 18, 59–62, 75, 80–82, 84, 89, 110, 113–114, 120–130, 133, 136, 138, 156
Peter, Paul and Mary 59
Plamandon, Pun 9, 15, 16, 19, 51, 66, 69–71, 75, 78–85, 100, 102, 106, 119, 129, 133, 135–136, 139, 143, 145, 151–153, 163, 166–167, 176, 178, 180
"Poison" 118
Port Huron Statement 55
Prairie radicals 63
Presley, Elvis 25
The Pretty Things 60
profanity 119–120, 128
punk rock 18, 19, 58, 88, 140, 154–158
Purity/Accuracy 126

Rage Against the Machine 19, 64, 84–85, 175
Rainbow People's Party 74, 78, 151–152
Rationals 62
Rebel Without a Cause 25
Reed, T.V. 182

Index

Rhodes, Jane 67, 69
Richard, Little 79
Rock and Roll Hall of Fame 140
"Rocket Reducer No. 62" 115–117
Rolling Stone 35, 90, 126, 154
Rolling Stones 12, 46, 59–60, 92, 133
Rose, Tricia 180
Rossinow, Doug 161
Rubin, Jerry 68, 81–82, 107
Rudnick, Bob 80, 145
Russell, Bertrand 164

Sales, Kirkpatrick 67
Samways, Alec 8
Sanders, Pharaoh 61, 92
San Francisco scene 32, 62–63, 157
Seale, Bobby 82
"Second Great Migration" 39
Secret Service 126
Seeger, Pete 59
Seger, Bob 61–62
"selling out" 8, 22, 184
Sempliner, David 44
Sex Pistols 19, 64, 84 155
sexuality 10, 113, 115–117, 124, 128, 161, 179
Shannon, Rev. William (*Catholic Sun*) 25
Shepp, Archie 44, 61, 92
Sheppard, Doug/*Ugly Things Magazine* 43, 45, 47, 49, 60, 89, 115, 117–118, 120, 137, 158–159
Siegmeister, Elie 170, 181
Simmons, Michael 10, 40, 43, 45
Sinatra, Frank 26, 35
Sinclair, Dave 102
Sinclair, John 2, 14, 15, 16, 17, 19, 33–35, 37–38, 43–48, 50–51, 54, 60–62, 65–86, 87–93, 95–102, 105–107, 114, 116, 119, 121–122, 126–129, 131–136, 139, 141–146, 151–153, 158–160, 163–166, 172, 175, 178–180
Sinclair, Leni 9, 15, 16, 19, 43–44, 51, 65–66, 69–70, 72–75, 83, 85, 91, 96, 102, 125, 135, 139, 144–145, 151–153, 159, 162, 174
Small, Christopher 20, 169, 171, 177, 179, 181, 182
Smith, Fred "Sonic" 4, 9, 40–41, 91–93, 102–103, 122, 124, 134, 149, 151
Smith, Suzanne 40–41, 64
Snow, David 13, 34–35
social location/social identity 13, 20, 23, 31, 33, 167

Sonic Revolution: A Celebration of the MC5 104, 109
Sonic Youth 19
Sonic's Rendezvous Band 149–150
Springsteen, Bruce 29
Steal This Movie! 108
Strausbaugh, John 29–30, 66
"Street Fighting Man" 115
Students for a Democratic Society (SDS) 14, 16, 34, 57–58, 63, 65, 67, 74, 78–79, 109, 125, 131, 160, 162
"Subterranean Homesick Blues" 12
Sugrue, Thomas J. 14, 39–40, 42
Sullivan, Ed 25
Sun/Dance 132
Sun Ra 58, 61, 92, 157
Sun Records 11
System of a Down 175
Szatmary, David 24–25

Tankian, Serj 175
"Teenage Lust" 116
"teenager" 24–28, 117
"temporary autonomous zones" 178, 182, 185
Thomas, Richard 39
Thompson, Dennis "Machine Gun" 7, 9, 40–41, 49–51, 53–54, 60–62, 88–90, 92–10, 103–104, 109, 112, 121–122, 124–125, 127, 131–132, 13, 142–143, 147, 149, 159–160, 162, 164, 173, 176, 180–181
Thunders, Johnny 148–149, 155
Time Magazine 33–34, 40, 128, 131
"Tonight" 117
Trans-Love Energies (TLE) 16, 18, 45–47, 51, 66, 70, 72, 74, 78, 98, 116, 128, 141
transistor radio 53
Turner, Tina 127
"Tutti Frutti" 116
Tyner, Rob 4, 7, 9, 40–41, 43–45, 47, 49, 51, 59–62, 73, 75, 77, 89, 94–96, 98–99, 102, 106–107, 115, 117–118, 120, 122, 124–125, 127, 129, 133, 137, 147, 149–150, 155, 158, 173

Uncut Magazine 90, 92, 110, 126, 179
Underground Press Syndicate (UPS) 133
United Auto Workers (UAW) 39
University of California–Berkeley 63
University of Michigan 119
usable rebellion 9, 11, 17, 18, 20–22, 29, 33–34, 37, 53, 66, 76–77, 85, 87–88,

Index

94, 104, 114, 117, 119, 130, 132, 137, 140, 159, 163, 168, 171–172, 176, 180, 182–184; rise of/tie to youth 23–36

Vietnam (War) 12, 14, 34, 46, 49, 52–54, 62–63, 65, 88, 90–91, 97, 109, 112, 118–119, 144, 155, 161–162, 164
"Volunteers" 115

Waksman, Steve 10–11, 75–77, 168
Walley, David 92–93, 125
Walser, Robert 157
Watergate Scandal 161
Waterhouse, John 83
Waters, Muddy 59, 116
Wayne State University 43
"We Shall Overcome" 12
Weather Underground/Weathermen 12, 16, 78–79, 106, 131, 153, 163
White, Al 50, 120
White, Jack 140
White Panther Party (WPP) 1–2, 4–5, 7–11, 13–20, 21–22, 28, 32, 33, 36, 37, 38, 151; band perspectives on 87–111; development 47–58; interaction of music and social change 66, 69, 71–82, 117–120, 168–185; legacy 154–167; organizers' perspectives 64–86; perceptions of authorities 93–101, 105–109, 113, 119, 121, 126, 128–132, 135–138, 140–145, 147, 153, 178, 181, 183; propaganda of 69, 88, 95–97, 102, 106–108, 110, 112, 114, 119, 130, 132–136, 180; relationship to New Left 78–84, 160–167; split with MC5 139–153
The White Panther State/meant (Statement) (Manifesto)/10-Point Program 21, 48, 51, 54, 65, 71–73, 89, 134
The White Stripes 140
Whitely, Shelia 179
The Who 59–60, 92, 133, 159
Willis, John 62
Wilson, Jackie 127
Wilson, Samuel 101
women's movement/rights 50, 56–57, 164
Woodstock 121
working class background 41–42, 62

The Yardbirds 42, 59–60
"Yellow Power" Movement 56
Yippies 16, 18, 53, 67, 80–82, 99, 106–109, 129
Young, Neil 20

Zappa, Frank 182
Zedong, Mao 79, 82, 95

www.ingramcontent.com/pod-product-compliance
Lightning Source LLC
Chambersburg PA
CBHW020913230426
43666CB00008B/1437